LOOKING BACK
Living and Writing History

Oliver MacDonagh

Oliver MacDonagh, *c.*1976

LOOKING BACK

Living and Writing History

Oliver MacDonagh

1924–2002

Edited and introduced by Tom Dunne

Foreword by Roy Foster

THE LILLIPUT PRESS
DUBLIN

First published 2008 by
THE LILLIPUT PRESS
62–63 Sitric Road, Arbour Hill
Dublin 7, Ireland
www.lilliputpress.ie

ISBN 978 1 84351 143 4

1 3 5 7 9 10 8 6 4 2

A CIP record for this title is available
from The British Library.

Set in 10.5 pt on 14 pt Sabon by Marsha Swan
Printed in England by MPG Books, Bodmin, Cornwall

Contents

II. INTERVIEWS WITH HISTORIANS

III. STYLE AND SUBSTANCE: THE BUSINESS OF WRITING HISTORY

Foreword

'As men draw close to their end they care less for disclosures.' Newman's dictum seems questionable at best, though it is quoted approvingly by Oliver MacDonagh in the following pages. And it is only partially borne out by the autobiographical reflections that make up most of this book. They constitute the impressionistic childhood autobiography of a remarkable intellectual, and incidentally supply the record of a developing historical imagination. MacDonagh took self-deprecation to an art form, but the intensity and insight of these memoirs convey a Wordsworthian sense of the man he would become.

They also constitute an essay in the social history of 1930s provincial Ireland (with a late swerve into wartime UCD). We are shown a social anatomy of the position of 'the Bank' and its adherents in a small town. The cuisine of a gifted home cook is described with opulent sensuousness. A character like Aunt Fluff might have stepped from the pages of William Trevor, with her brisk habits, her stories of dinner with Lord Mayo, her optimistic subscription to the *Writers' and Artists' Yearbook*, her disastrous past and her sad future. But there are also decisive pointers towards the social and intellectual influences that made MacDonagh one of the most distinguished Irish historians of a distinguished generation, and – though he hotly denied it – one of the most influential. Tom Dunne's introduction makes the case powerfully, and it need not be elaborated here. But it is illuminating to read that profile of MacDonagh's career before immersing oneself in his account of the childhood that preceded and conditioned it.

What emerges from these memoirs is a *habitus* that is instinctively Catholic (note the marvellous chapter on his altar-boy career, and the evocation of Benediction on a dark winter evening) and firmly Fine Gael, albeit in a town whose Fianna Fáil ethos recalls Colm Tóibín's depiction of 1930s Enniscorthy in *The Heather Blazing*. And yet the intellectual influences are as much British as Irish. MacDonagh's models of style remain the writers of English he read in his youth, notably Stevenson. 'He is the supreme narrator, and it is with stories that we all begin. His English is as clear as glass, straightforward, all sinews and muscle, free from every shadow of redundancy, or the contrived. His words are simple where simple words will do, but, where not, the right terms duly take their place.' This remained a touchstone for MacDonagh's own writing. In an absorbing profile of his intellectual interests, his love for Trollope and Austen is fixed early on, and he returned to the historical significance of both writers at the end of his life. But his first archival explorations come from exploring runs of Victorian periodicals in an Irish parlour on a wet day – echoing, oddly, the way that Standish O'Grady described his own induction into Irish history.

MacDonagh's career was divided between Ireland, England and Australia, and he left an enduring mark on the history writing of each country. Ireland is in his debt for the definitive biography of Daniel O'Connell, and one of the most brilliant short treatments of Irish history. For Britain, he redefined the history of early Victorian government, setting many hares coursing in various directions. And he supplied the controlling intellect behind the enormous bicentennial history of Australia, *Australians* – profitably bringing to the project the lessons hard-learned on the *New History of Ireland*, an enterprise that had sometimes resembled a cross between Mr Casaubon's labours and Henry James's *The Madonna of the Future*.

All MacDonagh's books cross borders. Significantly, his own favourites among his books were his study of Sir Jeremiah Fitzpatrick, who lived between Britain and Ireland and epitomized the interaction between them; and his surprisingly (to some) passionate reflections on Anglo-Irish relations, *States of Mind: A Study of Irish-Anglo Conflict 1780–1980*. The subtly coloured but closely observed memoirs gathered here show the dedication to combining clarity and nuance which distinguished everything MacDonagh wrote. He would have emphatically rejected the endorsement adopted by students of Theodor Adorno, that any profound reflection necessarily needs to be expressed in difficult language. By the same token, as he mischievously put it, he found all that he needed in Fitzpatrick rather than Foucault. But a laconic style and a tough-minded scepticism about loosely conceived theories do not imply simple empiricism (remember, as he did, his Aunt Bee's conclusion that the MacDonaghs were 'eejity with brains'). The intellectual heft and historical imagination of his work speak for themselves, and so do the reflections on his own thought processes prised (with some difficulty) out of him for the two interviews reproduced in this book.

The other qualities evoked by this, his last publication, are his humaneness and his scrupulous avoidance of recrimination – truly the mark of the man. The vivid gallery of 'characters' gathered around his childhood are all named with affection, but the (few) cruel teachers he encounters at school are permitted a decent anonymity as 'Sister X' and 'Mr Y'. And the powerful empathy whereby he identified with a Jewish refugee child spotted in a harrowing 1936 newspaper photograph is summoned up as painfully as if six decades had not intervened. 'Feeling is a sort of knowledge,' as he quotes elsewhere from *Adam Bede*. Oliver MacDonagh was a great scholar, and a good deal more. Early on in the book, referring to his father's reputation in Roscommon, he discusses the Irish (as opposed to English) definition of a 'gentleman': 'courtesy, modesty, decency' and – though he does not articulate it – a certain gentle authority. It is impossible not to read these absorbing memoirs without realizing how well the description applies to their author: a scholar and a gentleman.

Roy Foster (2008)

Oliver Ormond Gerard MacDonagh, 1924–2002*

Tom Dunne

At a crowded reception in Iveagh House in Dublin in 1989, following the awarding of honorary degrees by the National University of Ireland, one of the 'honorands', Oliver MacDonagh, a very modest and private man, seemed nonplussed by the compliments that rained upon him. Yet he was clearly delighted also to be thus honoured by his old university, forty-five years after he had graduated with first place in the BA, around the corner in Earlsfort Terrace. Since then, apart from a brief period in Cork, he had lived outside of Ireland, and his major reputation had been made in the area of British administrative history.

* This is an expanded and updated version of the tribute, 'Oliver MacDonagh', which I published in the *Festschrift, Ireland, England and Australia: Essays in Honour of Oliver MacDonagh* (edited by F.B. Smith, Canberra and Cork, 1990). Given this origin, it is not surprising that it is an admiring rather than a critical appraisal, and this also seems to me to be appropriate for this, his last book. I am grateful to Oliver's widow, Carmel, his son, Oliver, sister-in-law, Honor, and close friend, Niall Meagher for sharing reminiscences and letters with me, and to Ian d'Alton for his comments on the text.

Even among Irish colleagues the full extent of his contribution to scholarship was not widely understood, and he was relatively unknown to the general public. This conferring, therefore, in the company of Seamus Heaney and Tony O'Reilly, had a special significance, not only for him, but for those who had long admired the man and his work.

But to one non-historian present, a contemporary of Oliver's at Clongowes, there was something else to be celebrated, and he broke into the circle of family and friends to recall a poem that the new Hon. D.Litt. had published as a schoolboy, and which had made such an impression on this man, that he could still quote from it. This he proceeded to do, to the mingled amusement and embarrassment of the erstwhile poet, before disappearing again into the throng. The incident was revealing – not only of a hitherto unsuspected aspect of Oliver's past – but also of a major reason for honouring him. Even when his many contributions to scholarship have receded into historiographical perspective, and have been overtaken, as inevitably they must be, by later research, he will still be read for the literary qualities of his work; his gift with words will continue to make him remembered and memorable. He is that rarity among historians, a fine writer, who can be read simply for the pleasure as well as the profit of the experience.

Oliver MacDonagh was born in Carlow in 1924, although his father, Michael, an official in the National Bank, was then stationed in Limerick. His mother, Loretto Oliver (herself formerly an employee of the Bank of Ireland), came from Carlow and returned there for the birth of her first child. The Carlow connection, and especially his mother's family, continued to be of great importance to Oliver, throughout holidays from school and university, and ever after as a vital centre of family connection. It was symbolic of that tie that he was given, as his Christian name, his mother's surname. His first publication, at nine, was a poem in the local paper, *The Carlow Nationalist*.

Oliver spent his boyhood in Roscommon, an experience

vividly captured in his memoir, 'Clouds of Glory'. As the son of a bank manager he had a more privileged life than most, with a large bank house and garden, and the services of 'Tom the porter'. While aware of the deference paid to his father, he was also fully integrated into town life, a student in the rough-and-tumble of the local Christian Brothers' School, bookish and diligent, but capable of 'mitching' with some tougher companions. He became an omnivorous reader under the tutelage of Aunt 'Fluff', who lived with them, but was also a sports enthusiast, brought to rugby games by his father, and to the Galway Races, where he was introduced to agonized modest betting by his mother. In Roscommon too he was introduced to politics, learning 'in the immediate aftermath of a civil war, that politics was a really serious and divisive business'.

The strong religious sense also inculcated by his parents (and by his experiences as an altar boy) was further strengthened by his move, as a boarder, to the Jesuit college of Clongowes Wood, outside Dublin. The Jesuit influence meant that his Catholicism was, at the same time, strongly traditional and intellectually sophisticated. It was to be of fundamental importance throughout his life, and he maintained strong links with the Jesuits, both in Ireland and Australia. He was very happy in Clongowes, recalling in letters to another contemporary there, Niall Meagher, the library, 'which seemed to me the acme of civilized leisure', and his 'Gothick visions of what went on behind the closed doors and forbidden staircases' of the old castle. He won the Gold Medal for English Essay and represented the school in debating, thereby laying the basis for the powerful, yet richly modulated lecturing voice, that often surprised friends, used to the unassuming low key of his conversation.

He went on to University College Dublin, intending to become a barrister, and was active in the famous debating society – the Literary and Historical. In an article for its centenary history a decade later he evoked its wartime politics and personalities, praising its role as 'a medium for instinctive undergraduate aspiration'. UCD was a lively and stimulating place in this period, despite Ireland's wartime isolation. Oliver's generation, which included Garret FitzGerald, Charles Haughey, Anthony Cronin, Paddy Lynch and Desmond Williams, was to be prominent in Dublin's political and intellectual life over the coming decades. UCD also had its own distinctive traditions, especially from its origins in Newman's Catholic University (which James Joyce had attended, also after a period in Clongowes), and some of Newman's writings continued to be read as set texts. For MacDonagh, they became much more – seminal philosophical and theological readings to which he regularly returned, and by his own account, the principal models for his literary style as well as 'a supreme exemplar of the historiography of our modern age'. History soon became Oliver's main focus, and in UCD it had a special air of excitement and innovation, presided over by the volatile, stimulating figure of Robin Dudley Edwards, the pioneer, with Theo Moody of Trinity College, of a new and more professional school of Irish history, and soon to be joined by the enigmatically impressive Desmond Williams, fresh from Cambridge, where he was the first of the long line of UCD history graduates to do research at Peterhouse – the next 'generation' being Oliver, F.X. Martin and Kevin B. Nowlan.

While still an undergraduate, Oliver also enrolled as a student at King's Inns, and was called to the Irish Bar in the year after graduation. His legal training informed his historical writing from his early study of Victorian administration, to his sympathetic life of Daniel O'Connell. It also shaped his many contributions to the institutional life of the different universities in which he served. Apart from his literary offerings to student magazines, Oliver's other surprising extra-curricular activity in his UCD years was as a tipster in the racing pages of *The Irish Times*. Knowing nothing of horses, he told me that he culled his information from the English press, and so successful was he at this example of applied research that his record was second to none. His own sport, however, continued to be rugby, an abiding passion best exemplified for me by witnessing his transformation into an excitable and voluble touchline supporter of an Australian National University (ANU) team, featuring two of his sons.

Now firmly committed to history, Oliver moved to Cambridge in 1947, on the award of a travelling studentship from the National University of Ireland. His research topic, first registered as 'The state and Irish emigration' – under the supervison of D.W. Brogan – was ultimately to lead to his major work on Victorian government, but already he was publishing. His first scholarly article, on the Catholic clergy and emigration, appeared in *Irish Historical Studies* the year he went to Cambridge. In Peterhouse he also supervised in the Preliminary Examinations and in both parts of the Historical Tripos, a factor in his election in 1950 as fellow and college lecturer in history at the nearby St Catharine's College, where he succeeded E.E. Rich as director of studies in History a year later. At the time St Catharine's was embarking on its post-war expansion, with History as the largest of the Arts subjects, and Oliver's role was a vital one, not only as teacher and director, but also (from 1952) as college librarian, helping to build up one of the best undergraduate libraries in Cambridge.

His years in Cambridge were happy and stimulating ones on a variety of levels. Again he was lucky to find a vibrant new History school, with Brogan, Herbert Butterfield, M.M. Postan and Dom David Knowles in Peterhouse, J.H. Plumb at Christ's, and Kitson Clark at Trinity. In Cambridge too he met his wife, Carmel Hamilton, a statistician; they married in 1954 and five of their seven children were born while they lived there. They were a remarkably close couple, with her vivaciousness and theatricality providing a fascinating contrast to his shy, often awkward personality. His devoted attentiveness to her was striking. Family life was the bedrock of all else. His sister-in-law, Honor, recalls him often writing at the kitchen table when the children were small, dealing patiently with questions and minor crises.

St Catharine's too remained 'family' for him. He never lost his links with the college, and, in another characteristic example of *pietas*, he contributed an essay to its quincentenary history, published in 1973. He was visiting fellow there in 1985, and was elected honorary life fellow two years later.

MacDonagh also became a university assistant lecturer in 1959, the year after the appearance of his article, 'The nineteenth century revolution in government: a reappraisal', in the first number of *The Historical Journal*. It had evoked a remarkable response, much of it hostile, leading MacDonagh years later to compare himself to Byron in 'waking one morning to find myself infamous'. Originally a sensation, it has become a classic, one of only five 'of its most prestigious papers' recently highlighted by *The Historical Journal* in an anniversary promotion. Two years later, his first book, *A Pattern of Government Growth 1800–60: The Passenger Acts and their Enforcement*, confirmed his reputation as an exciting and innovative new force, and launched both a historiographical revolution and an academic 'industry' as important and extensive as that surrounding the Tudor government thesis of his Cambridge contemporary, Geoffrey Elton.

The impact of the MacDonagh model as a 'paradigm shift in the historiography of Victorian government' was well described by Roy MacLeod, in his introduction to a volume of commemorative essays on one of its key elements, *Government and Expertise: Specialists, Administrators and Professionals, 1860–1919* (1988). This book, MacLeod argued, 'is not, however, a traditional *Festschrift*, for that would be both premature, and given the enormous range of his scholarship, patently incomplete'. Instead it was offered as 'an interpretative instalment', and the editor pointed especially to MacDonagh's own contribution to the volume, seeing him 'still in the research front with us; a strategist who has no sympathy for Chateau generalship'. It was indeed a feature of the extensive debate on the MacDonagh thesis that he remained involved, despite his growing absorption in other research areas. As well as further testing and refining his model in a number of articles on the regulation of the coal industry, he also took account of the work of critics and supporters alike in producing a new synthesis in 1977 under the title *Early Victorian Government, 1830–1870*, and thus crowning the passage of his thesis 'from revolution to respectability' (MacLeod). MacDonagh's interest in this area had been sparked off originally by his earlier work on Irish emigration – work that had already produced the still important contribution to Edwards and Williams (eds), *The Great Famine* (1956), and was later to throw new light on the Irish in Australia.

Throughout his career, the seemingly unconnected elements of MacDonagh's large output continued to feed off one another. The questions that led to his model of government growth were also partly inspired by his reading of early-nineteenth-century fiction, while his writing on social, economic and administrative history later informed his highly original insights into the novels of Jane Austen. Perhaps the most fruitful example of this cross-fertilization was his pushing back of the administrative revolution thesis to the last decades of the eighteenth century, and focussing it on the colonial problem of Ireland, in his engaging and oddly neglected 1981 volume, *The Inspector General: Sir Jeremiah Fitzpatrick and Social Reform* – a book that also introduced him to some of the challenges of writing biography and was later described by him as 'one of my favourite children'.

Before moving on from his Cambridge years, it is worth pointing to another example of his eclecticism – his dramatic eruption into the controversy over the nature of the nineteenth-century empire, begun by two more contemporaries, Ronald Robinson and Jack Gallagher. MacDonagh's article, 'The anti-imperialism of free trade', had its origins in a piece of *joie de vivre* produced for a seminar, but its insights made a major contribution, as can be seen in its regular reprinting in volumes on the 'new imperialism' debate. While still in Cambridge he embarked (together with the Caius economist, S.R. Dennison) on a commissioned history of Guinness since 1886, a project that was to consume much of his research time in the 1960s. The book, a major study, was completed, but the company vetoed its publication, mainly it appears, because its critical, complex analysis, including an emphasis on the Unionism of successive heads of the firm, did not fit the corporate image then in vogue. It seemed a sad waste, despite articles on the origins of porter, and the interaction of government, science and industry in the nineteenth century that were by-products of his Guinness work. It thus gave him particular pleasure when the company, now part of a multi-national group, withdrew its objections and the book was published, albeit in truncated form, by Cork University Press in 1998.

In 1963 Oliver decided on a break from Cambridge, at first a temporary one, but in fact it was to determine the shape of his future academic career. He went as visiting fellow to the Australian National University's department of Demography, and liked the experience enough to move in the following year to the chair of History at the new Flinders University in Adelaide. His four years there, as foundation professor and chairman of the School of Social Sciences, allowed him little time to publish, but they provided a baptism of fire in different areas, in which he was also to excel: curriculum development and university administration. His diplomacy, courtesy and ability to master a 'brief' made him a key figure in the success of the new institution, and he was soon to have the same skills tested in a very different environment, when he returned to Ireland as professor of Modern History in University College Cork in 1968. The decision to return was taken partly for family reasons, his mother-in-law having recently died and his parents and father-in-law were elderly. However he also welcomed the opportunity to pursue his Irish history interests more fully, having written in Flinders a masterly reflective survey of the period since 1800, published in 1968 as *Ireland* and expanded and republished in 1977 as *Ireland: The Union and its Aftermath*. Still perhaps the best short introduction to the subject, its strength comes in part from the sense of distance and comparative perspective, which his years in England and Australia had given him.

His time in Cork was also comparatively brief, and, in terms of his work, not altogether happy. He found that the requirements of teaching and administration in a small department often made excessive demands, and allowed too little time for writing. Yet what was a burden to him proved a blessing for the college, then beginning a period of rapid expansion and modernization under a dynamic new president, M.D. MacCarthy. MacDonagh's recent experience and range of skills were often called upon, and in the words of a colleague, 'he played a significant, if characteristically unobtrusive and self-deprecatory role in college committee work in these formative years'. There were consolations also. He enjoyed his family and social life in Cobh, where he was especially active in the local tennis club, and where he and Carmel developed one of the most important friendships of their lives, with local GPs, Niall and Dolores Maher, to whom Oliver dedicated *The Inspector General*. He also developed an enduring enthusiasm for the particularly firebrand version of rugby associated with Munster. He did manage to get some writing done also: a short survey, *Emigration in the Victorian Age* (1973) and the innovative O'Donnell lecture, *The Nineteenth Century Novel and Irish Social History: Some Aspects* (1970). This pioneered an interdisciplinary approach to history and literature in Ireland, as well as opening up for MacDonagh himself a new area of research, culminating in his work on the novels of Jane Austen. MacDonagh's influence on the history school in Cork was also profound. Coming as the first professor with specific responsibility for *modern* history, he did much to break the traditional moulds in which the subject had been taught. In particular he gave a new prominence to British history, and had a lectureship in economic history established. The appointment of John O'Brien to this post also meant that courses were now taught in Australian history. MacDonagh himself was an inspired teacher of undergraduates, in his honours option encouraging original research on nineteenth-century parliamentary elections in Cork. He was also a generous and demanding research supervisor and extended the Peterhouse connection by 'sending' Ian d'Alton and the present writer there for further research in 1972.

MacDonagh went back to Australia the following year as W.K. Hancock professor of History at the Institute of Advanced Studies, Australian National University. Here, in the ideal conditions of the Research School of Social Sciences in Canberra, with 'wonderful historians and colleagues', notably Ken Inglis, Allen Martin and F.B. Smith, he was to blossom again as a prolific writer, with the variety, yet coherence of his range of interests coming more clearly into focus. In administrative history, while developing his new synthesis in *Early Victorian Government* he also added a key chapter expanding on the idea of Ireland as a laboratory of social control, first suggested in *Ireland*. His search for the patterns of pre-Victorian government growth also focussed on Ireland and resulted in *The Inspector General*. His early interest in Irish emigration now acquired the new focus of Irish-Australian immigration history, and he did much to professionalize this rapidly growing area of study, and to prevent its takeover for nostalgic or political purposes. His own incisive demographic essays, particularly the overviews published in 1986 and 1987, also did much to set the agenda for further work. As the main organizer of a series of conferences on Ireland and Irish-Australia he brought scholars from both countries together in an interdisciplinary forum. A remarkable feature of these gatherings was the mixed nature of the audiences they attracted – academics mingling with members of local history groups, many of them from rural areas. The fruits of these conferences are to be found in the published volumes of proceedings (three of them co-edited by

Oliver, mainly with Bill Mandle) and also in the enhanced profile and prestige of Irish-Australian history, and the stimulus given to research. Within his own department, too, MacDonagh did much to promote Irish history, attracting research students and visiting fellows from Ireland, as well as encouraging local interest.

As was the case during his period in Flinders, distance from Ireland again led MacDonagh to important reflective writing on its history. The revision and expansion of his 1968 study, *Ireland*, was also influenced by the tragic events that had occurred in Northern Ireland since that date. The background was even more important in the radical series of interpretative essays that followed, *States of Mind* (1983), although the highly original focus on topics like concepts of time and place, and on various cultural bases of politics, may also reflect the influence of the *Australians* project, with its commitment to innovative approaches to old questions. *States of Mind*, which won the Ewart-Biggs Memorial Prize in 1985, is still considered essential reading for all students of Irish history, and is a particularly enduring part of the MacDonagh legacy.

His next project was to pose a very different challenge. He had long been fascinated by Daniel O'Connell, sketching a new approach to his career in *Ireland*, undertaking the section on 'The Age of O'Connell' in the star-crossed *A New History of Ireland* (finally published, ironically, long after the appearance of his two-volume biography), and publishing occasional pieces on aspects of his career. MacDonagh was unusually well equipped to undertake a full-scale study of O'Connell, thanks to his mastery of both British and Irish society and politics in this period. He also identified strongly with this pragmatist negotiating between different cultures, the man of religious faith in an age of growing secularization, the Catholic leader who was also a sophisticated European liberal, the lawyer finding wide application for his legal skills, the family man anchoring an over-busy life in marriage and children.

He was both encouraged and enabled to embark on a biography by the appearance of Maurice O'Connell's magisterial eight-volume edition of O'Connell's correspondence. Added to these strengths of expertise, empathy and insight, MacDonagh developed a plain narrative style, which would make the work accessible to the general reader, and yet encompass the complexity demanded by the specialist. The resulting two-volume biography, *The Hereditary Bondsman: Daniel O'Connell 1775–1829* (1988), and *The Emancipist: Daniel O'Connell 1830–1847* (1989), offers a brilliant blending of private and public lives, and a major re-evaluation of a whole epoch, as well as of its dominant political figure. It is dense and challenging, yet reads easily and communicates the author's sense of excitement and involvement – a triumphant stylistic achievement as well as a defining work of scholarship.

This flood of publications may reinforce the image of a pampered member of a research institute, indulging in the luxury of focussing only on his own work. The research environment and freedom from routine teaching were of enormous help to MacDonagh, but his career at ANU also reflected wider concerns, and a generous commitment of time and energy to the academic community. Besides being an active and often innovative head of department for various periods, he took a creative role in faculty business and was in the higher reaches of the ANU administration. He became, in the words of a colleague, 'one of the most trusted people on the campus', a man with 'no reputation as a power-broker', but a respected senior figure, 'legally informed and precise, farsighted on what Government is likely to get up to, and humane in handling personal problems'. These skills were particularly useful in his contribution to key committees dealing with study leave and senior appointments and promotions. They were also evident, and perhaps even critical in the *Australians* project. According to his own 'personal retrospect' on the making of this great cooperative effort, he conceived the idea of a multi-volume history on first becoming head of 'the only "national" department in Australia, and the only department primarily devoted to research', as their contribution to the bicentenary of European settlement, then twelve years away. Greatly helping to shape the initial 'back-of-envelope scribble', and the policy decisions that ensured ultimate success was MacDonagh's own experience – positive and negative – of the ambitious *New History of Ireland* project, planned several years earlier, but only recently completed.

Oliver's account of his contribution to *Australians* was characteristically modest, stressing instead the importance of Ken Inglis's proposal of the 'slice' approach to the narrative volumes (i.e. examining a cross section of all aspects of Australian life at fifty-year intervals, rather than attempting an inclusive chronological account, 'a truly revolutionary device') and the decision to devolve responsibility for different volumes to groups based in universities and cities throughout the country – both features combining to produce a uniquely wide-ranging and collaborative attempt at 'history from below', expressing the life experiences of ordinary Australians as well as of the headline makers. Ultimate organizational and business decisions were taken by the management committee, which he chaired from first to last – having failed, as he put it, to carry the point of the minute he composed after the initial meeting: 'It was accepted that the author of these notes was, in effect, the pin in the grenade, to be discarded shortly before explosion.' It was a characteristic MacDonagh metaphor, except in missing its mark through a combination of modesty and wishful thinking! Having conceived the idea and devised the basic structures, he also proved prepared to see it through, and his diplomatic, administrative and legal skills were fully stretched in the protracted negotiations with publishers, funding agencies, editors, convenors and contributors.

The main debts owed to the *New History of Ireland* project were the reference volumes (in which, he believed, 'deep foundations have been laid for Australian historiography in general'), the idea of seminars for contributors to individual volumes, and the tough-minded commitment to replacing contributors, however eminent, who failed to deliver on time, and to adhere rigorously to the timetable for each stage. During this long process, colleagues were sometimes surprised at the strength of Oliver's firmness and resolve. In the words of one historian, 'He can be very tough in his courteous way.' The final product more than repaid the effort of all involved – five volumes of narrative and five of reference.

They stand as a monument to Australian scholarship and a challenge to historians elsewhere. Not the least remarkable feature of the project was the willingness of the older generation involved, exemplified in MacDonagh himself, to leave the main part of the writing to younger colleagues, and to accept radical ideas of approach and collaborative work from them. One of the first decisions of the management committee was to exclude all scholars over fifty-five years of age as contributors. This rather bizarre and arbitrary decision almost certainly excluded some whose scholarly contributions would have enhanced the project. Those so excluded who, like Oliver, continued to work on the organizational side, exhibited a self-effacement that was almost heroic, and is certainly rare. The commitment not only to recording but to reaching the lives of ordinary people through the systematic use of accessible language and a wide range of illustrations is another significant feature of the project, which historians in general might try to emulate. It was, above all, an immense collaborative effort, but in the words of a senior colleague involved, Oliver's 'managerial and scholarly contribution to the success of the series was immense'.

The same could be said of the roles that Oliver took on after his retirement from ANU – two years as executive director of The Academy of the Social Sciences in Australia, followed by two more as foundation professor at the Australian Catholic University, reprising his role at Flinders forty years earlier. Yet, he also found time to write, focussing especially on a long-cherished project, a study of the novels of Jane Austen. He began this work in a manner that typified his intellectual curiosity and eclecticism. Confined to bed by back trouble (a recurring condition that often made writing physically painful) he sought distraction by mapping the social geography of Austen's Chawton from her letters, and then comparing it with the fictional world of Highbury in *Emma*. The result was an article in *Historical Studies* in 1978, followed by a study of the church in *Mansfield Park*, and of the Regency era in the fragment *Sanditon*, both in 1987. The book, published in 1991 as *Jane Austen: Real and Imagined Worlds*, added to these a series of essays on the other novels, each on a specific theme, and each combining the well-honed skills of the social and economic historian with sensitive and original readings of well-loved texts. Here again can be seen his enduring concern with style.

In the original version of this introduction, written for his 1990 *Festschrift*, I speculated that perhaps he might combine his scholar's knowledge with boyhood memory to recreate the rural Ireland he knew in the 1920s and 1930s – or reflect on student life in Dublin during World War II – or the ambience of post-war Cambridge. The debilitating illnesses of his final years – borne with fortitude and humour – explain why he only wrote on his childhood, but it was also a matter of choice and temperament. As he told Roy Foster – doubtless reflecting the bruising response to his *Historical Journal* article – 'I've always disliked controversy in history.' He once described his life to me as 'unexceptional', but clearly it was not, and it was lived through times of enormous change, in a number of very different countries, and in a profession that has altered almost beyond recognition. He made no great claims for these 'little wisps of things', as he called his childhood memoirs in a letter to me, which also explained why – health aside – he chose the particular form. 'I've always been drawn (artistically too) to the essay type of book ... I like the sense of circling the wagons, shooting arrows from different directions, rather than a bull-headed direct assault.'

Those privileged to have known him will remember the man, unfailingly kind, generous, supportive and truly unassuming, a man of great charm, warmth and humour, of strong convictions and infectious enthusiasms, of great erudition and endless curiosity. While much missed by those who loved and admired him, he will live on through his writing. He was clear that 'history writing' was a 'literary craft', and he was conscious in every book he wrote, particularly as he got older, that each presented literary and stylistic challenges as well as those of evidence and interpretation. What he wrote of Newman as historian could also be applied to himself:

> Style in history is commonly regarded as an ornament or decoration; it may even be denigrated as showiness or affectation. Nothing can be further from the truth, and especially so in the case of Newman. With him, style is the literary outpouring, the outward and visible sign, of his prodigious mental energy and power ...
>
> He was a master of style, description and characterization. But he proved to be an *anima naturalitur historica*, into the bargain. The supreme quality in a historian is, I suppose, the capacity to discern the decisive moments or stretches of change, as well as its causes ...
>
> [Finally] there is the Fall and its consequent tangle of cross-purposes to be considered. The historian gripped by such a teaching has been handed a clue to the fundamental dualism of his enterprise. For history writing at its highest – so it seems to me – proceeds at two levels, that of actual happening and that of unrealized potentiality. Historical judgment, even historical evaluation, depends on the measurement, normally the silent or tacit measurement, of the first against the yardstick of the second. Moreover, a thorough grasp of what Newman calls the 'heart-piercing, reason-bewildering fact' that 'the human race is implicated in some terrible aboriginal tragedy' – this should furnish the

> breadth of mind and depth of sympathy of which our calling stands so much in need. Such, at any rate, is my own particular concept of the duty which we owe the dead – dead institutions, dead ideas and dead cultures no less than the faithful and unfaithful departed.

It was a duty he discharged with passion as well as style.

He began this essay on Newman by responding to the idea of the *Festschrift* in which it was to be included with 'a sort of embarrassed disbelief'. In explaining why he felt that he was 'almost the last historian who should be marked out for [such] an honour', he focussed especially on the fact that he had written so many different kinds of history. He had 'a horrid vision' of himself 'as a sort of pinchbeck *ultimas Romanorum*, a last general practitioner among consultants, a chance survivor from a vanquished world'. In an era of ever-narrower specialization, and of academic historians writing mainly in esoteric publications for one another, MacDonagh's wide-ranging curiosity, and willingness to experiment and engage with different audiences, without compromising his integrity, offer a challenge and a model.

Acknowledgments

The editor is grateful to the family of the late Oliver MacDonagh for their support and encouragement, especially his widow, Carmel; son, Oliver; sister-in-law, Honor McSweeney and her son, Paul. Oliver's friend, Niall Meagher, gave valuable advice and shared Oliver's letters to him. Catherine O'Brien's interest and encouragement was also important.

At The Lilliput Press, Antony Farrell was a supportive and helpful publisher, and it was a particular pleasure to work with editor, Fiona Dunne, who did not let filial respect get in the way of academic rigour. Siobán Devlin was an excellent proofreader, and Helen Litton provided the index.

It is also a pleasure to acknowledge a grant-in-aid of publication from the National University of Ireland, whose support for academic publishing is exemplary.

I
MEMOIR

EDITORIAL NOTE

What follows is the largely unpublished text of the memoir of his childhood that Oliver MacDonagh wrote in his final years, to which I have added his recollections of an important aspect of his undergraduate experience in UCD, and a series of reflections on his career as a writer, given in interviews, in an unpublished address, and in some of his published work. I also include two examples of his academic writing that throw particular light on his literary style. His introduction to his study of the late-eighteenth-century reformer, Sir Jeremiah Fitzpatrick, reveals much of his own approach to history writing, and of what he admired in such unsung heroes. His most important literary exemplar was Newman, and his paper on the Apologia pro Vita Sua, *reproduced here, reveals much of his own approach to historical research and to the importance of developing a literary style to match the subject matter. As the focus here is on MacDonagh as a writer, these examples of his academic work are reproduced without the references that accompanied them originally.*

Clouds of Glory: Memoirs of Childhood

Preface

My boyhood coincided, more or less, with the 1930s; I was just sixteen years old when war broke out in 1939. These essays (or fragments or pieces – call them what one will) are generally contained within the decade's boundaries. But I have not kept to these slavishly. Whenever it seemed sensible to go backwards or forwards a little in time, I have freely done so.

Although this is not an autobiography, even a truncated one, all the essays are autobiographical in nature. What I have written is true, though not of course the whole truth – whatever is? Exactitude, however, was not always possible. For instance, most of the dialogue reported is 'to the best of my recollection', rather than what I could testify to, in a court of law, as unswervingly accurate. At the same time, there are numerous recollected phrases which I would swear to – and when it comes to words and speech, as against faces and actions, I lay claim to a first-rate memory.

As the work is neither chronologically arranged nor aiming at comprehensiveness, it is better, I suppose, if I introduce the principal location and my immediate family before embarking at all on my narrations.

I spent almost all the 1930s in a small town, Roscommon, in the west of Ireland. It was a very small town, with a population of just under two thousand persons. It was also a very Catholic town. There were only four Protestants that I knew of – apart from the little floating world of Bank of Ireland Protestants – among its inhabitants. Yet it possessed a moderately sized Church of Ireland church (any other denomination would have called it a chapel) as well as a dilapidated Masonic lodge. Both must have been filled with ghosts; there can have been few others.

Roscommon had had, and even still had, some claims to distinction. It could boast the extensive remains of a Norman castle; some ruins of a medieval abbey (in which lay the tomb of the last King of Connacht, Rory O'Connor); an enormous but near-deserted jail-cum-barracks; a standard Georgian-type courthouse; a grey workhouse; a grey hospital and the central administration of the county. It enjoyed, therefore, a far from negligible past. As to the present, it may have been one of the smallest county towns in Western Europe, but county town (with all the accompanying appurtenances) it was, nonetheless.

The people could also take pride in the large, handsome, limestone Catholic church, with remarkable mosaics about the apse, which tended to their spiritual needs. Three banks, two commercial hotels, a saddler, a forge, a petrol station, numerous pubs and every sort of shop – how on earth did they all survive? – served them materially. The saddler's simply called itself 'Saddler', the forge had no need to advertise; but the grandiose Victorian titles for businesses were often used. The chemist's was called 'Medical Hall'; the bookmakers were 'Turf Accountants'; the butchers were generally 'Victuallers'; and each 'Drapery' was a 'Haberdashery' as well. All we lacked was 'Cigar Divan' for the tobacconist.

Although still only in his thirties, my father was manager of one of the banks, the National, and we lived over the office in what was effectively a commodious, five-bedroom house with an acre-large garden. My mother too had been (to use their own terminology) a bank official; and they had met in Limerick in 1921 or 1922. My father was then twenty-eight or twenty-nine, my mother six years younger. He was already amazingly advanced professionally for his age and epoch, being accountant (or second-in-command) in a major office; she was professionally lowly, but socially to be envied at the time, as a 'lady junior'. Her bank, the Bank of Ireland, was the doyen of the establishment in Limerick as well as all other places; his the National Bank, was probably the most plebian of all, although it was also true that gradations in status between the banks were, even at that time, pretty minute – perhaps observed, or at any rate valued, only by the staffs themselves.

My parents' first encounter, as it filtered down to us children when my mother fondly reminisced, was at once unromantic and romantic. She was engaged in the humble duty of 'Exchanges' – delivering to other banks cheques drawn upon them which had ended up at the Bank of Ireland and collecting from the other banks cheques drawn upon the Bank of Ireland in return – when she caught my father's eye farther up the counter. The dark and lovely girl (as we supposed her to be, and indeed she must have been) was then summoned to the great man's grille, and the two fell deeper and deeper into whispered conversation until at last they self-consciously sprang apart with a hastily agreed assignation for coffee at Kidd's Cafe. The rest (in the phrase that people set afloat fifty or sixty years later) was history. At any rate, we children were told no more.

Limerick was their, and my, first home, then Donegal. I was only six, and my sister, Pat, only four, when we moved again, to Roscommon, so that my memory of these early places (let alone my sister's) is very sketchy. Of course, my brother Donagh, who was seven years younger than I, had no knowledge of them at all.

Meanwhile, soon after we had moved to Roscommon, we were joined by my father's sister Florence (known to us children, for some reason long forgotten, as Aunt Fluff), who had just separated from her husband. She was accompanied by her, and my father's, nephew, Tony. He had been living with her in England since his mother died. Tony was two years older than I, a role model whom I wished in vain that I could emulate, especially in sport and popularity.

This is all one needs to know, I think, to follow the essays from the start. Everything else should reveal itself, in its proper place and order, as one goes along.

I have ended every preface that I have ever written with words of gratitude for my wife's care and love; and there is no reason why my last book should be any different from my first in this regard.

Oliver (front right) with his parents, Loretto and Michael, sister, Pat, and brother, Donagh

My Mother's Kitchen

My mother's kitchen, with two large windows, west and south, and a huge lagged boiler in one corner, was always enticingly bright and warm. She herself, though by no means a regular occupant, was its most powerful magnet. She was a superb *manufacturing* housewife. Dusting, shining and washing-up were great bores to her, but she was forever knitting, dress-making, smocking, crocheting, even upholstering in a slapdash way. It was, however, the kitchen that was truly her element; she was a cooking genius.

Of course, she was helped by having a big vegetable and fruit garden, well-tended by the bank porter whose official duties seem to have been few and – even more important – far between. He polished the brass knobs and opened the bank door, and did a quick round of the town with letters morning and afternoon but otherwise dug away or leant on his spade as the spirit moved him. What treasures he produced! I pass over all the dreary things I heartily disliked and struggled to evade, cabbage, cauliflower, parsnips, turnips and beetroot being my chief aversions. But summer brought lettuce, tomatoes, radishes, onions, new potatoes and similar delights. All these were 'pulled' just before they were washed for cooking; so too were mint and horseradish and other sauce-sources: in fact, the local hotel sent up respectfully for our fresh horseradish from time to time.

But fruit was our garden glory: pears (rather small and hard, I fear, but useful for gang fighting), apples (eating, cooking and crab, each of several varieties), red, white and blackcurrants, gooseberries, raspberries, loganberries, strawberries (if one beat the birds to it) and rhubarb. Blackberries were gathered from the hedges, on country roads, and mushrooms from the fields, in season. We bought nothing that could be grown in the west of Ireland, except for sacked potatoes to carry us through from January to June or July. Our eggs too were usually our own, and our fierily salted butter straight from a farmwife's dairy. Meat and bacon were 'prime' in every sense, never having undergone refrigeration; and our bought chickens arrived newly dead, always in pairs (we occasionally killed our own, a grisly process).

As a consequence, my mother had such materials for cooking as only, I suppose, the outrageously rich could know today. I should say 'simple materials' for it was all straightforward Western European produce. This matched my mother's cooking, which was simple and straightforward supreme. When we had roast chicken, for example – always a pair of chickens, by the way, and truly chickens for anything older went for boiling – she made her own stuffing and bread sauce from separate vintages of stale bread. Roast pork was accompanied by freshly-peeled and cored apples, just plucked from tree or storage shelf, and reduced to a silky cream – it would be an impertinence to call it sauce. Newly-gathered mint and home-made vinegar (and sugar) went with lamb, newly-gathered and chopped horseradish roots set off the roast beef and golden Roscommon – I cannot call it merely Yorkshire – pudding.

All these were managed and moulded with casual artistry. My mother did not weigh or measure things very much or seemingly pay a great deal of attention to the clock. She seemed to know instinctively the right quantities to use and the exact time to remove the various dishes from hob or oven. The apogee of this daily marvel was her cake and dessert making. Usually squinting through cigarette smoke, she flung sugar, butter and all the rest with apparent carelessness into her bowls, rolled sponges around brown paper, kneaded almond paste, spread hot raspberry jam (her own) on Russian Layer strips or filled her syringe with palely coloured icings. Yet somehow nothing was ever burnt or underdone or anything less than ambrosial in the end. Only her pastry excelled her cakes. 'It is the touch,' she used to say complacently, 'pastry comes from the hands'; and indeed power over the flour and milk and margarine flowed from hers, as her rolling pin passed backwards and forwards in just the right soft strength.

She spent her time with a princely extravagance. Chocolate éclairs meant the laborious preparation of the delicate cases, their cooking to the perfect medium of crispness and flexibility, the whipping and sugaring of cream almost warm from the dairy and the production of a chocolate icing soft yet quick-hardening enough for one sure bold stroke to lay a gleaming drip-less stripe along the top. Yet it needed only two or three great bites to obliterate one of these marvellous creations. Even at the time, I felt vaguely guilty at the gross disproportion between the craft and effort needed and the ultimate result.

Of course, everything was then labour-intensive, even the large coal-fired range. We always had a maid in those days, but there was still a lot for my mother to do, although she could – and did – more or less choose her own labour. There was also a need for help from us children. In the best tradition, though not quite in the usual way, this was largely seasonal. During the summer we were occasionally assigned to 'lift' potatoes, pick currants, raspberries and loganberries, climb apple and pear trees and pluck the fruit for the baskets and tin cans hanging on the branches, pull turnips and parsnips, clip the little box hedges around the vegetable patches, gather windfalls for the pigs' bucket, mow the lawn, go afield in search of mushrooms or gather blackberries in the country lanes. Actually, these duties might stretch from May to October but they were far from regular – depending as they did on both the immediacy of the need and (to some extent) the willingness of the conscript.

For much of this was, or soon became, tedious toil, to be evaded so far as possible. It was fun at first to climb apple trees; and testing one's weight on branches could seem at first a daring game. But with no end to the apples to be plucked the job soon palled. There was no fun in picking tiny currants. At the beginning it was quite pleasant to smell the dry and the damp earth, and the neighbouring mint, rhubarb and potato stalks – a cocktail of outdoor odours – at almost face level. This, however, palled even more quickly than apple-plucking: it seemed to take hours to fill a basin, and nothing ever stuck more obstinately to their bushes than these tiny, slippery balls that yielded so little fruit for the immensity of labour.

There was however one yearly chore which was never grudged – gathering the crab apples from branch or ground each September for making the jars of dark-pink unclouded jelly. The ritual of boilings in great aluminium pans, mashings, strainings through thick gauze fastened to the upturned legs of backless old kitchen chairs, watching the drips for the vital moment when there was enough extract to fill a jar – in fact, the whole procedure of turning the ghastly greyish mess of apple pulp into the most delicately flavoured, bitter-sweet and tenderest of all preserves was a – perhaps the – highlight of the kitchen year.

The red letter of my mother's cooking was not any particular meal or dish but one glorious summer in which she tried to pass on her skills to another. In 1937 or 1938 a missionary order transferred one of its bases from Doorn, close to the increasingly dangerous German–Dutch border, to a large country house, dignified as 'Castle', a few miles from our town. My mother put on one of her rare grand lunches to welcome the superior and vice-superior. I can't remember what exactly was eaten, but it was certainly days in preparation and every course represented the zenith of my mother's art. In the glow of stately, halting compliments from the German superior, my mother volunteered to help set up the new kitchen in the Castle: poor though their English still was, the priests had made it clear that their meals had been rough, and not particularly ready, since they had come to Ireland.

So began one of the excitements of her life. Once a week my father drove her over to the Castle – on one of her early driving lessons, as a girl, she had hit a cow and lost her nerve for good. The big kitchen was in charge of (I think that this was his name) Brother Schmidt. Merry, round and rubicund, surrounded by gleaming aluminium, steel and copper, he looked every inch a cook, as Hollywood then typecast cooks. But appearances were all. According to my mother, he could scarcely boil an egg. At any rate, the food of the west of Ireland was beyond him. So began her mission to turn Brother Schmidt into a Soyer.

He spoke no English, she spoke no German; at best they had a useful word or two in French in common. I gather – for I only accompanied her once or twice towards the end – that the first sessions were mostly pantomime. Each dish was cooked twice, first, with uncharacteristic slowness and methodicalness by her, and then repeated, with many halts and re-demonstrations, by him. They must have eaten full if not always well in the Castle those nights. Meanwhile, Brother had been adding new cooking words in English (phonetic, I suppose) to his little notebook as the lesson zig-zagged forward. Originally, my mother took with her great boxes of ingredients, but gradually Brother's list of words grew sufficiently for him to do most of his own ordering, except for meat for which, she held, the experienced eye, touch and scepticism about the butcher's assertions were perquisites in securing decent quality.

My mother returned exhilarated from each weekly visit. Of course, she said or implied, Brother would never really make a cook. His huge puffed hands would never acquire the touch for sifting or mixing or rolling or spreading. But he was exact, he was obedient, he never needed to be told twice; and as they developed between them a sufficient sort of kitchen German-English, the range of attempted dishes grew like wildfire.

Late in the course, I happened to be with my mother one afternoon when baked apples, apple tart and doubtless other more sophisticated apple sweets were on the programme. As everything was being laid on the big, scrubbed near-white table, she called for 'cloves' and, with Brother looking mystified, she sketched one (vastly magnified) in the air. He pulled out a pad, evidently long used in their communications, and drew, quite recognizably, a parsnip. After her wild head shakings, he tried again. This time it looked like an ice-cream cone, and he made his meaning certain by raising the paper to be licked by an undulating tongue. With more head-shakings, she now seized a loaf of bread and made imaginary small jabs across the top crust, mimicking cloves stuck into the pie pastry. Brother pulled out a skewer – 'nos' again, followed by her lifting up a great green cooking apple to jab at imaginarily in the same way. At last, an 'Ah' from Brother, and he scuttled off to rummage in a cupboard and produce triumphantly a small paper bag from which he drew a handful of cloves.

'Something – nelke,' said he; 'Nickel,' she answered; 'Nelke,' he corrected; 'Clove,' said my mother; 'Cloof,' he responded; 'Clove,' she repeated – very distinctly the second time. The notebook was duly produced and entered, and then they smiled serenely at one another, and set down to work. I suppose that this was typical of the three-legged fashion in which the whole course of instruction advanced.

I remember it as one of my mother's happy times. She felt that she was passing on 'the achieve of, the mastery of the thing', as well as seeing to it that a little group of helpless, bewildered, exiled men would end up being decently fed. She must have remembered it as very happy, too. On one of my last visits to her in hospital, the talk drifted onto the old days and the priests and brothers and the Castle, and when out of the blue she said, 'Mit nickel,' she laughed aloud with childish pleasure despite all her pain.

My Father's Bank

Even so staid an occupation as banking had its own language. Every office was a 'branch'. Every branch had its own number of 'hands'. Each 'staff' was headed by a 'manager' or 'agent', his chief assistant being an 'accountant', with the next in line the 'teller' or 'cashier', and the tail known as various sorts of 'clerk'. When the 'profession' wished to be formal or particularly dignified, it called itself, collectively, 'officials'. It was a very Victorian type of occupation, and not least in its concepts of honour and respectability.

After my father died, I met, either at his funeral or in the months soon after, four or five people who had 'served' under him as manager. Extraordinarily, each paid an identical tribute, though of course in slightly different phrases: 'He was a real gentleman,' 'He was the finest gentleman I ever met,' 'A gentleman to everyone in the office – and outside too, rich or poor.' I truly think that this expressed the *beau ideal* of the occupation at that time. Of course, no one thought of bank clerks as gentleman in the sense that the old Ascendancy and its satellites had been gentlemen. They meant that the 'profession' aspired to courtesy, modesty, decency, and similar humdrum but very comfortable virtues. As I remember them, his various staffs did not fall far short of their self-appointed mark. If this were really so, then he himself was certainly *primus inter pares*. Had he heard the posthumous accolades, he would have smiled deprecatingly, and demurred politely; but there would have been pride and a sense of fulfilment in his heart.

His five-handed office in Roscommon was quite a modern building, four-square, grey and ugly on the exterior, but bright, airy, cheerful and convenient within. All the door handles, and the openwork screens at which the public 'dealt', were of course of well-polished brass; the counters and cubicles were fashioned from a rich, dark mahogany, and the main floor laid out in large diagonal black and white marble squares. This was more or less mandatory bank decor in the 1930s. Some old-fashioned high leather-cushioned stools for clerks had survived and there was even an antique screw letter press gathering dust in a small back room. I seem to remember its still being used when I was very small – and fiendishly difficult it must have been to handle the heavily inked pad and flimsy, almost transparent copying paper. The results, in patchy virulent violet, could scarcely have been worth the trouble. Even the ancient practice of laborious transcription of letters and reports was surely preferable for the unfortunate clerk in charge. But doubtless Progress, in the shape of the screw copier, had been hailed and crowned at some stage in the mid-nineteenth century.

Quite soon after we arrived at the Roscommon branch – a big promotion for my father at the age of thirty-eight – my mother began to type his correspondence on a massive Underwood machine, which he had bought somewhere or other, secondhand. The office had not yet been provided with a 'lady-clerk' to do the typing work so that she was, in effect, an unpaid worker for the Bank. There were endless problems. She had often to stand by in the afternoon to hammer out the day's correspondence – or such of it, at any rate, as was deemed too important to be handwritten. She could never appear in the office itself and had to work upstairs, which meant endless journeys for my father up and down.

Her labours were meant to be secret: Bank confidentiality, if nothing else, should have forbidden them. It must however have been a very open secret in the office, if not further afield. Boxes of headed notepaper and carbon and copying paper were regularly carried up. Indeed, the accountant was occasionally tactless enough to reveal his thorough familiarity with what was going on. When he said things like, 'Perhaps there would be time for Mrs MacDonagh to redo the last paragraph,' my parents would anxiously deprecate the lapse later on. But what more could they do? Once they were thrown into scarcely bearable embarrassment. A visiting inspector, as he passed through the playroom where my mother typed, and caught sight of the decorously covered machine on a side table, jocularly remarked, 'So this is the engine room of the branch.' For days there was no end to the muttered discussions of what the inspector's 'joke' implied and portended.

Perhaps it was this which led on, though much later, to the Board's inquiry as to whether my father now needed a lady-clerk. Again, there were long, worried, marital confabulations. I find it hard to believe that my mother was really opposed to what would so obviously have been in her interest. But perhaps she was. Perhaps by now the interweaving of work had become an integral part of my parents' relationship. At any rate, the threat from Head Office was successfully beaten off or at least evaded for the time being.

At this stage, my mother acted as my father's constant counsellor, or at least sounding board. When he rose later to manage a big city branch, matters were much too large and complicated to be shared; but in Roscommon much of the business was well within her scope, especially as she knew, from having typed them, the contents of the main letters to the Board. Not that she was anything of a Mrs Proudie – no woman ever less so, in fact. Generally, it was the question of reassurance. 'Yes, dear' and 'You were perfectly right, dear' were the murmurs we usually overheard, as my parents slowly paced the garden, my father anxiously urging, my mother – I often suspected – struggling to suppress a yawn.

Occasionally, she had to undergo the trial of 'checking the tots'. This consisted of adding up immense columns of figures in pounds, shillings and pence. Why my father had to count, and recount, them in the first place was then, and still remains, a mystery. At any rate, to my mother was assigned the final tally. Everyone, except my father, seemed to know that she often skipped her dreary task and after various staged mumblings to herself and ostentatious movements of her pencil, pronounced all my father's totals to be correct. One winter evening, she burst in upon Fluff and us children in the kitchen, with her hand stuffed in her mouth, like a schoolgirl's, to suppress her laughter. 'The Boss', she told Fluff, 'has caught me out. He'd made a mistake twice over himself, and I went and ticked it without looking.' She and Fluff tried to appear appalled. Hypocritically, they deplored the mischance, as if they were terror-stricken. We all knew that really they thought it a tremendous joke.

Perhaps it was a faint, even if accidental, blow against masculine self-importance. Their private nickname for my father, 'The Boss', could not have been seriously meant; I have never known a less authoritarian or conceited man. But the very role of paterfamilias which had been thrust upon him invited a little feminine nose-tweaking when it could be safely done. In the end, whether from an extreme of nobility or from great naiveté, my father did not take the obvious precautionary step of concealing his own totals until my mother had provided hers. Instead, they went on exactly as before. Possibly, the whole business was part-charade, part the repeated sealing of a marriage.

Bank work must have been very tedious, especially in the lower ranks. But to me there was a certain glamour in the order, dignity and (one might even say) majesty of our office. I felt this especially when, now and then, I happened to enter it at night. If the moon was up, the place was patterned in silver and shadow. Even on dark nights, the street lamps reproduced this in a dimmer form; and the silence was equally impressive. I must have been a most romantic child. How many others would have felt in the combination of austerity and heavy opulence of a country bank something to stir the blood?

All the same, to grow up in a Bank house in a small place in the 1930s was to feel oneself half an alien. Nearly everyone else in the town seemed to have roots that went impenetrably deep. Even doctors and county agricultural inspectors, incomers though they might be, were there for life. As it happened, my family was comparatively lucky, and I perhaps most of all. Our stay at Roscommon lasted a full ten years and this spanned almost all my time of growing up. It also meant that my parents could develop fair degrees of friendship with some of the local families, and even ties of intimacy with one or two. To this they were all the more inclined because the other bank managers in the town not only came and went more rapidly but were also, for one reason or another, uncongenial people. One was miserly, another even suspected of that most heinous and disgraceful of bank-managerly offences, 'touting for business'.

Nonetheless, although we were, in our own estimation, quite well established civicly by 1940, to the natives we remained – and in logic had to remain – mere temporary abiders. I remember, as if it had come upon them only yesterday my parents' pain at overhearing bank clerks described as birds of passage. They only whispered the words to one another; they were too humiliating to be declared out loud. Nonetheless, they were true. Long though our stay in Roscommon turned out to be, there had always hung over us the threat (or hope, as it might be from time to time and person to person) of being transported elsewhere at a few weeks' notice.

Branch banks in rural Ireland are rarely if ever thought of as engines of social change, but so they had been in the later nineteenth century, and something of this effect lingered on into the 1930s. Most of the clerks came from the cities or large towns, most were firmly middle class in 'background'; many had been to 'good' boarding schools, many were Protestants – four or five times as many as would have been proportionate to the population as a whole. Although debarred officially from politics and practically from any public role, they thrived in tennis and golf and rugby clubs and as hon. treasurers of committees; and the managers at least were assiduous funeral attenders: my father's bowler was known domestically as his funeral hat, and indeed he never wore it otherwise. Thus, there was a dash of the exotic, a sense of living a larger than local life, about the Bank, which offset, to some extent, the lack of true native ties.

One tangible manifestation of the foreign element was the arrival, every three months or so, of a great wooden crate, bound with strips of tin, with large black stencilling on the sides: 'Chas Chambers, Stationers, Dublin'. Never was cargo more warmly welcomed by cultists than Chas Chambers's treasures by us children. When Tom, the porter, had snapped the metal bands and prised off the timbers of the lid, a magical hoard lay below us – blue ink, black ink, red ink, green ink, cartons of paper of all sizes, each with a sample of its kind pasted on the top, rulers (never, alas, of the gleaming ebony tubular sort usually employed in the office), bottles of gum, masking tape, blotters, pencils, pens with cases of variously gauged steel nibs, sealing wax – mostly pillar-box red but also black and woodland-green – cash books, well-wet ink pads in flat tins, reams of foolscap, and heaven knows what else.

We children – or at any rate this particular child – fell upon these spoils as soon as the chance arose, and made away with a due percentage of the items especially fancied. My own passions were for foolscap, green ink and ultra-fine steel nibs – a psychologist would doubtless have some fun explaining this melange. I was strangely free of any sense of guilt in counting off my self-allotted share. I suppose that I regarded it as a sort of *seigneur*'s levy.

I can't remember much about the Bank's supposed *raison d'être* (and source of profit), the 'customers'. These formed a mysterious and vaguely minatory background to our lives as children. We were meant never to listen when account-holders, especially if they were townspeople, were being discussed; and it was under the threat of utter family ruin that we were forbidden to speak abroad of any whispered confidences about them that we might possibly have overheard. In fact, we could not be unaware that various of the shopkeepers were Bank-attached, as these owned or ran the shops my mother 'dealt with' as a matter of course – whenever she could choose between two or more suppliers. It was also easy to guess attachment from the handful of other shops which followed the amiable if dubious practice of sending in small 'presents' at Christmas – a bottle of sherry (invariably Domecq's 'A Winter's Tale') or a box of Assorted Biscuits or a leg of ham or iced cake or something of the sort. This led to annual agonizing and debates as to whether the donors would be mortally offended (and perhaps even worse, remove their accounts) should the gifts be rejected or returned. In the end, however, it always turned out that – like Catherine the Great of Russia at the Partition of Poland – we wept, but we took.

If I knew comparatively little about our town customers, I knew even less about the farmers and proto-farmers and farmers' widows and cousins and uncles and aunts who made up the great majority of our clientele. The one salient fact about all of them, on their mostly miserable holdings in the desperate 1930s, seemed to be their struggle to survive. But there was one poor young farmer whom I remember clearly and particularly. I can even (I think) recall his name, Michael Cummins. He was a special pet of my father's, who much approved the dogged honesty with which he repaid that (horror of horrors), a Past Due Bill, for £15, at the rate of £2.10.0 every quarter. In earnest of his appreciation, my father supplied him with old *Irish Independents*; and I often walked out to him with these, with my friend Hal, on Saturday afternoons.

One day we cut across an unfamiliar stretch of bogland which seemed to offer a shortcut. We had scarcely turned in there from the boreen when a shout of anger at our backs lifted us almost off our feet. A hard-looking man with a shotgun roared, 'I know what you little curs are up to, lighting fires with those papers and setting the woods over there burning.' In vain we did try to explain our errand of mercy. He was Lord Crofton's steward, he said, and would march us both before him to the police barracks. Every so often he shook the gun menacingly, and we trembled and quavered.

Perhaps the thought of the long trudge to the barracks eventually dissuaded him. Perhaps he merely meant to terrify us out of a career as arsonists. At any rate, he let us go at last with fierce parting imprecations and assurances that he would use his gun unhesitatingly next time. We raced home, white-faced, without one single backward look. The poor young farmer did without his *Independent*s that Saturday.

In fact he must have cleared his Past Due Bill soon afterwards for I can remember only a few later Saturday excursions by Hal and me. The stoppage of the supply of *Independent*s was, presumably, the curious mark of his emancipation from his bondage to the Bank. But he remained our White-Headed Boy among the farmer-customers. One day, about a year later, my father came up to lunch from the office, smiling and rubbing his palms together, as he was wont to do when particularly pleased.

'Michael Cummins has been in to see me this morning and he tells me that he's getting married next month.'

'I suppose that means a new loan,' said my mother in (for her) rather caustic tones.

My father looked across at my sister and me, and then back to her, repressively. 'The girl does have a bit of money, I believe,' he replied – or, rather, thus evaded replying – to the implicit question before unlicensed ears. 'Anyhow, I think perhaps we ought to give him a wedding present.'

'A present to Michael Cummins?' My mother sounded amazed. But the thought of buying something – anything – always cheered her up, so she said no more about it, and instead began to interrogate my father about the age, looks, parentage and character of the bride-to-be. He however had no information to provide on these particular topics.

I can't remember – if I ever knew – what present was chosen for our Admirable Crichton. Appropriate selection was not my mother's forte. I would guess that Michael received the usual glass salad bowl with a silver rim, or something equally glittery and unsuitable. But the gift did not need to be intrinsically fitting to be remarkable. It was strange enough that it should have been given at all. That the Bank, in the form of its local suzerain, my father, should make a grossly impoverished customer a present – whoever heard of such an extraordinary thing?

Altar Ego

The altar boys were a tough corps to join at the age of seven. In my generation, the seniors enforced a mild form of hazing on the innocent recruits. My own initiation rites began with an assurance that if I stood on a pile of magazines (devoted mostly to the bloody conduct and consequences of Chicago gang killings), I could stick a wire into the electric socket in the servers' sacristy with impunity. I made the highest jump of my life, and yelled the loudest yell of shock, when I acted blindly on this assurance. Not many initiates were as credulous as I. On the other hand, unlike some, I did not take the dare to raid the priests' sacristry for a swig of altar wine. Nor would I take the dare to respond 'Make tay for us' instead of 'Pray for us' when the Litany of Our Lady was being recited in the church at Benediction. Even at the age of seven, I felt reluctant to dice with sacrilege.

There were no dire consequences for 'chickening out' except of course the very accusation itself. The big boys never laid a hand upon the smaller; the bullying, such as it was, was entirely psychological; and the fisticuffs were confined to boys of more or less equal age. Challenges to fight were, however, regularly issued after Evening Devotions on winter nights. The challenges were vicarious as a rule. One of the older servers would put forward one small boy and another put forward an opponent in a sort of proxy contest, the arena being the patch of ground behind the church which was lit by the blaze from the rear sacristy windows. My first bout (it was also my first fight ever) was, to my bounding delight, against a boy even smaller and skinnier than myself. I learned immediately that size can be a gross deceiver. I was trounced. I shall never forget how hard the knobby little knuckles struck against my face, again and again. I was too shocked even to think of escape by falling to the ground before, merciful Heaven, the sacristy light went out and the bout was over. My promoter led me away, snivelling in the dark, never to put me forward as his combatant again.

I redeemed my manhood, however, by becoming, briefly, the champion wrestler of my class – anything to avoid fists in the face at point-blank range.

When I first went on the altar, my great fear was to be rostered for a Mass said by the senior curate, a man possessed of private means, a bay hunter, an irascible temper, and dedication to the strict observance of every ecclesiastical ritual. I was not alone in this fear; rumour had it that he caned servers for misbehaviour and mistakes. I never actually saw this happening or knew anyone who actually claimed to have been beaten. But the cane itself was true enough. I saw it myself in one of the sacristy drawers under the maniples. Perhaps Father meant it to be seen but not used, to be held over us *in terrorem*.

At any rate, soon after I began serving, while I was still raw and trusting, a cabal was formed among the boys to protest against the shouts, clipped ears and dressings-down. They drew up a round robin, which we were all forced to sign, and I (on the ground of being the youngest!) was appointed to deliver it to the Monsignor. I was not so young or ignorant as not to recognize a poisoned chalice when one was forced upon me. But my fear of being jeered at and despised was more powerful than any other – or at least more immediate, as I was ringed with altar boys when the grubby envelope was gummed down.

The Monsignor was squat, powerful, scarlet-faced and grizzled; he might have been master of a tramp steamer or a racehorse trainer or boxing promoter or anything else that suggested toughness, shrewdness and habitual command. I did not think that he yet knew who I was although I had served tremblingly at one or two of his Masses already. My instinct told me that this would be the worst possible way to come under the great man's notice. So it was as if I were walking to the gallows that I slowly took the gravel path that wound its way from the church to the presbytery, watched from a safe distance, probably from behind the rhododendrons, by the rest. I knocked and rang, almost together, in the feverish hurry of desperation, as soon as I reached the teak front door. No sound: was I to be spared after all? Then the door swung open on noiseless hinges, and the housekeeper peered down at me with suspicion. I had forgotten – if I had ever known – that she existed. Instead I had visualized a direct confrontation with the Monsignor all the time. 'He's out,' she said before I could open my mouth. Dumbly, I thrust the letter in her hand, and fled away to my companions only to find that they had fled before me.

The sword of Damocles fell unexpectedly on my neck when I returned for lunch from school next day. My father awaited at the back door in a state of extreme agitation and occasional bursts of fury. The Monsignor had been to see him during the morning, and told him of my unexampled impertinence. But I had been ordered up to the Parish House at once so there was no time for me to be dealt with as I deserved. (Looking back, I feel sure that my father was much relieved by the royal command; otherwise, he would, out of paternal decency, if nothing else, have been forced to wallop me instead of merely shaking my shoulders back and forth unceasingly until my teeth rattled my head – so at least it felt like.)

With sobs and tear-stained face I made my second via dolorosa along the gravel path behind the church, this time unwatched and hopeless. It was the Monsignor himself who opened the door in response to my faint ring. Without a word, he pointed me to his study on the right-hand side of the hall; without a word, he sat down in his desk chair and stared at my face. At last, the impossible question, 'Well, what have you to say for yourself?' 'Nothing,' was the only possible, though silent, answer. 'You're beginning your insolence and irreverence young. I pity your poor father if this is the track you're taking.' Silence, except for my sniffles and his heavy hand beating the desk rhythmically. Then, at last, 'I suppose it was those big fellows put you up to it. They are too cowardly to bell the cat themselves.' Bells and cats were a mysterious irrelevance to me; but I felt that I could, without fear of altar reprisal, agree to such a general attribution of guilt. 'Alright,' said the Monsignor, as if suddenly bored, 'don't you ever dare set yourself up against a priest again – and you can tell your father that I've dealt with you. You can go now, and don't be late back to school.'

Dinnerless but dizzy with joy, I ran along the gravel path and up and down the streets, panting in through the school gate just as the after-play bell stopped ringing. I did not of course escape jeremiads from father, mother, maid, porter and everyone else at home; nor did they cease when night fell. I was made to feel even next day that I had disgraced my father, my family, my breeding and The Bank. But everything passes and so did this; I was careful not to mention it to any other boy and for once an episode failed to be passed about the town as 'news'.

About two months later, when I made my First Communion, the Monsignor, happening to visit our house that day, called for me and gave me, not a homily, but two little books published by (how romantic the name sounded to me then) Raphael Tuck. His choice still leaves me in amazement for no man ever seemed less of a sentimentalist or *litterateur*. The books were *Gulliver's Travels* and *Alice in Wonderland*. No further word of the round robin passed between us on that day or any other. Despite appearances, he was surely out of the ordinary run of parish priests. When I looked in the maniple drawer again the cane was gone, though I cannot say that Father ever abated his imprecations.

It must not be thought that menace and violence (harmless though these really were, at least in retrospect) impinged much on even the new altar boys. Far more important were the fun, prestige and solemnity of the office. At first the new servers were merely part of a crowd scene. Four or six or eight boys served at a time on Sundays, kneeling, or sitting hunched, on the lowest altar steps in even balance either side. But one graduated in time to candle-lighting (a nervous business in the beginning), receiving the Monsignor's biretta, pounding the great steel 'bell' at the Elevation, holding the incense boat, swinging the thurible, bearing a pole of the canopy and, ultimately, leading processions. Even from the start, however, the sense of participation in an immemorial ritual, the mystery of the rites, and the colour, drama and unremitting regularity of the solemnities entered the mind's pores, to be absorbed forever.

Much my favourite serving-piece was Benediction. It usually belonged to night-time when all the altar place looked richly bright – gold monstrance, gilt cope, brass candlesticks, soutanes of scarlet and white surplices, all against the background of an immense curved church-end of glistening mosaics. From the blaze of the altar, the nave stretched away in growing dimness. I loved too the noble roll of the Benediction hymns 'O Salutaris Hostia' and 'Tantum Ergo'; to my ears they were the most heavenly of all. I knew their every word by heart long before I understood them in the least. Now in English they sound sadly tame, but then the very voice of God.

I liked Benediction least in late spring and summer when the evening light robbed the ceremony of its glow and warmth; but this was precisely the time of year when I enjoyed being 'on' for the early morning weekday Mass. 'Early' is a relative term; in a west of Ireland town, where the opening time for some shops depended on when the owner happened to get up, 7.30 am was 'early'. Even so, on fine mornings I would dash off soon after seven to catch the sweet clear air and brilliant sun-glances off the windows in the empty street: it was as if the world were beginning all over again and I was the only person who knew what was afoot. When the church bell would suddenly break out, it seemed as if it were clanging the announcement.

It was chill at the altar on even the brightest of these mornings, quite different from the tone and mood of winter Benediction. The altar itself was drained of colour, the nave pierced by shafts of pale dust-dancing sunlight, the priest murmuring at speed, the pair of servers treading discordantly on the heels of his Latin prayers, as if in a game of verbal Snap: '... *ad altare Dei*' was not properly out before being overtaken with the happy gabble, '*Qui laetificat juventutem mea*'; and then we all scampered away into the responses. Only a rare cough or shuffle broke the peace of the sparse congregation; nothing broke the sense of quiet joy, the feeling that, for once, all was right with the world, which blessed us for that magical half-hour.

Most of the altar boy's life was governed by a seasonality as repetitive as the tides, with Christmas, Lent and Easter ceremonies intricately complicating, though still forming an immutable part of, the annual pattern. But it was also shot through by unusual occasions. The bishop appeared every two or three years for Confirmations; but we never saw him otherwise so that crozier-and-mitre drill had to be periodically relearnt. The priests seemed to find him much more awesome than the servers did – on the principle of big fleas and little fleas, I suppose.

Funerals of course were unforeseeable if common happenings. Whatever about other boys, the reality of death did not impress itself perceptibly on me when I 'served' a funeral, despite the proximity of the coffin and the ghastly waxiness of the flowers. Occasionally, I felt a *frisson* during the endless sad chant of 'Dies Irae' or at the first scuffle of earth upon the coffin in the open grave. Perhaps it was all too usual and formalized to touch me yet. I was much more affected by the sight of the funeral processions winding their way in the distance towards the graveyard. Our kitchen was high, on the second storey, and one of its big windows commanded a view of the road, leading upwards from the town, along which these processions passed. It was too distant from the road for any sound to reach us. Somehow, I found it inexpressibly saddening to watch the silent, ragged corteges making their slow final journeys. I kept trying to hold back the moment when the last car or straggle of people passed out of sight under the trees that screened the cemetery itself; it was as if life left the body then. It is curious that I was quite free from this kind of feeling when I was myself a server at a funeral. Self-importance and small bits of business are great antidotes to gloomy thought.

Missions too were different if attended as an altar boy and not a whey-faced presence in the midst of a sea of whey-faced presences. The altar boy was on the side of the Redemptorists, not that of the congregation. Neither metaphorically nor geographically were the pulpit words directed at him. Especially was this case on the women's nights of the retreats. One was swept up in a glorious wave of male solidarity when *they* were castigated. I seem to remember one missioner bawling at them, 'Now, tomorrow I don't want to hear your husbands' confessions, I want to hear your own.' Perhaps I read or heard of this much later. At any rate, it so impressed me as to be embedded firmly in my own altar boy recollections. For once, the serried rows of hats, scarves, berets, bonnets and shawls had to cop it sweet – and, best of all, silently.

I went on altar-boying on the odd occasion for many years after I was grown up, when on holiday in a remote part, at conferences when there was a priest attender, and the like. The question from the altar, 'Can anyone serve?', was like a trumpet to a warhorse long since put out to grass. The old procedure always came back to me as smoothly as pouring cream. '*Introibo in altare Dei*,' and away we swept. Wearing ordinary adult clothes, and tinkling tea-bells instead of beating gongs, did nothing to break the charm. The years were telescoped. For twenty or thirty minutes spring was renewed.

Vatican II of course changed all that. The age of Latin, the Tridentine Mass and the gabbling, bustling altar boy disappeared. Instead, straggling vernacular responses, portentous acolytes and (on Sundays at least) caterwauling choirs have replaced the once-familiar rite. I am, like all my surviving comrades of the little soutane and surplice, a liturgical and ecclesiastical dodo. John XXIII opened the windows, and as Mihailovich said sadly of himself and his comrades, we were blown away in the gale of the world.

Artless Dodger

Some of my remembered doings seem so unlike me that I must have been possessed occasionally by another spirit. When I was seven, one of my Christmas presents was a fire engine, one of my sister's a foursquare doll's house made of plywood. For some reason, I happened to be alone in our playroom after breakfast on that Christmas morning. Hurriedly, I took off the house roof, filled the two upstairs rooms with balled newspaper and tried to set them aflame with spills lighted from the playroom fire. I had got no further than smoke-staining the inside walls when horrified discovery was made; I had not even had time to wheel up the tin ladder of my fire engine against a window. I can't recall my punishment. Perhaps it was so appalling that it sank to the unfathomable bottom of my subconscious. More likely, I was sent to my room for an hour or two; my father was no disciplinarian and my mother's heart was always soft towards me.

Among these extraordinary outbreaks from my role as a thoroughly good child was a spell of mitching (or, as the English would say, playing truant) from school, all the more extraordinary because my two companions were the roughest of rough town boys. I don't think that our adventuring lasted long. On the second or third day, as we wandered in the wild ground about a mile or two outside the town, I stumbled into a boghole. These can be quite big, twelve or fifteen feet square; and as this was winter it was filled with filthy water, and the sides were steep and greasy. The cold of the water struck me like a bolt of lightning. Even as I went down my eye somehow registered its amazing colour. From below, it looked – as nearly as I can describe it – liquid topaz. That was my sole detached impression. From then on, I was struggling for my life.

Each time I bobbed to the surface, the boys tried to grasp my hands or hair.

Once or twice they succeeded momentarily and I gulped

in air. As I rose jack-in-the-box-like again and again, coughing and vomiting water, they clutched at me; but their own hands were by now slimy and foul with mud. In the end, somehow or other, they caught the collar of my jacket and hauled me over the lip of the boghole. I must have been a truly pitiable sight, sobbing and shivering uncontrollably, smeared and sodden. My teeth so chattered that I could scarcely hear what the boys said, let alone answer them. I stumbled along between them wherever they went, this way and that.

I have no idea how they found the wretched cottage that at last provided us with a refuge. Perhaps its wild-haired, strapping mistress heard our squelching progress along the edge of the bog and called them in. At any rate, I must have moved her to kind pity for, without a word, she stood me before the smouldering turf in the hearth and pulled my clothes off one by one, flinging them onto the fire hooks and the back of the settle, and wrapping me in a filthy potato sack, which needed both my hands to keep in place. 'I'll give ye all a cup of tea,' she said, 'Ye look perished out and out, especially the little fella. What happened to ye at all?' She was fated never to discover. As the boys began to gabble out our story, their voices on top of one another, the half-door creaked open, and the small, puce-faced, unshaven, fiery-eyed old farmer or labourer who owned or rented the place clumped in. 'What the hell are those whelps doing in here, destroying the house?' he shouted, waving his stick in anger at us.

The wife, who can scarcely have been half his age, though fully twice his size, whispered and muttered about the 'drowned creatures'; but with one wary eye on him she began to gather my wretched garments from various points behind her back and to push me sideways from the fire. Treading on the potato bag, I fell before the raised stick and screamed for mercy. And a strained sort of mercy I did receive. Instead of the anticipated blows, we were merely driven with menace through the now-open half-door. Our impotent protectress brought up the rear with the dripping bundle of my clothes clasped to her apron. She punctuated our wet and hurried progress with a *sotte voce* litany, half-plea, half-protest.

Once outside the cottage, she turned whispering conspirator. 'Into the cowshed with ye,' she directed, 'Let the little fella dress there and go out quiet the back.' She then left my life, a well-meaning but ineffectual angel, while we entered the stinking, squelching gloom of the tumbledown barn. Now the boys rounded on me, mingling abuse with imprecations to hurry. How to hurry with numbed fingers, shaking arms and legs and body, still-chattering teeth, ice-cold damp clothes, in semi-darkness and with straw and cow-dung of many vintages spread along the floor? I don't know now and I didn't know then. Eventually, I covered myself more or less – part inside-out and back-to-front, no doubt – and was hustled away, arms held either side like a prisoner.

We weren't far from home, as it happened – perhaps two miles at most. The last stage, however, had to be made along my own street, gathering a small gaggle of sympathizers and mockers as we passed along. The boys pushed me up our front steps, rang the door and fled. I reeled and collapsed dramatically as the door was opened, and Bridie, the maid, screamed at the horrid sight that met her.

I was very lucky, in a way. I went down at once with bronchitis, then pneumonia, and thus in the end escaped chastisement or even very close inquiry. But when, on my return to school, the boys began to hint at a reward for saving my valuable life, and I reported this at home my mother responded fiercely, 'The cheek of those brats, after leading you astray and almost drowning you. I like that. Reward, how-are-you!' so the boys got nothing except presumably the cane, which I escaped through the long interval before my return to school. I never again saw the good wife or the ferocious husband.

Although I never afterwards mitched directly, I lapsed into substantive mitching on occasion later on. The spectacles, which I was condemned to wear from the age of twelve, served me well. While they were being prepared in Dublin, I invented an oculist's prohibition against my reading or writing without them, and simply sat in class with folded arms for a week. At nights I went through a short charade of 'homework' at the kitchen table, reading the *Champion* or *Hotspur* whenever it seemed safe.

I must have become besotted by this idle double life for when my glasses arrived in their glossy case from Dublin, I spun it out by hiding them each morning in a hallstand drawer (which was practically never opened) and rescuing them each afternoon as I sneaked in from school. I kept this up for almost another week before my nerve gave way. Amazingly, my crime was never discovered, although the prospects of my being caught either in a street encounter or by some chance school or home remark were so high as to make disclosure seem almost certain.

I put my glasses to use at least once again after I went to boarding school. Towards the end of a desolate, monotonous term, I turned a mild eye-headache into an (almost literally, I said) blinding pain for the benefit of the school Sister – to such effect that she told the Rector that I must go at once to Dublin to be examined by my oculist. Of course, my grand oculist, a severe woman specialist, tailored and tied and collared as near as possible to a man, could not see me immediately. But, her secretary told the Rector over the telephone, she would endeavour to find time for me during her lunch hour in two days' time. Few moments of my life equal the simple joy with which I walked a mile to the village, Clane, to catch the Dublin bus: I was alone; I was free; eight silver, empty hours stretched out before me. Even the coming thundercloud of Dr Mary was still too far away to cast a shadow.

When at last I broke into her lunch hour, she did prove rather thundery. I was told bitingly that she had been led to think that my very vision was in peril, only to find that my short-sightedness had merely deteriorated slightly, as was bound to happen at my age. But she must have known something about schoolboys. Assuming, correctly, that it was a temporary escape from school that I had really sought – and carefully refraining from forcing me to admit as much – she became virtually an accomplice in my crime before the end of the consultation, writing me both a new prescription and a note to baffle and appease the Rector. I have never judged acidulous, mannish, elderly women harshly since.

I had a sweet hour or more to spend among the bookstalls on the quay before my bus left from there. I picked out and began to read the middle of an unknown book by an unknown author. It was Trollope's *Framley Parsonage*, a thick, fat reprint, priced one shilling. Of course, I became entrapped and bought. The jolting journey back to Clane passed in a dream. Even the approaching shades of the prison house could not force an entry into an imagination locked into south-west England, amid leafy lanes and sun-bright hedgerows.

The wages of sin were far from repaid on this occasion. I was even able to employ Dr Mary's supposed concern as a reason for moderating my class and study work for several days before the replacement spectacles unfortunately turned up.

*Words Without End, Amen**

I was born and grew up under lucky verbal stars. They say that one never forgets the number of one's first car. I don't: ZF641 forever. Nor shall I ever forget the name of my first proper book, *Treasure Island*. Not that I read it myself at the age of four. It was my father who read it to me, night by night, at bedtime. He was an undramatic reader. The colour came from

* Published in *The Irish Review*, 26 (Autumn 2000), 109–13.

the written, not the spoken words. Yet I strove desperately each night to stave off the snap with which he closed the dingy, limp red volume that had been his own school text twenty-odd years before.

'Please, Daddy, please, please, please. You can skip tomorrow if you'll go on tonight. Please, Daddy, just this one. I'll never ask again!'

He must have been well accustomed to this sort of plea. It was after all (in childish language) what he, as a country bank manager, must have heard a dozen times a week from debt-drowning customers in the 1930s. He almost always said 'No' to me also.

Yet it is the nightly thrills of fear that I remember best. From its very beginning, *Treasure Island* is – or was for me, at any rate – a terrifying children's book. How my heart thumped – like hammer-beats echoing the tap-tap-tap of the blind beggar's stick upon the road. I supped fullest of its horrors when, in imagination, I crouched in that apple-barrel with Jim Hawkins while Long John Silver, almost close enough to hear my faintest breath, set out his treacherous schemes. It was certain death to have been discovered. All the same, I went on sleeping soundly once the lights were out, panted to have more, and fell into a lifelong love of words.

I was very lucky that it was Stevenson that was first read to me. I can't think of a better sort of writing for a child to hear. He is the supreme narrator, and it is with stories that we all begin. His English is clear as glass, straightforward, all sinews and muscle, free from every shadow of redundancy or the contrived. His words are simple where simple words will do, but, where not, the right terms duly take their place. What could be plainer, yet more seductive in its rhythms, than the opening scene of *Treasure Island*?

> I remember him as if it were yesterday, as he came plodding to the inn door, his sea-chest following behind him in a hand-barrow; a tall, strong, heavy, nut-brown man; his tarry pigtail

> falling over the shoulders of his soiled blue coat; his hands ragged and scarred, with black, broken nails; and the sabre cut across one cheek, a dirty, livid white. I remember him looking round the cove and whistling to himself as he did so, and then breaking into that old sea-song that he sang so often afterwards: *Fifteen men on the Dead Man's Chest – yo-ho-ho, and a bottle of rum!* in the high, old, tottering voice that seemed to have been tuned and broken at the capstan bars.

My second stroke of fortune was a Montessori kindergarten education, which taught me to read early on. I can still hear the class of 'b'y, t'y, j'y', the local variant of 'boy, toy, joy', and see the ever-changing letters on the blackboard. Almost anything printed was grist to my crude little mill. I became one of those dreadful children who read even what is written on labels for want of anything else in sight. Or, to look at it in a better light, I had acquired a beneficent addiction.

'Comics' (as the earnest schoolboy weeklies, devoted to soccer heroes and English public school hi-jinks, were curiously called) were, of course, my early staple diet. A few children's classics came my way. *Lamb's Tales* I found hopelessly complex – *Alice in Wonderland* a bewilderment, but *Gulliver's Travels* just right for a very literal-minded child: I loved its exactitude and the solemn interplay of scales. I worked – or rather tore my way delightedly – through the William and Biggles stories. But the first really substantial book I read myself – as I counted substance at the age of twelve – was another Stevenson, this time *Kidnapped*. Its language was more difficult than *Treasure Island*'s and, the narrator being a Lowland Scot, necessarily more idiomatic. Yet even this was gain: who could forget Alan Breck's 'auld, cauld, dour, deidly' courage, so superior to the pedestrian English, 'old, cold, dour and deadly'. At any rate, the old magical Stevenson prose and rippling run of narrative worked on me as powerfully as ever – or rather very much better, as I had by now some rudimentary concept of composition.

Although I scarcely knew the word, let alone thought the thought deliberately, I was already groping about for a style. Heaven only knows what dreadful purple pages, misused foreign phrases, pomposities, latinities, jams of piled-up adjectives and swollen gerunds I floundered through as my fancy swung crazily in tune with whatever I happened to be reading. It might be too much to say that the murky waters turned crystalline and hardened. Yet, by the time I left school I had my own magnificent seven, the stylists who made me cry out, almost aloud, 'the achieve of the mastery of the thing' – Swift, Austen, Hazlitt, Newman, Belloc, Orwell, Waugh: steely, driving, brilliant, epigrammatic, enchanting stylists, all electric, in one way or another, with writer's energy. I suppose that they are still my magnificent seven, although I have to own a sneaking liking for one who is their polar opposite, the convoluted and absurdly over-mannered Meredith. But it was *Treasure Island* and *Kidnapped* that began all this.

My third happy chance in learning about words was my childhood stammer. It was quite bad by the time my aunt Florence – we children called her Fluff, most inappropriately for she was thin, wiry and darting – came to live with us. I was then about six years old.

'You can't possibly let that child grow up with that affliction,' she announced in her brisk way. 'I know the way to cure him – teach him poetry.'

By poetry, she meant jog-trot verse, mostly Longfellow and Kipling, with a lacing of Tennyson and de la Mare; and this she proceeded to drill into me, day and night. The really strange thing about Fluff's system was that it worked; within six months my stammer was virtually gone. In this process, I had acquired, willy-nilly, countless lines of mediocre poetry. To this day, I can reel off 'The Runaway Slave' and 'I remember the black wharves and the slips' and 'If' and 'On the Road to Mandalay'; and it is surprising how useful it is to have quotations of any sort that rise unbidden to the surface as occasion calls.

I had also acquired, willy-nilly, an unfailing ear for poetic rhythm – at any rate, of the simpler sort. When the time came, I seemed to scan lines automatically, wincing at wrong emphases or an infelicitous order in the words. And this spilled over, though less surely, into the more subtle harmonies, and cunningly contrived discords, of prose. Fluff's system was full of un-convenanted gains. The disease proved well worth the cure.

My final piece of fortune was to grow up in a world where Synge's English was still often to be heard. Of course, it was not to be heard with anything like the density or extravagance of Synge's peasant language. But the underlying constructions, cadences and range of words survived, albeit in much milder and more occasional form. 'The flies is woeful arrogant tonight,' said a farmer saluting us on a summer evening's walk. 'Ah, 'twas only like a daisy in the mouth of a bull,' said a labourer deprecatingly when congratulated on the speed with which he lowered a pint of Guinness. 'Can he eat? And we only passing one another on the stairs with trays,' said the sister of a tiresome invalid. 'Abroad in the haggard,' said everyone, indicating 'outside in the barn'. Thus I grew up steeped, unwittingly, in a variety of vocabulary and imagery quite outside the ordinary run of words and word-use. It bred in me a habit of always feeling about, without consciously thinking much about it, for fresh or arresting ways of saying things.

All this welled in time into an itch to write myself, and even to be published. As things turned out, I was to be my own first publisher. When I was about nine, I published a newspaper for my elementary school. Every word of it was written by me, with the letters in childish imitation of typeface; I drew the illustrations, execrably, as pseudo-photographs. The bannerhead ran the *National School Weekly*, the production run was two copies and the price only one penny. There were no sales of either the first or second (and last) edition.

A year or so later, I had turned poet and actually attained the glory of paper print. The owner-editor of the *Carlow Nationalist*, an uncle's friend, was persuaded in a kind, weak moment to publish one of my effusions, signed 'Oliver MacDonagh, aged 10'. Doubtless fortunately, I can remember only the opening line: 'Oh, Vale of Avoca, where grows Tom Moore's tree.' At least, it meant the sale of an extra dozen copies of the *Nationalist* – to my foolishly proud parents.

All through my school days, my passionate affair with words continued. I read with gluttonous indiscrimination, but also a simple faith in the then canon of 'great literature'. I slogged my way through lines of Complete Works, such as those of Scott or Thackeray, the very thought of doing which would make me feel faint today. I tried to get parts in plays, though my words on stage were usually confined to 'Ho, sirrah' and the like. Above all, I went on scribbling lines.

In time, my early doggerel turned into jingling verse, and jingling verse into poetry of a sort. In my last year at school, two of my poems were published in the *Irish Monthly*, an old and honourable Jesuit journal in which, legend has it, Yeats's earliest poems had appeared. For a night or two, I was the hero of the senior school, who were granted – remember these were unregenerate days – the 'privilege' of evening 'smokes' in honour of the achievement.

When I went on to university in Dublin, I gravitated naturally towards the writing set. We all had manuscripts hidden inside our jacket pockets, to be inflicted tentatively, sooner or later, on one another. We all sat timidly on the edges of groups in the literary pubs where the giants of the day, such as Flann O'Brien and Patrick Kavanagh, held surly court. We all looked on editors as so many St Peters with the key to heaven. Early on, I had a poem published in the university magazine and it received mild (but perhaps also deadly) praise as 'clever'. I began, and re-began, and re-began a novel. But gradually it was borne in on me that it was all no good. Gradually, I realized that I was totally lacking in creative imagination; I had never had, and never would have, the divine spark.

So I became an historian, went off eventually to Cambridge, and lived happily ever after that. My love of words, however, was unabated. I could exercise it only in the lower pastures, not on the bright, sun-glanced uplands. But even that has always been good enough. The verbal good fairies who blessed my childhood and adolescence did not cast their spells altogether in vain.

*Clouds of Glory**

Rugby was the deepest joy and the most acute anxiety of my youth; indeed, it still ranks pretty high on both counts. The town and its surrounds, however, were almost exclusively Gaelic football and hurling territory, and 'Ruby' (as it was then known locally) was resisted and resented as a 'foreign' game. I was its solitary supporter and aficionado among the boyhood of the place. This of course made me the focus of the school opprobrium of the supposed 'West Briton' form of football. Nor was it only the boys who made me their target. The Brothers too derided rugby; and if they refrained from open mockery of my perverse adherence, they made it clear that it cast my Hibernicity in doubt. One of them laughed long and gleefully when, in 1934, to celebrate the half-centenary of the foundation of the Gaelic Athletic Association, I had to march, togged out and carrying a hurling stick, together with the remainder of the school, along the festive streets. Perhaps I had the last laugh on this occasion. A photograph of the procession of boys, taken from a high vantage point and published next day in the *Irish Independent*, happened to cut me out except for the arm carrying the stick. But did my dedication to rugby really compensate

* Published in *The Irish Review*, 26, Autumn 2000, 103–8.

for missing the glory of a newspaper appearance? It was hard to say.

That dedication probably began with my father's love of the game. My first rugby memory is of being taken, at the age of three or four, to a match in Limerick – probably between his club, Bohemians, and their deadly and much better known local rivals, Garryowen. I carry from it only a single specific recollection, but that most vivid. The match was almost over and a kickable, all-important penalty had been awarded. I, lifted by my father onto a higher bench in the stand, was directly in line with the kicker and the goal posts. Suddenly, an old man in the row beneath me dropped to his knees, rosary in hand, and began to pray. I can recall nothing else, whether the kicker was successful, or the kick concluded the match, or even who won the game. But the tiny earlier sequence has remained sharply incised on my mind – perhaps because it impressed on me once and for all the awful, the tremendous, the soul-rending quality of rugby.

Others may find it difficult to believe that the old man dropping to his knees really happened but I do not think it at all unlikely. I question many of the mind-pictures of my boyhood but never this. When I was eight and nine and ten years old, listening to the static-ridden broadcasts of Internationals in which Ireland was engaged, I too prayed frequently during each great crisis, cried with unassuagable pain when we lost, cried out of sheer happiness when (much less often, alas) we held out against all the odds, and won. There must have been others gathered around the wireless on these occasions, but, in memory, I always seem to have suffered or been rejoiced alone – so utterly wrapt was I in the emotions of the hour.

It was not that I did not follow other games with passion. As one of the characters in the *Irish RM* observes, 'Indeed, if it was only two cocks ye see fightin', on the other road, yer heart'd take part with one o' them.' Roscommon was at that time an easy-beat at Gaelic football, and our close neighbouring county, Galway, a hated rival. But Mayo, west of the west,

I loved. So it was with every sport, from Kilkenny for hurling (because one of my aunts lived there) and Steve Donoghue among jockeys (because he was Irish born) through Australia at cricket (because they alone could beat England) and the Englishman Fred Perry at tennis (because he alone could beat Americans), to Notre Dame at gridiron (because they were the 'Catholic' team) and of course Ireland at hockey (a game I had never seen or wished to see or understand). I even backed soccer teams because of their romantic names, Tottenham Hotspur, Partick Thistle, Shamrock Rovers. All this was serious commitment. I grieved at failures, I rejoiced at victories. But rugby was on an altogether different plane. It was a tragic love, as against a casual affair; it alone gripped my very heart, and double-gripped it with Ireland playing.

When my father told me that he would take me to the next International at Lansdowne Road, I was first flooded with fear, fear that my dream world would be shattered by the actuality. But when the day came round, all that was as if it had never been. My heart danced with my feet on the short way to the station. The train to Dublin was almost empty; rugby was a matter of indifference, at best, to nearly all the town's inhabitants. One unlikely follower, a hardware dealer, entered the same compartment as ours, and after a few polite preliminaries which included me, talked to my father all the way so that I could play over and over the entire match in my mind in anticipation. All I can remember of their conversation was the drift over – God knows how – from Ireland's prospects in general to Ireland's prospects of producing the next Pope. 'Wouldn't it be a wonderful thing for the country, and wouldn't it be a fair reward? Look at the Eucharistic Congress,' they said to one another. Since Dublin had rated only the appearance of a papal nuncio at the Congress of 1932, the odds were obviously very long. But they went on canvassing the chances, instead of the vital question of the day, almost until we arrived in Dublin. Perhaps their thoughts had been running rapidly downhill on the lines of improbability ever since they had opened up on Ireland's chances of success that Saturday.

It was a fine rawish winter day, and since we arrived in Dublin much too early for the match, my father decided that we should walk from O'Connell St to the ground. I had been to Dublin several times already, but never before along that noble way of dark-red eighteenth-century brick, limestone facings and purse-proud Victorian villas. As we drew close the pedestrians began to thicken into crowds, the lamp posts bore newspaper legends about the game, rosette sellers were to be heard, in rasping Dublinese, before even seen, and a kiosk or two – of the exotic Parisian type – sprang up on the corner of the turning down to Mecca.

When we pressed past the railway crossing to the entrances, the moment for parting came. My father lined me up at the Schoolboys' entrance and gave me a shilling for a ticket, another shilling for any substance I could find within, and a casual instruction to meet him as near as I could get to the farther post of the railway crossing gate after the match. The Schoolboy 'stand' was a rising mound behind one set of goal-posts. It was more than half-filled already with knots of boys who, unlike me, seemed to know everyone about them. At first, my heart was light, and the time passed in noting ambiance. The winter sun made the carpet of turf gleam. The crowd chanted 'All alone' at a young girl walking along the side line and 'Knobbly Knees' at the boy scouts acting as stewards, and 'Take off your hat' to an alickadoo (the contemptuous word for a rugby official at the time). The No. 2 Army Band thumped out 'Let Erin Remember'.

Gradually, this palled, and it came over me that I never felt more acutely shy in my life. If only I knew some other boy, any other boy, anyone. Listening to a match on the wireless might be a proper matter for inward-turning passion, but – I now discovered – presence at a match demanded companionship. As I stood alone half-way up the grassy slope, other boys filled up the empty spaces in little groups and coalescences. I was the only isolate. As the groups pressed more and more closely on me, I took a desperate plunge and actually spoke to one, who happened to knock against me, about the Irish team. O blessed youth; he answered kindly the questions to which I already well knew the answers, and from there talked on. He merged me in the crowd; I was no longer a drop separated from the moving water. I could chant with the rest 'Hairy Legs' at the scoutmaster acting as steward for the side line benches and 'Where's the wife?' at the old fellow with the pretty girl being escorted to their seats below.

And when the supreme moment arrived at last I could shout in maniacal unison, 'Come on, Ireland, come on, Ireland,' when the small green figures came scampering out one by one from the distant pavilion at the ground's farther end. Was there ever a colour more vivid than that emerald? Were white shorts ever more white? Was there ever a kick more towering then McMahon's as he tested the wind and loosened his body in preparation? Was there ever a hesitation more delightful than that of the lazy yellow ball as it turned slowly over at the top of its flight? The English team, emerging close by us to the left looked heavy and slow by contrast; the all-white togs seemed to puff them out in size and likely clumsiness. But the Irish, neat and sparkling, their irrepressible individuality marked out by each man wearing his own club stockings, looked clean, crisp, natural rugby players from head to toe. The Schoolboy stand yelled out its pride and hope.

The roar soon subsided into isolated, agonized cries, as the English pack pushed the Irish about without apparent effort or concern. The English out-half and centres, fed a rich diet of clean ball, broke through seemingly at will; they did not even bother to use their bulky, flying wing three-quarters, who had been marked down beforehand as the leading danger. The tries came, three of them in the last ten minutes of the first half; and worst of all, Parker, England's unknown (to me) fullback, converted every one, from whatever angle. By half-time Ireland was down 23–0, a deficit scarcely credible in an era of 0–0 draws and 3–0 and 6–3 victories.

The Schoolboys were stunned, silent at first, then hiding their shame under would-be cynical remarks about their heroes. But we had despaired too soon. It was the green jerseys that swarmed and ran most often in the second half. Ireland was now attacking the distant posts, and with boys jumping with excitement on every side, I saw only snatches of the play, and could tell when a try was scored only from the leaps and cheers at the opposite end. But half a second afterwards we were all in the air or hugging each other in an ecstasy that could not be more acute had we actually seen what had happened. Four times that half we whistled and danced in a glorious moment; strangers flung arms about each other; I knew for the first time the insensate joy of mob emotion. When a fifth Irish try was disallowed, I howled protesting like the rest, although I had to be told by my neighbours what it was all about. I said 'Sssh' like all the rest when Parker, the English fullback (who, bad cess to him, kicked almost every goal – eight in all) ran up to take conversions and penalties: it was then a sacred obligation to maintain utter silence for kicks at goal – even, indeed particularly, for opponents' kicks. It was after all a game for gentlemen.

Although Ireland outscored England in the second half, the result was a 36–14 thrashing, defeat upon an unheard-of scale. Nonetheless, I was so caught up in the dramatic course of events (with eleven tries scored in all) and the uncovenanted comradeship, in joy and sorrow, of the superior beings – Dublin sophisticates – on every side of me, that I thought nothing of my reunion with my father until the final whistle blew, and my new-found friends rushed away to be lost in crowds seeking the closest exit. With space suddenly about me I began to panic. How vague were my father's directions! The railway crossing had four corners; which should I aim for? Was it really the crossing and not the railway bridge that he had meant? What would I do if I could not find him – dusk was not far away and I had only two shillings and a few pennies in my pocket? Did I dare accost and throw myself at the mercy of some kind-looking spectator, another sophisticated Dubliner, even if perforce a gentleman because he had been part and parcel of an International?

With thumping heart, I, too, flung myself onto the tail of the retiring crowd, bobbed in the crush at the gates like a cork in a choppy sea, and with great struggle turned myself to face towards instead of away from the railway crossing. It was at that moment closed, as a jam-packed train clattered slowly through, and the people on the road before it – including me, far back – were pressed together as if tinned. As the railway gates opened, the foremost shot through, then more and more. Part of the rushing tide, I had not the slightest chance of choosing my crossing post. I was lucky even to be swept near enough to the farthest one, on the city side of the tracks, to grasp it with both my arms and hold fast until the press of bodies slackened. Then came an infinity of time (I suppose that it was in reality only two minutes or three) while I peered wildly at the still-moving faces in search of my father's. The relief to see him at last sauntering along towards me unconcerned was almost agonizing in its force.

'Well, how was the Schoolboys? How did you like the match?'

'Oh, I loved it, Dad. Do you know' – such is the mind that I had been making my calculations even while gripped with terror lest I should be abandoned – 'do you know, if England hadn't made any of their conversions, and we had made all of ours, we'd only have lost by a point, 21–20.'

'Yes, by Jove, that Parker fellow was the clincher: never saw such kicking in all my life. But Ireland were shocking in the first half. I never saw George Morgan play such a bad game.'

George Morgan, the scrum-half for whose appearance and performance the adjective 'immaculate' might have been newly-minted, was my hero of heroes. He might well have been the best player in his position in all the world at that time; but I did not dare to defend him then, lest the criticisms became specific, and I myself was forced to assent to them secretly in my heart.

'Where were you standing, Dad?'

'At the far end, just above the sideline benches near where the chap went for the referee for disallowing Bailey's try. It was a good try, you know. Still, you can't have that sort of thing; Lansdowne Road isn't Paris.'

My father had once watched Ireland in France, before that country was expelled from the Championship, and much enjoyed recounting his outrage at the crowd's behaviour: 'Bugles, trumpets, whistles, even women or somebody shrieking and screaming when Crawford began his run up to kick.' I loved this story, but instead of elaborating as usual, my father said,

'Well, you must be hungry. Did you buy anything to eat at the ground?'

'No, Daddy, I was too afraid of losing my place to go looking.'

'I'll tell you what: we'll take trams from Westland Row down to the quays and have two mixed grills at the Clarence. You needn't tell Mummy about it unless she asks.'

We did. I could never have dreamt that a day on which I saw, with my own eyes, Ireland being beaten 36–14, would turn out to be one of the happiest of my life.

The schoolboy (left), with his friend, Tony

Galway Races

The lay festival of our year was the Galway Races. The last Wednesday and Thursday of each July were the sacred days. Roscommon had its race meetings too; but these were, at the time, shabby, down-at-heel affairs. Fields of four or five old stagers were the best that could be expected. 'Selling-platers', my mother contemptuously called them – the selling plate being, in her mind, the lowest form of racing life.

She followed the horses fervently, though spasmodically. Eight races, the Grand National, the Derby, the four other 'classics of the turf', the Cesarewich and the Manchester November Handicap, had her poring over lists of runners and jockeys and the betting forecasts, and mulling over the chances with us children. I always picture this happening – as more than once it did – under the great pear tree in the garden on a sunny afternoon: it would have been the afternoon before the Derby. Half of my mother whirred away at her old Singer sewing machine while the other half peered through spiralling cigarette smoke at the racing page of the *Irish Independent*.

'The Aga Khan has never had a bad horse yet,' she would muse at times like this, 'nor has Dorothy Paget many, for that matter.' Or 'Tommy Weston rode the winner of last year's Derby and there is a horse called Easton running this time. I think I might have a bet on him. It's such an extraordinary coincidence, isn't it?' Or 'How many horses are there with eight letters in their name? Eight has always been my lucky number, you know.' Once someone (my cousin Tony, I think) put in, 'But Steve Donoghue and Gordon Richards have eight letters in their names, too.' Taken aback, she answered slowly, 'Yes, I suppose that's true. You wouldn't really know what to do, would you?'

At this point, Tom the porter, digging slowly, but leisurely and steadily, in the back garden, was usually called in for consultation. At such times, he would remove his cap with great deliberation, stroke his thick, black, strong head of hair for a little while, and then pronounce judgment. Although my mother professed deep faith in his racing wisdom, she never submitted to it humbly. Instead it tended to enlarge either the area or the intensity of her indecision, depending on whether Tom's seal was placed on some fresh choice or on one that was being toyed with already. By this stage, the extreme course of shutting her eyes and sticking a needle into the runners' list might be resorted to. Yet, so far as I remember, she often won – or perhaps it is only rare triumphs that I recall.

Tom's treat of the year was to be taken by my mother and father to a chosen day of the Galway Races, usually the first. Although (to use today's language) as mechanically challenged as the rest of the household, he signalled the onset of the annual excursion by preparing our car as if it were to head some triumphal procession. Scorning children's aid, he would push it out of the garage single-handed; he was quite mechanical enough to manage the massive handbrake. Next came the lustration rites, with buckets of hot water handed down from the kitchen for endless washings and dryings, and finally the polishing with strips of old cotton sheets. Tom polished as he would have curry-combed a horse, sibilant 'Pssts' accompanying every downward sweep.

The crowning preparation was pumping up the Rexine-covered air cushions of the seats. These had no doubt been trumpeted as a technological advance when my father bought his dashing Riley in 1930. But they punctured easily, deflated steadily and slid passengers from one side to the other at full curvature. Long practice had given Tom a mastery over all these vagaries; and he made sure that the odious cushions struck the right balance between rotundity and sagging centres on the race-day mornings.

For some reason or another, I was the only child to accompany Tom on the back seat of the Riley for the opening day's racing in 1936. Already I knew the road to Galway almost by heart. Every promising Sunday in summer, we drove *en famille* to the sea at Barna, then a little place of half a dozen houses three miles past Galway city. First, we would clear Roscommon by a twisting railway bridge with Tom's own little house close by on the left, then to Athleague, the last outpost of our county, before heading for Ballygar, the first outpost of the next. We children thought grandly of crossing the invisible county border and indeed, compared with Athleague, even Ballygar seemed urbane and lush – though I doubt if the combined populations of the villages would have topped one thousand in those days.

To the blasé traveller, the road from Roscommon to Galway might have seemed quite flat and featureless, but to us it was a journey through the ever-romantic west. Every turn, every rise, every kink, every fall was familiar. Along one stretch of the road, statues of the Sacred Heart and Our Lady were cemented into the gate-piers of the small farmhouses, each in a little box protected in front by glass. We had even got to know which statue was coming next. How strange this was; who could have first thought of such a thing?

The best moment came when we crossed a small bridge close to Galway itself. Just upriver from the place (as my father had recounted when we first drove the road) our great-grandmother had been drowned. An aged lady knitting on a rocking chair close to the water's edge one sunny day, she had apparently over-rocked – or perhaps fainted – and tumbled in. We always fell into a solemn silence when we came upon the bridge. It was if she had died a soldier's death. Finally, we would pass on through the Sunday gloom of Eyre Square and the winding city streets into wide Salthill and on, ultimately, to stony Barna, redolent of salt, seaweed, tar, turf-smoke and flourishing potato fields, the smells somehow inimitably mixed.

On this occasion, however, we never reached even the fatal bridge, let alone Galway city, but turned off early and tamely to the racecourse road. After the regulatory roadside races picnic of chicken and ham sandwiches, rock cakes and thermos tea brewed down to the lowest common denominator of strength and sweetness, we bumped at last into the crowded field designated 'Car Park'. There we parted. Tom and I were destined for the outer grounds, for which there was no charge, my parents for the stands enclosure. Economy ruled, but much to my satisfaction as I enjoyed Tom's conversation no less than his negligent surveillance.

Having bought us a programme first, my mother dug in her purse for half a crown while my father jingled about in his pocket for another. 'There you are,' he said, 'five shillings in your pocket. You'll have to find a winner if you're to have enough to back the last race.' But he smiled as he spoke, as if in no doubt of his son's gambling acumen.

My capital fell, however, well before the first race was begun. I succumbed to the yells of the stall girls, 'Apples, oranges, ripe bananas!'; I bought a Cadbury Nut bar; I rolled pennies down the little chutes in the vain hope of one toppling over clear within the lines of profitable square. By the time for serious business, my five shillings had shrunk to little over three. Tom disapproved strongly of my frivolity, although he had bought a grisly packet of crubeens for himself. 'That's very foolish of you, boy, and you'll regret it, I can tell you, when time comes round to bet.' Nonetheless, he counted into my hand the pence needed to restore my stakes to a wagerable sum, though merely now four shillings.

Tom believed in past form and caution, and caution meant that he always bet each way. I was foolish enough to choose horses for the euphony of their names, and wished to bet to win. So we fell out over the very first race, and since I thought that no bookie would accept a child's shilling, I had to compromise. I kept to my sweet-sounding choice, but Tom backed it for me at a shilling each way. It was never to be glimpsed throughout the whole race, only thudding past far down amongst the also-rans as it passed us at the rails.

The great race of the day was the third, a steeplechase,

the Galway Plate, for which, come what might, I must reserve my remaining two shillings. There were two romantic sounding names amongst the runners, Cottage Fire and Yellow Furze; the rest were the usual ugly and obscure compounds. My mother had been loud in her praise of Cottage Fire on the journey down, but Yellow Furze seemed to me to have a wilder, freer, more venturous sounding ring, and my money would follow where my imagination led.

By the time the Plate came round, I had discovered that bookies – in the outer ground at least – had no hesitation in grasping bets from children even younger than myself. So, Tom being momentarily distracted, I dashed up to the nearest bellower of the odds, holding out my money and stuttering, 'Yellow Furze'. 'Two-bob-Yella-Furze-to-win-six-to-one-the-field-bar-one,' he chanted without even turning his head in my direction. In fact, I had changed my mind and meant to follow Tom's injunction and lay my bet each way. But I dared not interrupt the scarlet-faced giant on the fish-box a second time. My fortune was all staked on a win. 'Aren't you the stupid boy?' said Tom when I tried to explain what happened. His heart wasn't in the reproof, however; he had backed Yellow Furze himself.

Like many other things, steeplechases look better at a distance than close up. As one peers down the course from the home rails, the horses taking the hurdles and fences appear like so many waterfalls, with the animals bowing steeply to the ground and the riders as steeply backwards. For a moment each pair seems a simple curved graceful being, even if it may all end in a twist, a fall and a spilt jockey, like a crashing wave. As the mounts toil up the slope towards the stands, however, with their sawing breaths, heavy hooves, sides and quarters glistening and running with sweat, and legs splattered to the knees with earth clods flying, the romance of the thing drains away. It is mere humdrum, commonplace prose, when the field passes before one's nose, part bunched and part straggling on behind, and so it stays until they diminish again into the distance and become a sort of poetry once more.

I don't suppose I had many such high-flown thoughts watching anxiously with Tom as the runners laboured past the first time round. It was all I could do to take in the placing of the leading knot – my mother's Cottage Fire was second – although I had no difficulty in locating Yellow Furze: he was last. Still, out of a field of fifteen or so, four or five horses had fallen already and it was a relief to know that at least he was not amongst the ignominious.

Even Tom's keen countryman's eyes could not tell what was happening on the back stretch and we really knew nothing certainly until the leader flowed over the farthest fence in sight for the second time. 'Yellow Furze, by God!' Tom shouted. Yellow Furze it truly was and the noble animal stayed far clear of the remainder until he lolloped along the white rails and past the winning post beside us. He was distantly attended by Cottage Fire, with the rest (as the racing people say) nowhere. I was bathed in a vast ocean of content.

I can't remember much more of that day's races, but I can certainly remember being handed down a crumpled orange ten-shilling note and two sweaty florins from the lordly John Joe Murphy – or whoever – under his curlicued sign, 'Turf Accountant'. My day was complete. I had not the slightest wish to wager any more. For form's sake, I might have let the florins go, but the hard-won crumpled note – never. I discovered that afternoon I had no need to bet to enjoy the races. The strangely innocent absorption, the gaiety, happiness, gravity, greed, tremors, murmurs, groans and cheering of the crowds, the white sweep of rails and circle, the easy beauty of horses cantering, their heart-gripping struggle in the straight, above all, the jockeys' brilliant colours and sharp, hard, desperate faces – these I could watch for hours as one can watch the ever-changing, yet ever-constant sea.

Besides, the programme proved an unfailing joy. There was

the derivation of the horses' names to be worked out, their ages, handicaps and previous season's form to be computed and the bizarre caps and jackets of the jockeys – 'amber and turquoise hoops, black sleeves, black and amber quartered caps', 'primrose, grey sash, scarlet sleeves, primrose and scarlet cap' and so on – to be assembled mentally. I don't mean to say that I was up to such deep studies in 1936; but it was then that the seeds of this absurd pursuit were sown in me (as the love of crosswords or chess is sown in more serious bosoms) to prove a stay and companion at many a race meeting of the future.

On the way home I played with a Dinky car which I had providently put in my pocket before leaving. I ran it up the hillocks and along the causeways of my Rexine cushion, cornering fiercely, and with the silent shriek of brakes when almost off the edge. I had been pronounced, or perhaps pronounced myself, much too old for Dinkies a year before. But don't we all have lapses, especially in celebration? I had small fear of being noticed by my mother or Tom for they were deep in race talk, he leaning forward with his cap hung from one knee, she calling back over her shoulder.

'Well, I don't care what you say, Tom, Cottage Fire wasn't given a fair chance. Two stone extra to carry that distance!'

'But isn't that what I always tell you, ma'am? You never pay any attention to the weights and aren't they what count at the end of the long haul?'

'But two stone! I ask you!'

'Isn't that always what I say, though? Those handicappers go to town altogether when a young horse has come home first the last time out. Did I ever bet on one? No – and aren't I in the right of it?'

And so it went on and on, my mother ceaselessly bewailing the injustice of the turf, and Tom steadfast in upholding masculine rationality. Meanwhile my Dinky zoomed around and around.

Two or three years later, I discovered *A Golden Treasury of*

Irish Verse. The editor had had the wit to include a nineteenth-century street ballad, 'Galway Races'.

The last two stanzas run:

It's there you see the jockeys and they mounted on most
stately,
The pink and blue, the red and green, the Emblem of our
nation.
When the bell was rung for starting, the horses seemed
impatient,
Though they never stood on ground, their speed was so
amazing.
There was half a million people there all of different
denominations,
The Catholic, the Protestant, the Jew and Prespetarian.
There was no animosity, no matter what persuasion,
But fáilte and hospitality, including fresh acquaintance.

I thought to myself, that about says it all – well, almost, anyhow.

Grande Dame

I have never been quite sure what *femme formidable* means. But I have no doubt at all that my maternal grandmother must have fully fitted the role. Family legend has it that, at the age of nineteen or so, she put her steely eye upon my grandfather; and he, who was also nineteen and intent on setting off for America, found himself instead standing at the altar in double-quick time.

In business as in courtship, she proved masterful. In between her numerous pregnancies – she ended up with eight children – she ran their butcher's shop. To my easy-going, sweet-tempered grandfather (the description is my mother's; she doted on him) fell the agreeable tasks of going about the country buying cattle and sheep, and fleeces for his wool store and fell-mongery. He was devoted to shooting and raising Irish setters – delights that could be readily combined with his rural expeditions. It was, I gather, a most happy marriage, which issued also in a prosperous concern. She was a born businesswoman, he a quietly contented man.

I never knew my Grandpa Oliver; he died when I was a very little child. Nor did I know my grandmother in her days of glory. I remember her only as a chair-bound invalid, the victim of a crippling stroke when she was still in her fifties. My earliest recalled encounter with her was not one calculated to fix my affection. I was sleeping in a little annex off her bedroom on a visit to her house, and woke up to hear her discussing 'Oliver' with my Aunt Bee, who minded her. Suddenly aroused, I heard her say that, altogether, she could never take to me, that I was too quiet for my age (then five or six), that one could never tell what I was thinking – and much more in the same strain. Aunt Bee, however, had more of the fabled heart of gold than anyone else I have met in life; she both thought and said the best of everyone. Now, she demurred, 'Ah, Mother, he's only a small child and is probably a bit frightened, away from home on his own for the first time. And then, remember, all those MacDonaghs are eejity with brains.'

The first of these sentences is only 'to the best of my recollection'. But the second is absolutely her very words: 'all those MacDonaghs are eejity with brains' burned itself into my memory. Aunt Bee had said it in pitying tones, and meant it only as a palliation of my seeming coldness and reserve. But while half of me felt proper shame at the awkward and socially debilitating qualities which unfitted one for the practicalities of life, the other half felt a quite improper pride in my family's superiority of mind. At any rate, one way or other, from that moment onwards, I loved Aunt Bee fervently for what she intended to be a gallant defence of the oppressed. Conversely, I became still more tongue-tied and unprepossessing in Granny's presence. Although she rarely chided me openly, my initial eavesdropping kept me in constant fear of the accusation direct.

I saw a good deal of her when I was a small boy. I was often shipped off to stay with the good Aunt Bee during holidays. Granny always sat in a big chair dominating the drawing room, which was the hub of the house. The room was very large, the place for work or play or reading or games when, as commonly, the rain spilled down; and it was convenient to have me as my grandmother's messenger, to clatter up and down the stairs for her various requests and queries. She had largely lost her capacity to concentrate – except in pursuing some domestic malefactor – and her principal pleasure was watching life go by from the big window at which her chair was placed. Since her house was directly opposite the main post office, and since she had lived in Carlow all her life, this kept her interested and entertained – as well as *au courant* with patches of the local gossip – for comparatively long stretches of time. But she was often bored too, and when bored testy, and when testy liable to turn tyrannical in a petty way.

One summer I arrived to find that Aunt Bee or some other lucky projector had stumbled on a way to keep her amused, and even happy, for almost the entire day long. For two or three months past, my grandmother had taken to (or perhaps one should say, been taken to) the turf. Every day she backed not one but at least half a dozen horses, and this often in a complicated way with each-way doubles and accumulating stakes, all in shillings, florins and half-crowns. It was very puzzling then but I think now that the reason for such extraordinary betting was that, although she set out to make a single choice, she could not bear to let go any mount on which her vagrant fancy had alighted. Hence the gambling cat's cradle with which she daily ended up.

But there had turned out to be a difficulty. My grandmother could not bear to lose. When this happened (during the first day or two, of course), she had apparently sobbed like a child bereft. Aunt Bee told me, in her graphic way, that the front of Granny's grey silk dress was wet from the tears that had coursed all the way down from her eyes. Then someone – it was surely too duplicitous to have been Aunt Bee – found a quick solution to the problem: my grandmother must always win, and win handsomely into the bargain. That way lay happiness in the home.

The thing proved quite easy after all. My grandmother could still read after a fashion; but she was easily muddled by the more esoteric horses' names and could be readily confused as to who was riding which horse and what starting prices were predicted. A little sleight of hand could eventually substitute the day's winners for her original misguided selections.

I was initiated into these counter-tactics soon after I arrived and appointed a sort of punter's mate to my grandmother. The morning began with my reading out from the *Irish Independent* the names of the day's favourites (she never backed outsiders), their riders and the odds, and the tipster, Captain Keen's selections and especially his Naps (or special choices, one for every meeting). These were accompanied by various mutterings and enjoined pauses while Granny scribbled with her pencil on a little pad. What she wrote trailed off into illegibility after the first letter or two; but it mattered little as in the end I was told (with many retreats and changes of mind) what the day's betting programme was to be, and transcribed it all laboriously in my round childish hand. Next, Aunt Bee was summoned; the 'take' money was extracted from Granny's purse (the only time it left her hand during the morning); and list and cash were at last borne away, ostensibly to be lodged with Mr Rickard, our nearby bookie.

There matters usually rested until the *Herald* arrived from Dublin in the evening, with the day's results. Then began the process of rigging Granny's hypothetical bets to match the actual winners and second- or third-placed runners, and to obfuscate the odds at which they had romped home or barely fallen short. She was easily overborne if she protested that she had never heard of this or that horse's name, or if she seemed to fancy that she had scribbled this or that loser on her list. After all, she was being agreeably deceived in her own imagined interest; and she hated to lose any race at all, let alone five or six. So, once the results had been gabbled out, the *Herald* was quickly shuffled aside; then, the great business of calculating the day's winnings could begin. These were usually considerable, two or three pounds at least – smiles and congratulations all round.

I doubt whether Mr Rickard really kept his betting shop open until 7 or 8 pm. But Granny needed little persuasion to believe he did. Accordingly, she gracefully received her little pile of notes and coins with her evening toilette. Mr Rickard was always promptitude itself in yielding up his losses! The only remaining problem was that, in next morning's afterglow of success and with the rich feel of coin and note under her hand, my grandmother was apt to distribute presents to whoever who happened to be nearby at the moment of rejoicing. I received a half a crown, the maid another, Aunt Bee a ten-shilling note and so on throughout the household. All these distributions were gathered in by Aunt Bee during the course of the day, to be slipped back into Granny's purse when the chance next offered, or else retained if this was necessary to keep the whole crazy cycle in balance.

For me, as for any siblings or cousins who were also staying in the house, the role of bogus beneficiary was painful; the loss so palpable, the return of the gain so swift. But one became inured in time to the robotic transfers, the left hand taking with relentless regularity what was scarcely yet warm from possession in the right. There was trouble occasionally, when a strange child or some impoverished adult visitor was unexpectedly endowed. But, outside the range of the family, what could be done? Better simply write it down as a business loss, an unfortunate hazard of the game.

Nothing charmed my grandmother more than Mr Rickard's supposed sporting reaction to his daily train of losses. Whenever she saw him below her on the opposite side of the street, she waved and knocked with what strength she could muster against the window. Mr Rickard did not notice her at first; but once aware of the smiling, gesticulating old lady above him, his eyes were drawn mesmerically towards her whenever he approached or left the post office. He began to look apprehensive, even 'hunted' in an indeterminate sort of way. Meanwhile, Granny expatiated on his 'generosity' – but with tongue in cheek. What was one to think of the professional acumen of one who could devise no countermeasure to staunch an unremitting stream of misfortune? On the other hand, she believed Aunt Bee when, in a moment of hilarity, my aunt presented her with an old costume jewellery, 'diamond' ring found down the side of an armchair, telling her that it had been sent in to her by Mr Rickard as a token of respect for her fidelity as a client. The ring – precious trophy – never left Granny's little finger after that. Ah, but it was the pride which, we are told, always precedes the fall.

On very fine days, Granny was wheeled out in the afternoon for an hour or so, the wheeler being Nancy, a girl of about sixteen, the niece or daughter of someone in the household entourage. On this particular ill-fated summer Thursday, I and an even younger cousin who was also holidaying in Carlow, were directed to accompany the promenaders on their journey to the riverside and towpath. Scarcely had the cortege turned the first corner, however, than we beheld Mr Rickard approaching us rapidly with his little shuffle. He saw us at once – I suppose with horror – but short of his turning tail, or dashing through traffic across the road, we were not to be avoided. Then my grandmother suddenly recognized him, gave little cries of joy, and held aloft her left hand while pointing to the ring, in a stabbing motion, with the index finger of her right.

Mr Rickard had seen us too late; we were upon him before

he could retreat other than to the gutter. Defeated, he half-raised his greasy trilby hat in acknowledgment of Granny's mysterious cries and gestures.

'Your ring; you see I'm wearing your ring. You are a very foolish man, that's all I can say – but generous, very free.'

Rickard was lost but game. 'Thank you, Mrs Oliver, but I'm afraid I'm not certain what you're talking about.'

'The horses, the horses of course. The winners and the prize you sent me for picking the right ones nearly every day. See, I'm wearing it, you silly man.'

So the crazy interchange went on, as if they were two blind crabs trying to advance upon each other on an open strand. Gradually my grandmother's role as punter was revealed to Mr Rickard; he was amazed but unexpectedly suspicious too. Both amazement and suspicion grew by leaps and bounds as Granny rattled madly on about her triumphs and his reported rueful admiration. She became irate at last at his apparent incomprehension. In turn, he somehow came to believe – or so it seemed – that either she or he was being tricked out of tens, or perhaps even hundreds, of pounds.

'I think that you are being tricked, Mrs Oliver. I think that I am being tricked, Mrs Oliver. You had better look out at home, I tell you, oh, yes, had better look out. And I can tell you I'll be looking out, oh, yes, I can warn you that.'

As Mr Rickard's unexpected tirade mounted in shrillness, my grandmother turned whey-faced and began to shake. Nancy and my cousin and I were frozen by shock. Then, as suddenly as he had broken forth, Mr Rickard stopped and turned on his heel, back the way he came. Absurdly – like a mechanical doll – he kept doffing and donning his trilby to Granny, who was now behind him. At last, she whispered that she wanted to go home; and, as if a fairytale spell had been lifted, we all snapped back into life and motion.

That night, she told Aunt Bee (who had already been made the confidante of our party's horrified accounts) that she was tired of the horses, and that Mr Rickard was rather a mean scut after all. She kept, however, a tight hold on her final 'winnings'. Nor did the 'diamond' ring ever leave her finger, during that holiday at least.

Fluff

Fluff was the hygiene teacher in our family. She taught us – in my case unlasting – lessons in ferocious cleanliness. For herself, cleanliness was well up with godliness; and she tried to inspire everyone within her orbit with the same enthusiasm. She saw to it that we children bathed at least three nights a week, and that we worked vigorously at bathing with no idle lolling in warm water. She made her own soap, mainly fag-ends of old soaps boiled down, with some mysterious aromatic additions of her own; she was justly proud of its latheriness, although this meant that it disintegrated almost at the touch. Under her direction, we were reared to change our underclothes with a frequency ill-suited to the climate; and woe betide anyone caught wearing a vest under pyjamas, however merciless the winter chill of our beds might be. Fortunately, she did not demand of others the obsessive dusting and unremitting tidying that she exercised daily on her own room.

Fluff was also devoted to sweet-making, a much more endearing addiction than washing. Here she had mixed success. Her toffee sometimes stuck blackly to its trays, her fudge sometimes fell apart when handled, her creams sometimes failed to crystallize. Hardly ever, however, were Fluff's creations so wide of the mark as not to be seized on and gobbled down. Otherwise, apart from the laundry and linen duties, which she performed with Prussian solemnity and efficiency, Fluff had no domestic interests. She was much too possessed by the artistic temperament to enjoy routine in anything except her few chosen fields of household endeavour.

She had once had a house and a husband of her own, a GP in a Norfolk village. She had been both childless and comfortably supported by one or two or whatever the appropriate number of servants might have been to run her presumably modest establishment. Then came the tragedy of her life. Her husband was cited as co-respondent in a divorce case, his partner in shame being the wife of the local squire and, worse still, one of his patients. In the event, the squire got his divorce, but the doctor did not. Fluff had been so deeply mortified that she would yield him nothing, which meant that he, as the 'guilty' one, would have to wait many years before he could hope to remarry. Meanwhile, possibly with her approbation, he was struck off the Medical Register for misconduct. He could earn no money until he was restored and Fluff received nothing more from him either then or after she came to my father, her brother, for support.

Fluff was in many ways an exotic creature in our midst, a diamond surrounded by moonstones, a show jumper among harness horses. In a society in which talking was a leading art, she stood head and shoulders above the rest. In a society which abounded in storytellers, she was still remarkable. 'Did I ever tell you about the time I sat next to the Earl of Mayo at dinner?' she would ask before launching into one of her Norfolk tales. 'Well, when he heard I was born in Limerick, he threw back his head and laughed. As a young man, he said, way back in the 1890s, he did a sort of Grand Tour with another bright buck like himself. At one stage they landed up in Constantinople where his uncle or some relation or other had once been a crony of the Sultan, Ambassador or Plenipotentiary or something. Anyhow, the Earl got permission to tour all over the Sultan's palace, though perhaps not quite everywhere, I suppose. At last, the two young fellows got down to the kitchens, which were vast, stretching the whole length of the basement underground. The place was filled with dozens of Turks of all sorts and sizes but suddenly he saw one face turkey-red from toiling over an oven – and it was female too! He turned politely to ask his guide who she was, when she herself stepped forward, grabbed his hand and declared, "The Earl of Mayo, is it? Well, there you are, I'm Mrs McGrath from the Windmill, Limerick." He never discovered more; the guide whipped them both away. Now, isn't that a nice mystery for you? How did an old woman from the Windmill, Limerick, end up basting fowl in a Turkish cellar? And the Earl said she looked as happy as Larry with it.'

Of course, words down in black and white cannot begin to convey Fluff's vivacity, charm or effortless command of attention. Nor can any repetition of her narrations convey a tithe of her wit, sharp thrusts or suppleness in the use of words. She seemed glittering in readiness at all points to become a writer; and indeed this must have been her hope of reshaping her life after she came to live with us in Roscommon. Later on, I guessed the significance of two volumes, on her bedroom mantelpiece, the *Writers' and Artists' Yearbook*s for 1930 and 1931. I suppose that she found there the names and addresses of publishers and agents, and other signposts and directions for the literary trade; but whether or not she ever used them I have no idea.

From some guarded remarks of my parents from time to time, I came to understand that, when she joined our household, it was expected on all sides that she would take up the business of authorship. After all, she arrived (according to the account on which we children were reared) trailing the distant glory of having won Second Place in English in the Junior Grade Examination for all Ireland, immediately behind her elder sister who had come first. Alas, this early achievement was translated by my innocent mother and father into a sure recipe for being able to compose books; and to them – happily unliterary people – publication would follow composition as surely as the night the day. But despite Fluff's wonderful dexterity of tongue, and genius for throwing off comic verse and doggerel at high speed, I doubt if she ever wrote more than a page or two seriously, let alone canalized usefully her torrential speech. She was blessed, to the point of brimming over, with the artistic temperament. But she was also a sad exemplar of the abyss, so commonly to be found in the Irish of her (and indeed my own) generation, between the artistic temperament and the artistic achievement. Fluff was a songbird who never sang.

She was nonetheless my literary inspiration. Apart from embedding in my mind, when she first arrived, great stretches of sing-song poetry to cure my stammer, she took me with her from the start on her weekly trawls of our public library up the street. This was a remarkable repository for a town of less than two thousand inhabitants, remarkable even as the headquarters of a county service. At least, so it then seemed to me. It was the inexhaustible Aladdin's Cave of my youth.

Fluff quickly became the darling friend of the librarian, even to the point of calling her by her improbable – for the west of Ireland – Christian name, Gladys; and whether because of this or because it was the general practice we were allowed to take out six books apiece each week. At first, my choices were all children's, then boys' books, on which Fluff merely cast a casual eye. But gradually one of her passionate, if short-lived, reading interests, international affairs, began to wear off on me. I took to glancing through her borrowed books on Goering, Ciano, Manchuria, Abyssinia and the like, then looked harder, and finally toiled my way through some of them for myself.

There is still an attic in my mind filled with dusty, arid, unused and unusable shards of information on the continental happenings of the mid-1930s. Only one ever kept its pith and warmth for me. It was a *Daily Express* photograph of a young Jewish refugee walking the tarmac at Croydon aerodrome, with the snub-nosed sixteen-seater passenger plane that had carried her from Germany in the background. She was a very lovely girl, I thought, with thick plaited hair, a big-buttoned overcoat, ribbon-crossed white stockings to her knees (a thing I had never seen before), and some sort of Teddy trailing from one hand. The newspaper reported her to be fourteen years of age; I was twelve. The gap in ages did not seem quite impossible to bridge. I simply fell in love with her there and then. I secretly saved the page and kept the cutting for a long, long time, fantasizing about tracking her down in England when I was eighteen years old and she was twenty. But somewhere or other along the line the winds of time must have whipped away my picture. Even yet, though, her image rises true and full and faithfully to my mind's eye.

Fluff's main, steady reading, however, was contemporary novels. Doubtless, she had had her fill already of reading 'great' works. At any rate, while she preached them to me incessantly, she hardly ever practised reading them herself. Waugh and Graham Greene apart, the authors and fiction she sought were almost all upper-middle or middlebrow in quality. Writers such as Somerset Maugham and Galsworthy, and currently celebrated novels such as Cronin's *The Citadel*, Priestley's *The Good Companions*, du Maurier's *Rebecca* and Mitchell's *Gone With the Wind* were now her choices.

She talked enthusiastically about these books to me (she had to talk to someone) but scrupled about letting me loose among them. So she tied together the pages that she thought too indelicate for my tender eyes with red knitting wool, and left it to my honour to pass by these dangerous passages unread. I was obedient; in any case, I could never hope to retie the red wool so neatly as to deceive her. Besides, I was not really much interested in the novels that she favoured at that time.

Things went smoothly for a time with my knowing just enough about her books to satisfy her need to vent her enthusiasm upon an informed listener. Then one fatal Saturday I, by mistake, returned one of her red-tied volumes among my own. Only as Gladys accepted my armful of books over the desk did Fluff notice that the shameful woollen bindings had never been removed. She started to explain but after a few confused words fell silent. Meanwhile, Gladys put the book on one side for later investigation. 'You idiot, you stupid boy,' hissed Fluff in my ear as we descended the library steps, 'She'll think I'm a horrible woman, tying up all the *risqué* parts to snigger over them again. Oh, my God, how shall I ever face Gladys now? Ohhh, you are a stupid boy.'

That ended my early run in modern fiction. The ball of red wool was put away, and Fluff had to content herself with giving me occasional quotations and synopses. Fortunately, Waugh survived as permitted, indeed encouraged, reading, although I remained puzzled as to why the hero of *Decline and Fall* was sent to prison – the white slave traffic not being a familiar topic in our household conversations.

Even if our reading paths, which had been momentarily conjoined, diverged again, Fluff remained my mentor. She had an extraordinary ear and eye for the slightest failings in either grammar or syntax, and even for solecisms or verbal infelicities which she found hard to pin down exactly but knew instinctively were present and offensive. She guarded jealously against such encroachments as that of 'presently' upon 'at present' (or 'now') or 'disinterested' upon 'uninterested' or 'convince' upon 'persuade' or 'like' upon 'as if'. As for the grosser confusions to be heard on or seen in the modern media – 'mitigate' for 'militate', 'imply' for 'infer', 'flout' for 'flaunt', and so on – she would simply have refused to believe that such things could be among supposedly literate people.

Fluff was also a thoroughgoing snob (or elitist, as she herself thought) in the more obvious sense. Well before U and non-U became current coin, she insisted that we say 'napkin' instead of 'serviette', 'lavatory' instead of 'toilet', and 'sweet' or 'pudding' instead of 'dessert'. We were as well drilled in table etiquette as any waiter in the Ritz, and knew how to lay out the knives, forks and spoons for six or seven courses in their proper order. We could all have dined comfortably with the Earl of Mayo, no questions asked.

Fluff never seemed happy after we moved from Roscommon to Waterford in the early 1940s. Perhaps she felt an accepted eccentric in a small town but un-personed in a strange if uncrowded city. In Roscommon there were two or three people, like Gladys, who, in part at least, spoke her own language and could give her a good game or two, if not a full set, in her own particular sort of verbal and intellectual tennis. In Waterford, she knew no one outside the home and seemed too dispirited even to try to find a kindred soul. Suddenly – at least to me, who was then in Dublin – Fluff left for London where she, probably for the first time in her life, went out to work, taking a job in some canteen or factory.

Was this a sadder or a better course for her? I do not know, although on meeting her again several times when I was a research student in London later on, she spoke of parts of her new life with all her old familiar gaiety, sarcasm and wit. Lucky her co-workers! She must have blazed like a meteor across their skies. But in the end, I fear, I let Fluff down. One of the traits of which I am most ashamed is proving so often to be an eleven- instead of an eleventh-hour labourer in the vineyard – not someone who comes to work only for the final hour, but, much worse, someone who works until the final hour but lacks the perseverance to last out until the end. My retrospect is darkened by missed deathbeds after long attention and the final fatal unanswered letter after years of dutiful replies. So it was with Fluff. I met her less and less as I became absorbed elsewhere, and even postponed the inquiry that I should have made when (as things turned out) she was actually dying. Fortunately for Fluff, she had a niece more considering and larger-hearted than this particular nephew. As with all my failures, it rises up to strike me now and then. Fluff gave me so much in the beginning; I gave her back so little at the very close.

Thin Air

We never knew what we might find when we ran home from school at lunchtime. Once it was a salesman of the newly-invented electric carpet sweeper. Even before seen, he could be heard pounding out his spell (it may really have been the famous 'It beats as it sweeps as it cleans') above the deafening drone and sinister rattle of the Electrolux my mother has just bought. Another lunchtime the eight volumes of Newnes' *Pictorial Knowledge* were laid out, spines gleaming upwards, on the dining-room table. Their purchase was still in doubt, but fortunately the pleading eyes of us children decided the question in their favour. Thank God for that. Much of what I remember from early days, especially the most interesting parts, I trace back to *Pictorial Knowledge*. This is especially the case with such rags and tatters of scientific information as have ever come my way – I must have been the last boy in Western Europe to have missed, or escaped, any teaching in the natural sciences. Deeply imprinted in my memory is the illustration of the digestive process, with little men in white coats, stirring and adding, level by level, as the food descended and thickened on its journey bowelward.

Then there was the day on which I arrived home for lunch to find an itinerant upholsterer stripping away all the material from our drawing-room sofa, armchairs and pouffes. When I came back to lunch next day, it was to find my mother standing appalled amid the wreckage of her treasures, her face tragic as Dido's among the ruins of Carthage. My father, foolishly trustful as usual, had advanced the upholsterer a pound, most of which he had already drunk before lighting out of town by the evening train.

But the best lunchtime surprise of all was the installation of our first radio in 1933 or thereabouts. To us, it was, of course a wireless (strange name when one remembers the complication of its intestines) and its travelling assembler 'the wireless man'.

Our wireless man must have been a notable pioneer. Apart from some mysterious fiddling with the silver lungs called valves, I don't recall any repairs being needed in nearly a decade's constant use. The machine was actually put together and linked up to the aerial during our hour for lunch. For once, we did not put eating first, but waited and waited and waited for the magic voice. And come it did before we had to race back along the streets to school. After fusillades of static, it announced itself as emanating from Athlone, full twenty miles away.

The wireless immediately became our most venerated household god. It stood in state on our black oak dumb waiter in the dining room. This meant that it was always silent during mealtimes – the defences of civilization had not yet totally collapsed: not that that mattered greatly to us children for we ate always in the kitchen. Such abstinence was typical of the family's treatment of the god. Our wireless was not used in the fashion of a radio today. It never pattered and spieled, mostly unnoticed, in the background. Instead, it was employed, and then rather solemnly, only for specific listening. I can't recall which programmes my parents regularly heard; not many, I'm sure, apart from the evening news. I heard few myself. Sport of course predominated. But there were two weekly offerings to which I was devoted. The first was *Question Time*, followed eagerly by the entire household, on Sunday nights; the second, Austin Clark's 'workshop' (as we would say today) for would-be and beginning poets every Thursday evening – for which I was usually the solitary auditor.

It is strange how an apparently well-established and universal social institution can vanish totally. It must be fifty years since I saw or heard mention of *Question Time*, although in its day, in the mid-1930s, it must have been the jewel in Radio Éireann's crown. It appealed to all. Sunday nights were sacred to Joe Linnane's programme as it 'played' live in town after town throughout the land. It was really a very simple, gimmick-less, even primitive quiz show. The cash prizes were mere tokens. The contestants competed for honour only, for the five-minute glory of being pronounced the winner so that all the nation could hear one's name. But the game spread far and fast beyond the airwaves. 'Question Times' were soon being held locally to raise five or ten pounds for charity or some other public purpose.

Halls were packed as people trooped in to hear their fellow citizens astound them with their knowledge or their ignorance. Then matches between neighbouring towns began, each with its team of home champions and local polymaths. Meanwhile, Joe Linnane or Radio Éireann or both published little books of questions (graded 2 mark, 4 mark and 6 mark just like Joe's own on *The Big Time*); and these became standard practice, or test works for the ambitious.

It happened that my incessant random reading had left me with stores of information, which were quite worthless for all usual purposes, but possibly valuable for *Question Time*. Sometimes storybook beginnings actually occur, and so it was with my *Question Time* career. At one night session at our local hall, a contestant having been declared absent, my vicariously vain father pushed me forward to fill the missing place. Instantly, I became the Boy Wonder of the town, to be pointed out curiously next day by people in the street and jeered at as a show-off by the majority of my peers at school. I had almost won my very first contest, and went on to score two or three victories in a row. How the defeated adults must have loathed a ten-year-old whelp who had picked up so many fistfuls of heterogeneous facts! At any rate, they had shortly to endure my company, in the backs of cars and to the fore at supper tables, in the midst of their own covert courtships and heavy gossip, whenever Roscommon 'played away' in neighbouring towns such as Castlerea.

The *Question Time* craze soon died off, and with it my little turn of local fame, but not before Roscommon took to the air itself one Sunday evening. This was a towering event.

Before the great Joe Linnane and his huge hexagonal microphones and coils and festoons of wires, and his stage manager and entourage of recording engineers, we competitors shrank morally in much the same way as Alice shrank physically after eating the reducing cake. I think it was Joe's preliminary admonitions to bear in mind the presence and susceptibilities of the vast listening world that seemed to have broken our collective spirit. Together with all the oppressive paraphernalia of a 1930s broadcast, they certainly broke mine.

I suppose that I must have stammered a correct response or two when it came my turn to stumble over the cables on the floor on my way to the main microphone. But I remember none – only my shameful failures. Two of these were burnt poker-like into my brain. 'Pacific and Oriental,' I confidently replied when asked what the letters 'P&O' stood for – I should have said 'peninsular' not 'Pacific'; and I was dumbstruck when asked which Irish town had a palindromic name – I should have thought of 'Navan'. I have since known the correct answers for more than sixty years without ever being able to deploy them in a conversation. What a waste of useless information, and my very first venture into radio was – not surprisingly – my last for at least a decade.

Austin Clark's programme was, by contrast, a highbrow and a 'niche' affair. Its audience must have been tiny, mostly aspiring poets, I daresay; and even in the Ireland of the 1930s these were comparatively few. Clark was himself quite a serious poet, although everybody was a moon while the sun of W.B. still waxed. For the programme, people sent in verses for his appraisal, and Clark selected two or three for judgment on each occasion. Although he read them aloud in lovely tones and found sweet cadences in the most unpromising phrases, he was a severe critic. I hesitated long before I submitted one of my pieces to the scrutiny of 'content, language, imagery and rhythm' that the programme threatened. I need not have worried. Neither my first pieces nor any of its successors was considered worthy of appraisal – I think. For my friend Hal told me that he had heard Clark reading out my name and poem one Thursday evening when I was away on holidays. But Hal was a bit of a *farceur* and the last fellow in the world to listen voluntarily to a verse-speaking half an hour. Nonetheless, I could not bear but to ask him, 'And what did Mr Clark say about it? What did he think of it?' 'Not much,' said Hal, 'he thought it was pretty awful.' Though I did not believe him for an instant, I acted as if the death sentence had truly been pronounced. Austin Clark's postbox and programme knew me no more.

All this was really the bread and butter of our wireless set; and even transmissions from London came to seem ordinary fare. The glamour, the romance of the whole business belonged to the short-wave stations, even if these were only momentarily audible amid the storm of atmospheric shot and shell. My cousin Tony and I nursed the ambition of hearing American radio; and indeed we once caught snatches of a gridiron game between Notre Dame (our team, of course) and Navy. God knows where the broadcast came from – Philadelphia swims feebly to the surface of recall – but for us it mattered only that all that vast waste of grey Atlantic was being bridged. We never learned the score or the result but we did gather the perfectly correct impression that most of the time at an American Football match is not spent in play; one long interval seemed to be filled with a recruitment advertisement for the Navy, so far as we could decipher the message through the bursts of static. Never mind: we were hearing in between the horrid cacophonies, a voice speeding faster than any arrow, across three thousand miles of trackless air, setting off within us viscous impressions (cinema-derived, no doubt) of strange hybrids – huge-helmeted, wall-shouldered, little-hipped and thin-breeched creatures – charging inexplicably in all directions in an explosion of play before the commentary sank again to the even ground that signalled the restoration of inactivity. Mystery and marvel, it was both.

Our biggest coup should have been listening to the world heavyweight championship between Joe Louis and Max Schmeling. We had planned for this as if for a safari. The broadcast was scheduled for 2.30 am, our time, so we laid in rugs against the cold, and against hunger lemonade, Yorkshire Toffee, Kerry Creams and an orange and an apple each. Vicarious adventure would join hands with midnight feast. It all seemed much less enticing when the alarm clock ripped us into surly wakefulness; but struggle up we did at last only to find that we had risen in vain. The Madison Square Garden crowd-roars drowned almost every word of commentary whenever – and it was very rarely – that static did not drown the cheering and all else. Our feast was a gloomy affair after all, not even begun until we had finally abandoned our attempt in despair. Two days later, I was aghast to read that blacks had committed suicide in Harlem in their desolation at the defeat of their idol, Lewis. Somehow or other, I felt too a curious species of relief that I had heard nothing of a contest that had produced so tragic a result.

There was one sport, however, that I listened to alone; Tony although a gifted hurler, had no interest at all in cricket. My own interest in it far exceeded my knowledge of the game, for I had never seen it played apart from momentary glimpses in Movietone News. I had read about it in English schoolboy stories and knew the cap colours and careers of the great players of the day from the fronts and backs of cigarette cards. The rest derived from my native wit working on shards of information and impressions. Nonetheless, as soon as I discovered Test Match broadcasts I became their addict. Much later in my life, I came to realize that while watching cricket is usually an unmarred joy, and seeing it on television better still, listening to it being described on radio is the best of all. By lucky chance, I had stumbled on the right entrance gate.

Unhappy Days

In the best-worst Irish tradition, my memories of my early schooldays are mostly unhappy. I got off to a lucky start in Limerick. I began in the Montessori system; hence I read miraculously early and learnt not to feel guilty about taking a midday rest. Next, at the ages of five and six, I was taught, together with my sister, by a governess in Donegal. She seemed a very big and wise girl to us, but I suppose that she was really no more than fourteen years of age and merely an average school-leaver in days when school ceased at twelve or thirteen for the majority. At any rate, she knew a great deal more than we did, and successfully communicated much of it.

So when I turned up at the convent school in Roscommon I was quite up to scratch for my age, academically. But, believe it or not, I encountered straight away one of those fabulous nun-monsters, who seem, in retrospect, too fantastic ever to have existed. Sister X (let us call her that) struck terror into our seven-year-old hearts by lighting the end of her thin cane from the red oil lamp which burnt below the picture of the Sacred Heart hanging over the mantelpiece in our classroom. The most anti-clerical of Italian film directors could not have devised a more blood-chilling or blasphemous set of images. In reality, it was almost all smoke and mirrors. I can't recall anyone being struck or even threatened, except subliminally, by the smouldering stick. All the same, it produced a trembling and obedient class.

Although she was not at all to blame for it, it was also in Sister X's class that I received my most searing childhood humiliation. The Inspector arrived one morning at our classroom door. School inspections were long-dreaded events, akin to the visitations of the Czar's emissaries in the mid-nineteenth-century Russian countryside. This particular inquisition concluded in an examination of the class's singing – in Irish, of course. We were arranged in tiers, boys and girls together, along the raked benches of the room. The tuning fork quivered; the note was given; we began. Up and down the rows stalked the red-faced, cross-visaged Inspector. Suddenly, he shouted 'Stop,' and turned querulously on Sister, 'one of them is singing out of key.' Sister shrugged in silent disengagement.

'Arís,' the Inspector shouted; even our Irish was up to translating this as 'Again.' Now he passed along the rows more slowly, pausing and bending before almost every little singing mouth. He bent and paused longest when he reached the very end of the second top row. 'Stop,' he roared again, seizing me by the shoulder and force-marching me to the aisle, 'I think I've found him.' I was of course then ordered to be silent. The class began for the third time, now without me; the Inspector trod amongst them with a lighter, almost a jaunty step; he began to keep time with his hands; his frown faded in favour of a faint smile at first, then a decided smirk. 'Ah, yes, that was the trouble. Keep that boy out of the singing class in future, Sister, and things should go well.' He spoke with insufferable self-satisfaction.

For once, seven-year-olds felt, or at any rate showed pity. When the bell rang for the end of class, no one jeered, or even looked, at me in my shameful isolation. I don't suppose that anyone went so far as to speak to me that day. After all, what was there to be said? The priest had pronounced me a leper. Nevertheless, Sister would have none of that. Next singing class, she dragged me from the aisle into which I had automatically shuffled, and planted me down at the end of my usual row, with instructions to open and close my mouth as seemed appropriate to the words and tune, but to issue forth no sound. I suffered in silence in the midst of song.

Soon afterwards, towards the end of the academic year, the class was, as customarily, divided according to sex, and its male half marched off to the Boys' National School. Conscripts following the sergeant to their barracks of induction must have felt much the same as we did. Not that Brother Francis, who led our straggle through the town's streets, was at all a martinet. If Sister was Sister X, he was Brother A. I can recall him on occasions, in later years, setting aside our dreary rote choruses and drills for an afternoon, gathering us about him in a circle and reading aloud stories from Hans Andersen – o rare, o blessed hours. Nor was there much of the tyrant about our first boys' teacher, Mr Foley. He was a mild man, a distantly friendly near-neighbour to my parents. It was this mildness which was – almost – to produce my next most desperate hour of shame.

Summer holidays had quickly followed our transition to the Boys' National School; and that year my father, for a miracle, took us 'overseas'. Rhyl in north Wales, instead of Tramore, Co. Waterford, was chosen for our ritual fortnight by the beach. To my sister and me, who had never seen any but Ireland's shores and were never to do so again until after World War II, the journey was as marvel-full as riding in by camel train to Samerkand. But in fact, the cross-channel passage apart, we merely travelled, crowded and third-class rail, the short distance from Holyhead to Rhyl, where we stayed put.

On the day after our return, Mr Foley caught sight of me across the street, and called me over to tell of my adventures. Town rumour had doubtless exaggerated our excursion, and in my vainglory at interested notice by a teacher out of class, I swelled out the story wildly. I was deep into my imaginary, encyclopaedia-inspired London doings, when my father suddenly joined us from behind. There was time for only one great thrill of shame – but it ran through me from head to toe like an electric bolt – before Mr Foley piled terror upon terror by saying, 'The lad has just been telling me, Mr MacDonagh, about Madame Tussaud's and how you took him all over Nelson's *Victory* on the Thames.'

My heart ceased to beat; my lungs ceased to breathe. My face flushed in overlapping waves; my eyes were locked to the flagstone at my feet, my thoughts narrowed to a single prayer for immediate extinction. At last, my father spoke, 'Yes, he did like seeing over the *Victory*.' How sweet is salvation after the abandonment of hope: no matter how my father might rant at me or punish me or despise me in an hour's time, I had somehow escaped complete disgrace, final humiliation, before Mr Foley. Nor did it end there. My supposed tour of the Tower of London was next solemnly discussed between the men. At last the conversation turned slowly back to home affairs, and I could creep away, still trembling all over from the averted doom. And what a prince of chivalry my father proved – as always. Never, never did he say a word or so much as look a look about my stupid, braggart lies, not even to my mother, not even to myself.

Perhaps it was only common justice, however, that in the end I failed to escape Mr Foley's censure. Four days before school reopened – on a sunny Thursday afternoon – he saw and heard me across the street, pounding frantically on our hall door and sobbing as if my heart would break. When he reached me, and I turned my dirt-and-grief-stained face to his, he leapt backwards in his shock. For as I tried to speak, he saw only a grinning black mass where once my teeth had shone.

The explanation was – and indeed still is – complicated. At seven years of age, and as yet a relative newcomer to Roscommon, I was desperate to secure some footing among my peers. One avenue that led on to respect was of course taking 'dares'. Some 'dares' I daren't take – anything involving heights, for instance – but otherwise my passion to gain acceptance rendered me absolutely reckless. That afternoon, as some other boys and I played amongst the ancient tar machines and near-empty tar barrels at the county council roadworks up our street, we began to knead the sun-softened tar into balls to throw at one another. It proved a disappointing sport – the balls usually stuck altogether or for a fatal moment, in the thrower's hand. Then someone issued a 'dare' to taste and chew one of the filthy things. Madly, I took up the gauntlet, which all the rest had evaded, only to find that the ball filled all my mouth, that the tar had cemented my upper and lower teeth together, and that I could breathe only through my nose and make only horrid noises in my chest. Terror-stricken, I (doubtless wisely) gave no thought to possible salvation by my companions but raced for home. Thus it was that, at the callously unmoved hall door, a most pitiable creature came to startle Mr Foley out of his skin.

Meanwhile, my pounding at the door continued – vainly; for it was a half-holiday afternoon and everybody seemed to be out of doors. It took Mr Foley some time to grasp the situation, but once he did, he had no hesitation in leading me across to his own house and throwing the problem, literally as well as figuratively, into his wife's lap. Mrs Foley took it all coolly, calmed me down a little, scraped and poked with an assortment of pencils, steel knitting needles and sharp-ended vegetable peeling knives, and finally forced my teeth apart, and started to rub them one by one (God knows why but it seemed to work) with butter. As she rubbed, she hissed as if I were a horse being groomed; but it was decidedly a hiss of disapproval, not one of rhythmic labour. She was not amused. Nor did she particularly pity my terror, shame and pain. Neither did Mr Foley. He led me back in stern silence and handed me over as if from one police officer to another. I draw a veil (as they say) over the hullaballoos at home, the various, voluble and seemingly endless explanations, expostulations, recriminations and commiserations, and the renewed struggle to scrape bare my teeth, and clean and chill and soothe the rawness of my mouth. In time, all this passed away. But Mr Foley did not pass away. I had blotted my copybook irretrievably before I had even crossed his classroom door. I was lucky that his rule was mild and his resort to the cane only occasional. Otherwise, it would have gone hard with me that year, as he had written me down as a boy to be watched carefully and leapt on at the slightest wanderings from the straight and narrow path.

Two classes on, we fell into the clutches of the dreaded Mr – well, let us call him Y. If Sister were Sister X, he must have been Y or Z, sunk to the very bottom of the schoolboy scale. Poor man, I am quite sure now that he merited pity rather than hate. He must have been stricken already by some dire disease. His face was putty-grey, his voice whispering-hoarse, and, once hoisted into his chair on the rostrum with the aid of his walking sticks and one or two pupil-conscripts, he stayed there almost all the day. But we felt no pity for him. We were young savages, indifferent to everything except his lashing irony, his lightning impatience and his ready resort to the cane – even to punishing us en masse upon occasions.

I suppose that the various surrounding horrors – his hawking coughs, stained handkerchiefs and old shapeless clothes, and the dirty, dark, dank, dust-ridden classroom (all the classrooms of the Boys' National School were all of those but Mr Y's alone was without side-windows) – added much to our unreasoning daily fears. But our chief apprehension was that a universal round of caning would strike the class out of the blue – because of the failure of some unknown culprit to confess his crime, or the general worthlessness of the preceding night's homework, or disobedience of a command for total silence, or some other last straw falling unluckily on Mr Y's back. It was not that we suffered much physically. With a class of almost thirty strong, the strokes were only two apiece, feeble enough to start with, and rapidly diminishing in severity. It was the shuffle of the long line awaiting execution, and the steady whistle of the falling cane, regular as the guillotine's thud, which broke our collective spirit.

Strangely enough, I remember the one reprieve of that year much more clearly than the several mass punishments. I happened to be the first in line on that occasion. It was usually left to ourselves to form our own crocodile of ignominy and I had been the one pushed forward at the very moment when Mr Y lost patience with our shuffling and dodging, and beat 'Halt' upon his desk. We were being pre-examined ahead of the visit of the Religious Inspector next day, and had shown up very badly in the face of Mr Y's questions. 'All out,' he had ordered angrily, 'all hands out, the lot of you.' As I stood shivering in the foreground before him, he suddenly burst into a laugh and demanded, 'And what was said to the leper after he had been cured?' A tremulous, hesitant, ragged chorus answered him, 'Go, show yourself to the priest.' Mr Y's little joke was now complete. 'Go, thou, and do likewise,' he responded, indifferent to the mixture of texts, and snuffling at his own wit and our bewilderment. It seemed to take forever for us to realize that we were being mysteriously spared, and to begin to stumble over one another on the way back to the safety of our desks.

I'm not sure that the trauma of the eleventh-hour escape was not worse than half an hour of swollen and aching hands. Each made for its own particular version of unhappy days; but the escape left an inexpungible memory.

Yet, even as I write this, sun chases cloud. In my recollection, moments of ecstasy keep springing up, dissipating momentarily the black remembrances. The playground, with its cracked crumbling, concrete and mossy interstices, may have matched the schoolrooms for squalor, but it was there that I was once struck with a flash of exquisite delight: I had – a most improbable and solitary triumph – touched the end-wall first, to win the favourite game of our recess. The school may have been backed by only a small patch of greasy pasture and a single tree, but it was there that I wrestled with other small boys, loving the fun of it, rolling over and over, grappling, sweating, smelling from moment to moment the grass and earth at one's nose, sweet and pungent despite all the trampling feet.

I also remember fondly our little headmaster, Brother B (well, Brother C+ at least), whose humour we tickled when we reached his shores after emerging from the storms of Mr Y. Brother B was the only teacher I ever met who seemed to find his pupils funny – though not in a way that wounded our various *amours propres*: he was neither offensive about, nor perceptibly softened by, our schoolboy gaffes and howlers. We generously allowed him his amusement, and joined in it when we could – not so much from sycophancy as from the infection of his invariable good temper.

Warmest of all are the memories of those enchanted winter afternoons when Brother A crowded us around him near the glowing stove and held us spellbound as he read aloud the story of the 'Little Tin Soldier' or (an extraordinary incomer to the west of Ireland in the 1930s) the jog-along verses of *Around the Boree Log*. What could ever equal this for sheer, pure, cherubic bliss without alloy: instead of strain, ease; instead of giving, getting; instead of school, anti-school – at least, in our imaginations.

Perhaps then I should think of my first school years in terms of light as well as dark, of unhappiness shafted through with joy. But memory can't be reasoned with, and there the black has always predominated. Besides, who could be so insufferably affected as to speak of the *chiaroscuro* of the classroom?

Up de Valera and All That

Someone visiting the Aran Islands in the mid-1930s observed that the only English the local children knew – which they kept calling out as they surrounded him – was 'A pinny for sweets. Up de Valera.' This pretty well sums up my impression of the politics of Roscommon at the time. Almost the entire town seemed populated by de Valera supporters; and at school there were only two dissenters. One was the son of a Cumann na nGaedheal (or Treatyite) member for the county, and he was tacitly forgiven his offence, partly because he was wise enough never to mention politics and partly because even the most rabid Fianna Fáiler recorded that something was due to filial piety. I, who was equally an inheritor of my politics, was not so fortunate. I was forced to defend Cumann na nGaedheal and its successor, Fine Gael, *contra mundum*. This meant serving as a target for the jeers of the invariably triumphant de Valera-ites. Constant victories rendered them tolerantly contemptuous rather than nastily aggressive; and I could even safely answer back their mockery whenever they had been mellowed by some particularly glorious success.

My political pedigree was normal enough for an Irish Catholic family, though perhaps more various in its strands than most. My grandfather Oliver had taken the Parnellite side after the 'split'. He would, therefore, as a very young man, have striven on Parnell's behalf in the (for Parnell) disastrous Carlow by-election of 1891. My grandmother Oliver, however, was supposed once to have slapped her pocket and said that she supported whoever filled it. This was in response to her being rebuked by some perfervid spirit for supplying meat to the British army during their summer manoeuvres around Carlow. If uttered at all, her dictum was probably an expression of her innate pugnacity rather than a serious opinion; and in any event she would have been voteless at the time.

My other grandmother was a fierce Sinn Féiner during the Troubles; she was once hauled off to some barracks in Limerick in a lorry with a number of other protestors. Perhaps to her disappointment, she was not 'detained' there long; but at least she had the cachet ever after of having been arrested by the Black and Tans. I never discovered what the protest or demonstration was about, or how soon she was released. I learnt only that The Mote (as her children called her) had been vastly amused when someone in the lorry had started to chant 'God Save Ireland' and another roared, 'Shut up there or we'll miss the ride.'

I can't imagine my father ever following such a lead, but he had his radical moments. In 1918, he signed the national Anti-Conscription pledge to resist, by force if necessary, induction into the British army. There was not much to wonder at in this: most young Irishmen then did the same. More surprisingly, he was one of the five bank officials who founded the IBOA (Irish Bank Officials Association), which later proved itself a surprisingly militant trade union. But in national terms he was never a Republican but rather a passive and moderate Free Stater. My mother's family were solidly in the same tradition throughout the 1920s and 1930s, and of course she herself – without any interest of her own in politics – simply followed their lead. I was therefore bred up to be a Cosgraveite and Cumann na nGaedheal partisan. Or rather my parents' mild inclination was blown out by my childish enthusiasm into another of my 'causes'.

My first remembered general election was that of 1932, and my first political experience that of encountering a (to me) gigantic poster, erected at the corner of our street, and inscribed with the cryptic message, 'Remember the Seventy Seven'. The words were painted in red, with drips from the letters to indicate their bloody implication. It was Fluff, a sometime Republican like her mother, who explained that the 'Seventy Seven' were anti-Treatyite prisoners who had been executed by the Cumann na nGaedheal government in 1922–3 in a series of reprisals: they had now been adopted by the Fianna Fáil party as martyrs calling out for vengeance. Whatever its effect on the voters, the poster terrified me and haunted my dreams for nights.

Roscommon was traditionally a radical political county, many of its voters being small farmers struggling to make a living from poor soil. It had been to the forefront during the Land War of the 1880s, gone Parnellite in the 1890s and returned the first Sinn Féiner ever to be elected to parliament in 1917. Small wonder that revenge for the 'Seventy Seven' should be invoked in scarlet letters in the town during the passionate contest of 1932. Yet my childish impression of effortless Fianna Fáil supremacy cannot have been altogether right. Even as a small boy of seven I could sense the great antagonism and even hatreds generated by this particular campaign. In long retrospect, it forms a collage of the purple faces of shouting men, wearing celluloid collars, stringy ties and watch chains; planks laid on porter barrels to make platforms; sudden scuffles in the background; people hanging out of upstairs windows, safe above the stormy meetings; and flags, tricolours, everywhere, even on telegraph poles and the sides of lorries, gable ends of shops and houses, and on the bonnets, and protruding spare wheels, at the rears of cars.

'I hear Cosgrave will be coming on here from Athlone on Wednesday,' said my father as we walked home from Sunday Mass nine or ten days before the polling. I had been pestering him for a week with election questions so that this was a gracious as well as gratuitous sharing of information. He was ill-rewarded. I instantly turned suppliant eyes upon him. 'Can you take me to see him, Dad? And to hear him speaking? He'll surely be speaking, if he's here? Please, Dad, please.'

'Of course, I can't just take off to hear Mr Cosgrave or Mr Anybody Else – not that I'd want to in weather like this. And what about your school, Roll? I imagine it's in the morning he'll be passing through here.'

My father scarcely ever sounded decisive or even firm (he usually got his own way, very quietly), but this was one of the rare occasions. His face was set. I did not even try to argue with him. But for some mysterious and seemingly miraculous cause my mother then intervened on my behalf. 'No,' she said, 'I read that Mr Cosgrave won't be here till two or three. I don't mind taking Roll to see him; his heart is set on it. It won't kill him not to go back to school after lunch for once in a while.' To this day, I don't know what moved her to such nobility. In amazed thanksgiving, I threw myself upon her.

So it was that we were standing together at the corner of Church St and Main St at 2 pm on Wednesday afternoon, trying to face away from the icy wind blowing off the surviving patches of the morning's snow. We had scarcely taken up station when the first of a chain of cars began to chug and rattle past us; then another, and another, and another. I numbered them up to thirty before I lost count in my confusion; there must have been fifty altogether in the stream. It was – what I had only yet heard of vaguely as another American Marvel – a motorcade! Almost every car had a tricolour poster extolling Cumann na nGaedheal or Cosgrave hung on its bonnet or pasted to its doors. Which of them bore the Great Man himself, it was impossible to tell. The newspaper that morning had reported the poor fellow as suffering from a heavy cold and chest infection, and it was no day for open sedans. Still, to have seen at least a quarter of a mile of cars grinding past, all blazoned with battle honours, was a pretty fair compensation, I supposed.

Moreover, we did see Mr Cosgrave as we scuttled up the incline to the square where he was being presented with an Address of Welcome by the county council. I was astonished to see the platform crowded with men who were, presumably, his supporters. Where on earth had they been in ordinary times when almost every living being in town seemed to shout, actually or metaphorically, 'Up Dev'? Among the hundred or so people shuffling and stamping about in the square, chilled by the bitter north-easter and renewed snow flurries, there was only a solitary interjector, and he did nothing more than intone 'Up the Republic. Up de Valera,' at steady intervals, like a warning horn in sea fog. We pushed (or rather I pushed my mother) near enough to the platform to hear snatches of Cosgrave's speech of thanks. None of it was comprehensible to me. But I did take in clearly a thin face blue with cold, gesturing hands red with cold, hair rising in the cold like a cockatoo's and a deep collar turned right up about the ears against the wind. Maybe he looked a saint – the newspaper had also reported that he would attend Mass and receive Holy Communion in Athlone that morning – but, alas, I could no longer see him as a hero. He just didn't fit.

I suppose that the whole meeting lasted an hour at most but it seemed to me more like three or four before the coughing and spluttering of motors in the background signalled the imminent departure of the *caravanserai*. The next stage was a twenty-odd mile drive to yet another meeting in Castlerea, but it would not be quite the same procession as we had seen arrive. Some cars were heading back down Main St, presumably to return to their snug garages in Athlone. Others, local in origin, were joining the corps afresh. Had I thought of it, I would have found myself quite amazed to discover that even a few of Roscommon's handful of car owners were fervent enough Cumann na nGaedhealers to launch their vehicles into a wretched winter murk.

The last image that appears before my remembering eye is that of dozens of boxy old cars (like those on whose running boards once rode film G-men or the Keystone Kops) manoeuvring awkwardly in the square, amid clouds of exhaust smoke and steam. My mother, however, refused to wait for the formation of the second motorcade. 'I'm chilled to the very bone,' she said, 'We're going home straightaway.' I made no protest. Only too happily, I skipped down the slope beside her, my gloved hand in hers, though with no warmth in either. I had had my fill of Cosgrave and speeches and platforms. To get close to our glowing kitchen range with the damper out, and to feel life returning to my painful flesh, was at that moment my only passion.

It would be too much to say that I became forever disenchanted with politics in the course of a single afternoon, and while I was still only seven years of age. But without question the chestnut had lost something of its newborn gloss and glow. When Mr de Valera took in Roscommon a few days later, following an identical pattern to Mr Cosgrave (except presumably for the county council's 'Loyal Address' but with a few supporters on horseback added to his motorcade) I learnt of it all with complete sangfroid.

Strangely enough, for all the preceding noise and fury, Fianna Fáil gained no seats in the Roscommon constituency in that famous general election. As J.F. Kennedy noted bitterly much later, 'The quiet ones vote, too.' Overall, however, Cosgrave was badly defeated and immediately displaced. Thereafter, the decade was unremittingly de Valera's. He went from strength to strength, ultimately to be crowned and practically beatified as 'The Man who kept us out of the War'. All along this valley of tears I still adhered stoutly, and even, in the rare interludes of hope, fervently, to Cumann na nGaedheal and its successory party, Fine Gael. I had however nothing more than the glamour of a lost cause to sustain me, and I was too young in years and heart alike to embrace reiterated failure with enthusiasm. Perhaps Mr Cosgrave's drear February afternoon had killed off my zealotry forever.

Clio's Boy

Of all that I ever read in our encyclopaedia – Newnes's *Pictorial Knowledge* – nothing impressed me more than the fable of Thor and the Hag. Thor was the indomitable Norse god whose strength none could bend, the Hag, a crippled, decrepit, ragged old crone who stood in his way, denying him passage. Thrice Thor rushed at her, and thrice wrestled her fiercely back and forth. But her grip was so iron-hard and her force so much greater than his own that each time she drove him finally to the ground and pinned him to the underlying rock. On his third fall, he turned to depart, humiliated, when the Hag called out after him, 'Thor, do not be ashamed. You have fought the Invincible itself. I am Death.'

Although I was very young when I first read the fable, and felt only the vague sadness of it all, my feelings hardened over time into a glowing admiration of Thor's gallantry and pity for the pathos of his situation. Then, very gradually, some interior chemistry turned the story, for me, into a metaphor for history and history writing. After all, is not the historian wrestling ceaselessly with Death, trying to seize back what he can from the lost world that is Death's domain, yet knowing that a full or lasting victory is, in the very nature of things, impossible? Of course, I didn't reason all this out until I grew much older. But from the start I had a powerful sense that the story of Thor's duel with the Hag was telling me something of great importance about living and what lay ahead.

It was as a consequence of this, I suppose, that I was always susceptible to things that seemed to pitch me into the past directly. A century-old artefact or piece of writing (at least, one with some special known association), might virtually transport me for one instant into what I guessed had once been the actuality. This happened very seldom and was quite random in its working. But when it did occur it was as if something had been prised, if only for one moment, from the icy handhold of the dead.

So much for an early, perhaps accidental, predisposition. To it, chance added a strange form of historical raw material. Soon after we were transferred to Roscommon, when I was about six years old, my parents arrived home one day from a country-house auction with a carful of Victorian bric-a-brac. This included ancient series of duodecimo volumes and bundles of bound nineteenth-century periodicals ranging from the *Quarterly Review* to *Young Ireland*. The duodecimos were all eighteenth-century histories of England, by Goldsmith, Smollett, Hume and the like – dirty, faded, repulsive to the touch and incomprehensible in content. Most of the periodicals were equally unattractive. *La Belle Assemblé* for the 1820s contained nothing but tinted plates of impossibly long-legged, gauzy ladies with ringlets before their ears. *The Edinburgh Review* (our sequence ran from 1801 to 1820) was filled with long, heavy, black-typed articles on subjects such as Sanitation and Colonial Settlement, and Overpopulation.

So it went on; but there was one exception. I did like *Punch*;

and we had secured an almost unbroken set, in thin, bound, half-yearly volumes, stretching from 1840 to 1859. At first, it was the exquisite drawings and the mysterious alternative title '*or the London Charivari*' that fascinated me; and many a rainy hour – and there seem to have been many rainy hours in the west of Ireland in the 1930s – I spent turning over the stiff, age-waved pages, wondering at the fine line and enigmatic captions of the cartoons. In time, I graduated to reading the shorter pieces of text. I never read a whole crammed page nor found the laborious facetiousness very funny. Still, after all those wet idle days of leafing, gazing, guessing at meaning and venturing farther into the unexplored, I absorbed quite a good deal of the obsessions, interests, world-pictures, self-images and cocksure assumptions of the upper and middle classes – the classes who counted when it came to the exercise of power – in early Victorian England.

I do not mean to say that I really grasped the thrust or political implications of the cartoons or of the weighty skits or moralizing prose. But I did acquire, through the pores of my imagination, so to speak, a real sense of the time and place. It was as if I had been cast up on some exotic shore and forced to live among a tribe whose language and practices were at first scarcely comprehensible but gradually became familiar. Or as if I were travelling through an unknown country, the more of which I saw the more I could grasp its general contours.

When later on (and it was much later on for we studied only Irish and Continental European history in school in those days) I began to read nineteenth-century British history, I found that my *Punch*-derived map of 1840–60 was quite unorthodox. The published professional histories gave one no indication that, for example, the contamination of the River Thames, or the adulteration of cheap confectionery, or the drinking needs of the bona fide working-class Sabbath traveller, were of such passionate concern during this epoch as to merit full-page cartoons – no fewer or smaller than those devoted to the doomed Corn Laws, or the Papal Aggression of 1851, or the

Czar Nicholas hell-bent on instigating the Crimean War. One would never dream that hackney-carriage charges, or table-turning spiritualism, or photographers badgering worthy citizens in the streets, or the scandalous administration of the Blue Coat schools, were then held to deserve, week after week, long sententious columns of their own. My boyhood map of mid-nineteenth-century England may have been pretty blank on the established public and political features but it was rich in the little detail which came from seeing these years through the eyes of articulate contemporaries.

Curiously, and in a way similarly, even my father's bank played its part in turning me into an historian. Not only did it, all unwittingly, provide me with pens and paper ad lib – even in the quantities that needed to be wasted by a nine- or ten-year-old beginning writer – it was also the occasion of two of my critical formative experiences.

The first arose from my father's secreting away, and preserving at home, a single volume out of a nineteenth-century series that was being swept into the maw of some vandalizing paper drive during the First World War. It happened to be the Limerick Branch Correspondence Book for the middle months of 1841. Most of the letters (copies of the originals, written in the thin, slanting, elegant hand of some long-vanished junior) were, to me, dull records of cash in transit, accounts in debit, proposed overdrafts, staff absences and the like. But one struck home with me at once. For some reason it gripped my imagination from the moment that I first read it at, I would guess, the age of nine or ten. It was dated one summer Monday, in 1841, and reported sombrely that, on the day before, a clerk from the branch had been drowned in a boating accident on the river Shannon. He was seventeen years old, had joined the Bank at Limerick a fortnight earlier, could swim and had supported another young man in the water only to disappear himself before he too could be rescued. His body had not yet been recovered.

Although the letter began, 'I regret to inform the Board

...', it simply set out the bare facts of the tragedy, without any expression of personal sorrow or indeed of feeling of any kind. But the manager cannot have been quite heartless. He had the delicacy to make no mention of the replacement now needed; and he went on to 'submit' to the directors a request that the drowned boy's mother be paid £18.15.0, his full quarter's salary, although he had served two weeks only. His mother, the manager went on, was a widow with two younger daughters to support, and little income.

It would be much too much to say that I was haunted by the poor clerk. I never even tried to discover more about him by hunting through the *Limerick Chronicle* in search of a reported inquest, even at a time when I was working on the provincial papers for the 1840s. All the same, I lived over and over again that imagined Sunday. I supposed the raw new clerk to have been joyous when asked by youths whom he had just met to join them on the river; I saw the storm sweeping suddenly out of Clare across the broad river, and over the heavy clumsy yacht, filled with ignorant sailors; I felt the shock of the icy, amber water, the heart-pounding, arm-aching struggle in the whipped-up estuary, the desperate hauling-in of the rescued one, and the rushing final failure of strength of the other, my poor hero.

I was never in the least confused as to where fact ended and where my own imagining began. Yet the totality, the *tout ensemble* of actual base and suppository superstructure, was what always appeared before me. It was my first real *picturing* of the past. My elaboration of what the little letter said helped me to feel the reality of the happening, to resurrect something small, buried in history, so long ago – even if I knew full well that it was only an outflow of sympathy, and not a set of actualities, that I would ever know for sure.

Later on I had a second, confirmatory Bank experience. Roscommon branch had only one sub-office, in Creggs, then a down-at-heel, decaying village, not far from the town. The sub-office may have opened weekly for a few hours, or perhaps only on grand occasions, such as fair-days: I can't now recall. My father was of course far above so humble a duty as handing out and taking in the cash, and sanctioning the cheques at Creggs. But every so often – perhaps by way of a mild diversion – he took it on, driving out there with a padlocked box of money, forms and account books stowed in the boot, and guarded, from the safe situation of the front passenger seat, by the faithful Tom. Not that any highwayman had ever disturbed, or was likely ever to disturb, the otherwise uneven course of the Creggs run.

I accompanied them once, having clamoured for some time, I daresay, to be included in this mysterious excursion. As things turned out, it was as remorselessly wet a day as even Co. Roscommon could produce. The car halted outside the drenched walls of a pub in a miserable street already under two or three inches of water. Men, boys and cattle cowered under such shelter as they could find. Even the drumming rain, however, could not altogether overcome the voices raised in dealing, gossip, sarcasm and argument.

After much heaving and pushing by Tom and my father and the publican, we were damply established in a small room opening off the bar proper, with my father seated behind a seamed and battered deal table and Tom at the ready to hand him papers or banknotes from the box. I was soon bored by the succession of 'customers', in steaming raincoats and sodden caps, changing money or negotiating God-knows-what in confidential whispers. The morning seemed interminable. There was nowhere to go, nothing to do but sit on my hard chair in the corner. It seemed forever until the bank closed – sharp on 12.30 pm as if it were Head Office itself – and the table was cleared for our bacon, cabbage and boiled potatoes.

As we sat down to eat, Tom said to the publican, who had put his head round the door to see how we fared, 'Isn't this the table, Matt, where Parnell made his last speech ever.' 'It is,' Matt answered, 'My uncle often told me how the boys dragged it out and hoisted it up on a dray outside there in the front.

'Twas from behind it Parnell spoke in the teeming rain. There's a bit of history for you, boy,' he added to me.

He spoke more truly than he thought. I stroked the underside of the table reverently. Even already, a poignant image had begun to take shape in my mind – the image of the desperate, dying hero, hoarsely shouting, against the noise of the downpour, at perhaps two or three dozen farmers and labourers. Parnell was now truly the uncrowned King of Ireland – in the proper sense of being overthrown rather than that of popular adulation. Now he was humbled down to a roaring gutter in Creggs. When in after years I read the details of Parnell's last days, and especially the details of that fatal Sunday in Creggs, they seemed as intimately familiar as if I had been there myself, as if I had somehow imprinted on my mind a single but immortal and epitomizing scene. The table had proved the transmitter. History had become a living thing – paradoxically through a still-life picture of my own making – and the past could never seem unpeopled or inert again.

1998–2002

Oliver: going places

2. A Student at University College Dublin: Memories of the Literary and Historical Society in the 1940s

Though I have the temerity to write about the L&H in my time at University College, I cannot claim to have been an L&H man proper. I was never a successful speaker. In freshman innocence, I chose a night when J.C. Flood was in the chair to make my maiden speech, and never recovered from that first debacle. In my second year, I conceived the extraordinary notion that I might do better if my speeches were not prepared or thought about but left to the guidance of the moment. Heaven knows what miseries this delusion brought down upon my audiences and myself, but (partly from self-mortification and mostly through laziness) I persisted in it to the end. My sole term of office in the L&H was due entirely to the favour of that master politician, E.M. Walsh, and the peak of my career an occasion when I took his place in the auditor's chair, due to his having some bigger political fish to fry in the provinces. Nonetheless, I remained a pretty regular attender and listener throughout my years in College. However much, at the mandarin stage, I adopted a *nil admirari* attitude, I always knew secretly that the greatest glories of an undergraduate career were to be gained in that gloomy theatre.

I was at College from 1941 to 1946. Thus, in one sense, I belonged to a war generation. In another, nothing could be farther from the truth. When I went to Cambridge in 1947, it was to a world of ex-servicemen whose experiences might have belonged to another planet. My best friend there was a man who had been shot down after a raid on Ploesti, who had hidden for a week in Hungarian marshes, and been imprisoned in Budapest (in the charge of a Good Soldier Schweik character who could never quite make up his mind to help him to escape) until the Russians doubtfully took him over. Another man I knew, a research mathematician from Bonn, had been a tank officer in Guderian's command. He had crossed and recrossed the Dneiper, the Oka and the Don. Compared with them – and most of the undergraduates were men like these – our 'war' in Dublin was vicarious and dreamlike. It was something we read of day by day in newspapers. We followed the fortunes of the contestants with the same engaged detachment that men listen to a test match in Australia in the snugness and dark of a December dawn. It was all, so to say, two-dimensional: there was no element to make it pressing or palpable or to add perspective. If an Anglophile spoke of German concentration camps, half a dozen voices would tell him that it was the British who had invented concentration camps during their South African campaigns. And that would be that. Both houses were equally plagued, and we ourselves in Cromwell's phrase, 'totally uncommitted'.

Nonetheless, this vicarious war dominated our undergraduate life and our L&H. Though there were not, so far as I can recall, many motions directly concerning the conflict or the belligerents, these formed the background to most serious debates, even to debates on domestic issues. For domestic politics were at that time 'overshadowed' by 'neutrality', and in any event, many roads therein led ultimately to partition, and through it to the war in which Great Britain was involved. It is not possible to say simply that the Society was divided into an Allied party, a German party and a party of neutralists. There were, rather, three distinct, if overlapping, lines of political division in its ranks: division according to Irish party allegiance, division on the general Left-Right pattern of Socialism versus Fascism, and division in the attitudes adopted towards Great Britain. Much the most important and immediate was, of course, the domestic triangle of IRA, Fianna Fáil and Fine Gael, for the first two had by now fallen decisively and violently apart. There were a few supporters of the Labour Party (or parties, as they then were), and some obscure and minute division in the ranks of the doctrinaire republicans. But, broadly speaking, Left, Centre and Right, in a strictly national and constitutional sense, was the normal spectrum.

As a body, and particularly as a body of backbenchers the L&H hovered between Left and Centre. No doubt individually and in private, the overwhelming majority of members would have supported Mr de Valera in his constitutional definitions and national policy. But, in accordance with the natural law that governs students everywhere, they pretended in the mass to a degree of radicalism beyond that of their secret inclination. At any rate, it always seemed to me that the noise and votes of the L&H in wartime like the extreme socialist victories in all English universities in the 1930s, should be proportionately discounted. It must also be remembered that Fianna Fáil had been very long in power and appeared almost immovable. For the great majority of the society, who were quite innocent of political ambitions but young and healthily antagonistic to establishments, this was perhaps something of a stumbling block. Fine Gael, on the other hand, was at that time at the nadir of its fortunes. To our generation it seemed a gradually dwindling body of ageing men. As His Excellency's Opposition, as the alternative government waiting in the wings, it appeared to have no policy to offer but 'the same only rather less so'. Finally, it seemed pre-eminently and irremediably respectable. Subsequent history has shown this to be very false, but such was, I think, the prevailing impression of the time, and one ill-calculated to fire the blood. Nonetheless, many, if not indeed most, of the best speakers in the Society (in contradistinction to the solid and inarticulate body of the House) were Fine Gael in inclination. This may have been, in part, hereditary. A number were the sons of former or current politicians, or came of the legal, academic and bureaucratic families who had also formed part of the hierarchy of 1922. Perhaps, too, environment played a part. An extraordinarily large proportion of the most able leaders and speakers in the Society came from a handful of well-known Dublin schools. At any rate, it was a fact; and in consequence it is, I think, not unfair to say that in oratorical merit and administration the L&H inclined towards Fine Gael; that in collective sentiment it was pro-government; and that in collective voice and vote it was usually in opposition to the government and often (particularly on issues such as Roger McHugh's internment) positively Republican.

To a limited extent, the other lines of political division cut across all this. The very few socialists in the Society tended to support the Allies for obvious reasons, though one or two still maintained a Spanish Civil War tradition in which Popular Front politics for the Continent were combined with doctrinaire nationalism and hatred of Great Britain at home. Most, though not quite all, pro-Germans were extreme republicans. Some went to the length of wearing leather jerkins or long black raincoats like a Nazi admiral, or swastikas in their lapels, for though they were quite in earnest, there was something schoolboyish about it all. Though by no means numerous, this 'Mountain' of the L&H threw up two or three magnificent speakers. The best was Ciaran McAnally, who was not so much pro-German as an especially passionate and determined Ulster nationalist. For oratory of his own sort, wild, burning, yet ultimately controlled and intelligent, I have never heard his equal. It was one of the great experiences of the L&H to watch his slight, taut, immobile figure, as the knife-like sentences slowly built up to a crescendo of castigation, when he would bring his fists suddenly crashing down before the awed and silent House. There was, again, a British 'party', by which I mean not a party of Unionists, but a party overtly hoping for a British victory. For the most part this merely consisted of the 'nice boys' from the Law Society, but E.M. Walsh, for one, had developed a coherent defence of the current Commonwealth. He had, moreover, the courage or insouciance of his conviction. Remembrance Day once fell upon a Saturday; disdaining even to glance down at the poppy he was wearing, he faced the excited mob with cold indifference. As the war wore on, the Society's interest in, and conflicts over it declined. This was so as early as 1943, by which time the United States (whom none would oppose) was thoroughly involved in hostilities, an Allied victory was assured, and the charges of German and Japanese atrocities and breaches of faith could no longer be pooh-poohed.

In my own view two men, successive auditors, Walter Treanor and Eamonn Walsh, dominated the Society during these years. This they did, not by oratory or extraordinary intelligence (though both were able and ready speakers and competent if not especially ready students), but by elemental force of character and personality. Both were born politicians, born with the capacity for manipulating others and the instinct that could predict their likely movement. But the forms in which they expressed their powers were very different. Walsh, cool, inscrutable and impossible to face down, was on the pattern of the English Tory interloper, of the school of Beaconsfield and F.E. Smith. Indeed, I should be much surprised if he did not, in fact, take these two geniuses for his models. Treanor, on the other hand, was something of the American city 'boss'. He was a superlative leader, perpetually restless, and extroverted and ambitious. But there was nothing petty in his ambition. No one could have been less vain, and in many ways he was both disinterested and a romantic. More than anybody else I knew in the Society, he had a feeling for the L&H as a living thing, as a part of continuing history; and nothing that might enhance its name or preserve its past was too much trouble for him to essay. In style of speaking, there was a striking contrast between the two. Walsh was formalized and witty. Whether being urbane or denunciatory, he was detached. Walter Treanor had an infectious chuckle when he amused himself, a stammer when he was nervous, humour, devil-may-careishness and, on occasions, the invaluable capacity to move an audience.

The greatest 'private member' of the Society in these years was, I should say, Kevin Lynch. I do not mean that he was 'independent' in the political sense; indeed, he was a rather strong party man. But he had no ambition whatever to hold office, he never trimmed his sentiments to suit an audience, and he allowed no private friendships or feelings to restrain him in his holy work of denouncing auditors, committees and other powers that be. He was *mutatis mutandis* the John Bright type of radical, and similarly exasperating and incorruptible. He was not immediately popular with the Society, for his oratory was flat and plain. But, as he was gradually seen for what he was, he won a very general respect. He stood four-square before his audience, looked it in the face, and told it in effect that he was a Clare man and afraid of nothing. Another, but very different, independent was Charles Fitzsimons. Although he did once serve on the committee, he was essentially a lone wolf who belonged to no governing circle. He suffered, moreover, from a disadvantage that was not in the least his fault. His sister had recently and dramatically risen to film stardom, and he could never escape from the transferred notoriety. It was difficult for people to treat him on his own merits, and recognize that he was very intelligent and an abundant, if florid, speaker. That he eventually succeeded in imposing his personality on the house was, in the circumstances, a remarkable achievement.

An interesting contrast to the independents were P.R. Hogbin and Alec Hinkson. Both were fluent, classical in profile and dignified in demeanour. To revert to the parliamentary metaphor, they looked junior Lords of the Treasury – on the Conservative side. Neither was perhaps in the first class in debate, but they made (as in the case of Hogbin) or would have made, good auditors. Hinkson did not, in fact, become auditor of the L&H, but he presided over the Law Society at this time, and managed it mildly and extraordinarily well. In my very early days in the L&H the banner of Labour was carried by Rory Roberts, who seemed a person (I did not know him myself), and was a speaker, of enormous charm and gusto. Later, the socialist mantle fell on Anthony Cronin. Cronin was excellent in debate on most occasions. He gave the impression that he was not a 'natural' speaker, but nervous, sensitive and driving himself to his task: but this merely heightened the predominant mark of his speeches, sincerity. The reputed *éminence grise* of Labour was K.B. Nowlan. He certainly looked an *éminence grise*, but of what he was an eminence was by no means certain. I suspect that his intense interest in European politics was altogether academic. He did not often appear in the Society, but one at least of his performances was brilliant. Some time in 1945 or 1946 he consented to take the chair as M. Nowlansky, a representative of the Russian puppet government in Poland. After an early passage of arms with Frank Martin as to whether he belonged to the Lublin or Dublin Committee, he spoke for forty minutes of his experiences on the Russian flagship in the Japanese war of 1904, of his spell in the Duma, of his work as a political agent during the Baltic campaigns of 1919, and so on. It was much the best thing of its kind which I heard at the Society, compiled with the most intricate fantasy and grotesque accuracy of historical detail. For weeks after he was pointed out to one another by shocked and bewildered freshmen in the Main Hall, and we maintained the joke for a while in the *National Student*. One other of the serious debaters must be mentioned. This was Seán Flanagan who came to the L&H very late in his undergraduate career, but was, I should say, the best of all speakers on the Fianna Fáil side. In contrast to most of his contemporaries, who tended towards the diffuse and flowery, Flanagan's oratory was remarkably economical and planned. His speeches derived from clear thinking and were delivered in a confident, rather rasping voice. Altogether, a formidable man.

Of course, then as always, much that was best in the L&H came from the back-benches and the foolery of private business, I remember well one earnest speaker pausing for effect after a technicoloured and inaccurate account of the fall of the last of the Romanovs. The awkward silence was broken by a hollow voice from the top of the House, 'He ain't gonna reign no more, no more.' The entire Society broke into laughter. In my first year one or two of what seemed to us the very old guard put in occasional appearances at private business. My first memory of my very first meeting is of sardonic, mock-serious auditor-baiting by Patrick Lynch and a man called Monaghan. In our own times, the giant of private business was Ivar Boden. He looked Pickwickian, and played the part. He was not in the least mordant or satirical, but simply and irresistibly comic. One marvellous occasion was his polite cross-examination of (if I remember rightly) a bemused French *chargé d'affaires* on the subject of the pen of his aunt. His stock character was a Dublin gurrier who had a bee in his bonnet about George VI; and he maintained this for meeting after meeting without ceasing to be funny. In the generation which immediately followed, it was, I think, Kevin Burke and Frank Martin who approached nearest to Boden as private-business men.

No doubt, this picture of the L&H is most subjective, and many would disagree with my choice or categorization of persons. I can only plead that this is my recollection, and that even at so short a distance of time, memory is random and eclectic. I need hardly add that the shortness of the distance in time can be inhibiting in other ways. But the main point is perhaps that the L&H is recollected as a community and a thing to which the particular actors are subordinate. Why is this so, what was its special magic? Not altogether the oratory: some of those who seemed to me to rank highest amongst university speakers – Tom Finlay, Patrick Casey or Fergus O'Duffy – rarely, if ever, addressed the Society. Not the surroundings, which were, particularly at first sight, subterranean in general appearance, discordant in colour and forbidding. Not even the wit and intimacy and foolery: in these respects, it was sometimes surpassed by the smaller and more cliquey bodies such as the Law or Hall societies. Yet it cannot be denied that the L&H is a great society, perhaps in the very first rank of undergraduate societies, and one which leaves an indelible impression on any member of sufficient sensibility to take it. Even the blackboards, the scored, ugly benches, the patched and faded plush forms and the drab walls are impressed with this character, and form an accepted background for every memory.

If we put the question less fancifully, and ask why the L&H is a great society, there are, I think, three main answers. The first is one that we must struggle against rejecting out of hand for triteness. Though it is tedious to be told, it is nonetheless true that Irishmen are born speakers. To apply Huxley's observation on Gladstone, you can put Irishmen, at any rate young Irishmen, in the middle of a moor with nothing in the world but their shirts, and still be unable to prevent them from being orators. Even if some fish slipped through the net, the majority of good speakers was held by the L&H and the harvest was rich enough. Secondly and relevant to this, the L&H by some providence steers a mean course between many of the dangers which beset student groups. It is political without being obsessed by future careers or subject to illusions of political grandeur. With some, if not sufficient, cause, it regards itself as the chief undergraduate body in a separate nation, and the chief nursery of public men in a new state. But politics do not intrude into its own affairs. Whether a man is Fianna Fáil or Fine Gael or Labour is literally irrelevant to the auditorship or the holding of other office. Thus, the petty machines and premature party spleen that bedevil some of the English universities are avoided. Again, the private business of the L&H takes place within a loose framework of Palgrave and the Constitution. As befits our national character, it is decently legalistic and pedantic. But the forms are not taken seriously. The Society is not dominated, as many such societies tend to be, by irrelevant parliamentarism and procedural mumbo-jumbo, which, however appropriate to the real business of legislating, become absurd if applied exactly to the pretence of it. Correspondingly, foppishness and the imaginary 'parliamentary manner' are almost unknown in the L&H. It has, of course, its own compensating vices, but they are not so deadly. Finally, the L&H is both the nearest embodiment of a university that our undergraduates experience at their own level, and the field where our undergraduate achievement and past come nearest to those of even the most celebrated and ancient rivals.

I do not think it is only romantics or antiquarians amongst undergraduates who feel this hunger for a history, for a sense of belonging to some great and living organism well-rooted in tradition. I think it is a need of undergraduates of every sort and everywhere. In a non-residential university placed in the heart of a capital city, the bias towards loss of identity as undergraduates and faculty segregation is powerful. Of the counteracting agencies, the L&H is in my view incomparably the most widespread and influential, much more palpable and attainable to the great majority of students than, say, the SRC. It has, again, magical and prophetic names at its foundation and throughout its vicissitudes, a folklore, a hereditary ethos and a history that is ancient in the timescale of undergraduate organizations the world over. Because it is, in its context, so superior a medium for instinctive undergraduate aspirations, it taps the best in each undergraduate generation to a degree to which debating societies in other universities with multitudinous alternatives cannot. And each generation in University College not only draws on it for satisfaction; it adds to the living tradition in so doing.

1955

3. 'Peopling History': Reflections on a Life of History Writing

I have never received a greater honour than being chosen as an author at the Festival of Adelaide. Historians may not be two-a-penny even in these inflationary days. Historians worthy of the name of writer are however quite a different matter. Caesar, Aubrey, Clarendon, Gibbon, de Tocqueville, Carlyle, Macaulay – those are the sort of names that that phrase carries in its train. I excuse myself with the reflection that such a train, like the more common kind, must have its third- as well as first-class compartments. Even so, I know that I have little claim even to stand upright in the guard's van. But, like Captain Wentworth in *Persuasion*, I must brook being happier than I deserve, and confess that there is much more joy than embarrassment in being over-rated.

Apart from some painful schoolboy verses, I have practised only one literary craft throughout my life, that of history writing – and you all know what an old dog can't be taught. I shall therefore stick to my trade and try to provide you this evening with a history – of how I came to find myself in the field of biography at last.

At the end of his career Gladstone remarked that the history of his political life was really very simple. He had started as a Tory and learned gradually to be a Liberal. In an immodest comparison, I may say that I began life as an administrative historian and learned gradually – according to the invitation that brings me here – to become a writer. I started as a laborious student of the growth of nineteenth-century government; of the drafting, reformulation and amendment of regulatory statutes; and of the genesis of delegated legislation, administrative discretions and inspectoral autonomy. These fields of study have their own elusive charm; but they are not such as bring the human personality to the forefront. To compound the depersonalization, my own special interest was in abstract processes, and ultimately the construction of models to expose the interior momentum of government in nineteenth-century British circumstances.

I was not quite such a historical Gradgrind as this sketch of my first major undertaking may suggest. For one thing, it would have been quite impracticable as well as heartless to pass unseeingly over either the mass, or the particulars, of human misery that had evoked the enlargement of state power with which I was concerned. I was, so to speak, living in countries stricken by mass famine and disease, forced to the pitheads of terrible colliery disasters, compelled to follow out the swindling of the poor and ignorant. One does not spend one's days among such things, even if only in historical imagination, and come out the same person as went in.

Actual identifiable people also shouldered their way into my abstractive work. The mid-nineteenth-century bureaucracy was minute by modern standards. The two Whitehall departments with which I was particularly concerned, the Home Office and the Colonial Office, was each, despite its immense responsibilities, effectively run by six or seven people. Moreover, the field officers, the inspectors, who were my special interest, were also very few in number, less than a dozen even as late as the 1890s. Thus as I made my way through the mounds of correspondence, minutes, reports, drafts, comments and advices, I began to know certain of the characters (in their official bearing, at least) very well. This was all the more the case because most Victorian public servants were far from grey anonymities but irascible, sardonic, eccentric, full of zeal, bellicose or marked by some similar predominating humour. Almost all wrote good, and some glittering prose. Several were recruited from outside the service, from the ranks of barristers with insufficient briefs, or dons who wanted to get married. Some, even of the career men, devoted their spare – to say nothing of their official – time to writing books, tracts or plays. Some, like Sir Henry Taylor or Sir James Stephen, were already famous in their own day. Others, often quite as interesting, poured their talents into composing biting minutes or cross and trenchant answers to parliamentary questions. In short, my world of administrative history was quite soon peopled by a number of extraordinary individuals. As I wrote, I found myself having to make room for them in my book, even to the extent of building a whole chapter about a single emigration officer who was so idiosyncratic in words and action, that he might have stepped – no questions asked – out of Dickens's pages.

My surreptitious list towards biography was soon corrected. The next books were *seriatim* the history of a brewing company, an analysis of the politics and economics of modern Ireland, and a general survey of early-Victorian government. Each was, in its own way, a 'pattern' sort of book, concerned with rhythms of development or large-scale general movements in society. Individuals had of course a part to play in each, particularly in the history of modern Ireland. But these were generally familiar public men, to be encapsulated in a glib phrase or two and measured only as contributors or otherwise to the great sweeping processes of change. The brewing history (fated never to be published because the company was not enamoured of the image that emerged*) threw up a sort

* It was published in 1998.

of corporate personality in its managerial class, drawn exclusively for more than half a century from Oxford or Cambridge Firsts in the Natural Sciences. These men were fascinating as a caste but not susceptible to individualization, given the complete dearth of private papers. Early Victorian government in Great Britain did bring some leading players – even if (in my estimation) no heroes – to the stage. But it was their public personae only that concerned me. Indeed, rarely did they leave behind any other remains in the records. So for years my history was populated, with negligible exceptions, by masses and functionaries rather than people as ordinarily understood.

In a way, this reached its apogee in a book written in the early 1980s, which I called *States of Mind: A Study of Anglo-Irish Conflict* over the past two centuries. *States of Mind* was, appropriately enough, a 'think-book', concerned with popular mentalities and in particular with the cross-purposes produced by prevailing British and Irish concepts, imagery and assumptions as they bore on politics. I drew freely on all sorts of material to forward my various arguments, and, occasionally, a minute history of a particular individual seemed the most effective method of making the point I had in sight. In some ways, these were a species of 'Dictionary of Biography' entry I suppose – but an inferior species for they contained little personal data, and consisted essentially in the exposition of certain people's ideologies and their formation and effect.

Meanwhile, however, I had inadvertently taken a new step towards biography. It happened in this way. Some years before I found that my fresh research into nineteenth-century governmental records was tending to replicate my earlier work. I kept finding the same patterns as before. I was locked into my own ideas. Now there are historians who can spend their lives mastering more and more one special field. But I was not that sort of scholar. On the other hand, I did not want to leave my subject dangling. In the end, I hit on the notion of moving back in time, to the late-eighteenth century, in order to discover which elements making for the subsequent revolution were missing then. I shall say nothing here about my technical conclusions. The pertinent point is that, much to my surprise and far from my intention, the resultant book, *The Inspector General*, published in 1981, ended up with a sort of hero. Sir Jeremiah Fitzpatrick turned out to be the Pooh-Bah of social reform, Irish as well as British, military as well as civil, in the 1780s and 1790s. He worked for improvement (his favourite word) in prisons, transportation, emigrant ships, military hospitals, ambulance corps, soldiers' diet, widows' pensions, the regulation of slaughter houses, camp design and many other grave problems of the day. He had no master plan. His strange course began in serendipity and progressed by tangents. His guiding stars were the Enlightenment values of Economy, Rationality and Humanity; his general bearing that of a Don Quixote, although a Don Quixote with some alloy of ideological vanity and bureaucratic cunning. I had meant him to be no more than a medium through which the building-up of governmental forms could be laboriously traced.

But Sir Jeremiah would have none of this. Even in death, even in distant and fragmentary retrospect, he intruded, with the same thick-skinned pertinacity with which he had maddened lord lieutenants, chief secretaries and cabinet ministers all his official life. His obituaries named him 'the second Howard' (after the great prison reformer) and 'the Soldiers' Friend' (for his tireless struggle to make the lot of the common troops less miserable and brutal); but harassed administrators and politicians called him 'that Gadfly' or 'Nuisance' or 'the busybody Sir Jeremiah'. He was inescapable as a person; he could not be treated as a type or trigger or mechanism for producing change. He began to take over my pages as he had in life commandeered hospital wards and ambulance wagons without authority; and in the end reviewers of *The Inspector General* paid scant attention to my refinements of historical patterning and a great deal to Fitzpatrick's character and fortunes.

More or less accidentally, I had been blooded in biography.

I was, not at once, but soon, emboldened to take up seriously a project I had long had in distant contemplation. How had the culture of modern Catholic nationalist Ireland come to be formed? This was a fundamental question of – to me, at least – towering importance – yet one that no one had ever asked in earnest. There was of course the problem of how to grapple with so shadowy or fluid a phenomenon as a people's cast of mind and body of assumptions. But I had already hit on a promising solution to this difficulty. Daniel O'Connell seemed to me both the chief shaper of the modern Irish Catholic culture and, in his own career, the epitome of its rapid advance in the years 1800–50.

In 1984 I took the plunge and began writing the first of two volumes of approximately 130,000 words each. At this stage, I intended to use O'Connell's life, which I would trace more or less chronologically in the usual way, as the medium for a systematic analysis of cultural formation. O'Connell, however, soon changed all that. I started, (as is my bad composing habit) by tackling what seemed to be the easiest and most self-contained parts first – in this case at chapter IV which was to deal with O'Connell's courtship, covert wedding and efforts to conceal his marriage from the close-fisted uncle from whom he had great expectations. I was immediately and irrevocably caught up in the personal. It was simply the story of the man's life that I had to tell. My own ears can still hear, as an underlying beat in what I wrote, the universal themes of cultural evolution. But whether any other reader catches or has caught these grand inferences, is more than I can say. O'Connell himself proved large enough a subject to fill my two books down to the final lines. The rest must take care of itself. I had ended up a biographer *faute de mieux*.

My predecessor as head of department in Canberra, John La Nauze, had an often-repeated dictum: no historian should attempt a biography until he or she was well over fifty years of age, because they had not lived through enough till then. I smiled (inwardly, of course) when, in my thirties, I first heard this iron law laid down. But when, twenty years later, I sat down to write *O'Connell*, I saw La Nauze's point. Like O'Connell, I had reared or was still rearing seven children. Like him, I had groaned under the weight of so numerous a progeny, and felt the multiplication of both pains and pleasures, and desperate juggling with priorities, that go with running such a complex enterprise. Like him, I had been married many years, and knew multitudinous marital traffic and interdependence from the inside. I certainly cannot press these correspondences to the limit. O'Connell met his waves with wonderful dexterity and rode down their aftersides as if his cares were forever over. Yet the considerable similarity of structure between my life and my subject's did, I believe, sensitize me to a host of small actions and reactions which would probably have gone unnoticed if I had not traversed essentially the same ranges of experience. In all this, age was important. It was necessary not only to undergo, but also to establish the long perspective and to have time to turn things over repeatedly in my mind. 'For it seems to me,' George Eliot's Adam Bede concluded, 'it's the same with love and happiness as with sorrow – the more we know of it the better we can feel what other people's lives are or might have been ... the more knowledge a man has, the better he'll do's work; and feeling's a sort of knowledge.'

Moreover, age apart, there was much in my hereditary situation which resembled O'Connell's. Although he was, in late youth and early manhood, almost a stock Enlightenment figure and priggish deist, and although he remained in certain ways a Godwinite to the end, the real drama of both his public and private life derived from his Catholicism. In a miniscule way, the same was true of me. In middle age, O'Connell was drawn into the uprush of the second Counter-Reformation, as it affected the English-speaking world. I was born and bred in the last phase of this great modern historical phenomenon. I knew from the inside the nuances of feeling; of rational and irrational antipathy; of scruple, conscience and bad conscience; of piety and impiety, which gripped souls in this spiritual milieu. There was no intellectual virtue in the rapport. It was simply that I had learnt the same code, the same small language or set of signals. But the chance acquirement gave me a sort of microscopic vision for certain things. Again, my eye had been schooled by my circumstances.

Correspondingly, on the very large scale, I could see myself as part – albeit an infinitesimal part – of a vast movement which O'Connell had done much to initiate and shape. The Irish world in which I grew up in the 1930s was in many ways the apotheosis of O'Connell's endeavour. He would have anathemized the violence which had given birth to the Irish Free State, or Éire, as it was commonly called from 1937 onwards. But the profoundly constitutional and legalistic product of that violence – the two-party state, judicial system and public service copied almost without variation from Westminster and Whitehall, yet with both objective and subjective independence – was precisely what O'Connell had aimed for almost a century before. It was at last an Irish world in which a Roman Catholic felt no sense of inferiority or servility beyond the commonplace social snobberies that affected all. At the same time, I lived long enough ago to catch, in other English-speaking countries, the faint final manifestations of anti-Popish and anti-Irish prejudice – not much perhaps but enough to vivify O'Connell's resentment of (to use his own analogy) the condition of hereditary bondsman into which he had been born.

Perhaps I am arguing in a circle. Perhaps it was precisely because I could, or had to, identify with O'Connell that I chose to undertake his biography. It does not really matter. One way or other, I believe that the identification enabled me to write better books than otherwise.

In form, both of my O'Connell books were as straightforwardly chronological as I could make them, as well as focussed on a master individual who controlled his own life – not absolutely, of course, but to a very unusual degree. My latest biographical or quasi-biographical venture, *Jane Austen: Real and Imagined Worlds*, is altogether different. For one thing, I am not unmarried, childless or a woman, and there were correspondingly alarming calls upon my stock of sympathy. For another I use, not chronological sequence, but facets of character or experience as the organizing principle of the book; and I see aspects of Jane Austen's life side by side with particular pieces of her fiction. Thus, I treat, for example, Jane Austen's own Anglicanism and the Church of England as depicted in *Mansfield Park*, in a single chapter; Jane Austen's own social trafficking and that of *Emma* in another; and her own money (and lack of it) and the same theme in *Sense and Sensibility* in a third. Again, Jane Austen's was an extraordinarily passive life, with none of the *chiaroscuro* of O'Connell's; and only momentary gleams of those dramatic incidents that even the most monochromatic life affords, appear in the meagre surviving records.

For, unlike O'Connell's case, the body of biographical material for Jane Austen is very small – only some 130 letters written by herself, a handful of casual family or other contemporary references, a brief memoir and a one-line obituary notice in the *Hampshire Chronicle*. Thus, the Austen book was a polar opposite to the O'Connell. It demanded something like a medievalist's *modus operandi*, with sources fragmentary and haphazard, and the need for inference and hypothesis correspondingly profuse. Matching the novels and stretches of the discoverable life required a tedious petit-point type of composition; while the decision to relate each facet to a particular work or works, in the hope of a more concentrated and striking argument, called for almost a series of *tours de force*.

This last was in fact the hardest choice to make when I was planning the structure of the book. It could not be a biography proper. I doubt if the sources suffice for a full and rounded 'Life' to be written at any rate, on the scale and at the level of known fact that would satisfy a professional historian. On the other hand, certain aspects of her character and experience are sufficiently well documented for reasonable certainty of judgment. Thus, I was led to the idea of breaking the book down to facts. On the surface, this meant a fragmentary and disjointed treatment. But I was in hope that, taken together, they would eventually end in a near full-length portrait – not indeed of the realistic Rubenesque kind, but more a picture in which the unpainted (and unpaintable) bits of canvas would matter comparatively little against the strong brushstrokes of the rest. The whole would have to be merely the sum of the parts that I could manage; and I took heart from Jane Austen's own couplet,

> I do not write for such dull elves
> As have not a good deal of ingenuity themselves.

All this is, however, a little *post hoc*. Actually the book began in a double accident in 1976. The first part of the accident was my having to spend a week in bed with spondialitis – or, colloquially speaking, a bad back. As I read and reread alternately *Emma* and Jane Austen's *Letters*, I began to discern – or so I thought – common patterns of social comings and goings. I began to jot down times and dates and companies and associations, at first on the backs of cigarette packets and, then, in earnest, on foolscap sheets. In the end, I had numerous scribbled pages. The second relevant accident of 1976 was the retirement of John La Nauze from the History department, and my wish to give, in his honour, the sort of occasional paper that he would like. La Nauze was not a Janeite but certainly an Austenite; and no one, so far as I knew, had ever worked out the correspondences between Jane Austen's social routine and that of any of her novels. The upshot was a paper, 'Highbury and Chawton', in which the daily patterns of the elites of the imaginary and real villages were compared. Unwittingly, I had been launched on what would eventually issue in a book.

So far I had no more than an idea for intellectual amusement, a species of literary crossword. I had however become much interested in Jane Austen's religion and dissatisfied by the crudity of such categorizations of it as I had come across. In particular, these seemed ill-informed about the complex and burgeoning characteristics of the Church of England in the two decades 1797–1817, which contained the only direct record of Jane Austen's spirituality, as evidenced by her own letters. So, as a holiday from time to time, I began to collect and worry over the indications of her religious feelings and convictions – at the same time matching and comparing these with their equivalents manifested in her fiction. I had before me the pattern of Highbury and Chawton, the use of a single novel for a theme; and, in following their pattern for religion, the choice had to be *Mansfield Park*, much richer in ecclesiastical and clerical observation than any of her other books. Off and on, I worked on this over the years, in the interstices of various other things. In the end, I had a rounded and argued paper.

Even still, I did not think of a Jane Austen book. This possibility occurred to me only when I was embarked on a third essay trying to reconstruct her attitude to the contemporary world. This time, I found her unfinished fragment of a novel, *Sanditon*, written in 1817 in two months before she died, the most interesting illumination and expansion of views expressed glancingly and ad hoc in her correspondence. In *Sanditon* Jane Austen confronts modernity – not just in its literary but also in its moral, stylistic, scientific and material forms – and not just in a satiric but also, occasionally, in an appreciative vein. The fragment gives substance and sequence to the critiques implicit in the ironic commentaries on life about her, which continually thread her letters to her sister. At any rate, by the time that I took up this theme seriously – somewhere in the middle 1980s, so far as I recall – I began to think that I should carry the whole project (for such it had become by then) forward to make a book. I was at that stage deep in the writing of *O'Connell*, with much still to go. But I decided to adopt *Jane Austen* as a secondary task, to turn to when I reached impasses or found that I had run up a cul de sac.

This left me with three problems over and above the everlasting problem of writing anything at all. First, could I, and should I, adhere to the method of one novel, one facet of the life? Second, which other facets of Jane Austen's experience should I try to analyse? And third, in what order should I arrange any chapters? The problems were interconnected but I shall give my answers separately although this was not in fact how I reached them. As to the first, there was the argument for symmetry. All my work in store had already taken this form. A more substantial reason for not changing was my belief that the procedure provided a simpler, clearer and more artistically satisfying form than commingling all the fiction in random fashion. As things turned out I was not able to adhere absolutely to this plan. I could deal with family and *Persuasion* alone, and money and *Sense and Sensibility* alone. But with 'girlhood' I wished to bring out impressive though unexpected similarities between the heroines of *Pride and Prejudice* and *Northanger Abbey*, as well as to draw on a piece that Jane Austen had written when she was sixteen, called 'Catherine at The Bower'. Correspondingly, in the case of courtship, marriage and spinsterhood, I wished to show the changes which time and circumstances produced in Jane Austen's relative weighing-up and factors, and accordingly called on three pieces of fiction, divided by intervals of approximately ten years, the early epistolary novel *Lady Susan*, the fragment posthumously entitled *The Watsons* and, once again, *Pride and Prejudice*. Still, I felt that I had substantially met my self-imposed pattern, and was happy enough with the result.

As to the second question, which other facets of Jane Austen's life I should tackle, the answers presented themselves immediately – growing-up, courtship, family and money seemed rather obvious choices; and these exhausted the novels at my disposal. Moreover, the topics had to be such as received prime attention in the correspondence. I have been asked recently, and publicly, by a rather fierce feminist, 'How did you deal with Jane Austen's sexuality?' I could not resist the smart reply, 'The short answer is "briefly".' In a serious sense, however, even had I wished to write of this, it would have been quite impracticable because of the virtual absence of what I should regard as evidence in either her letters or any other source. The point is, of course, I had to confine myself to facets on which there was sound and copious enough personal material on which to arrive at a conclusion.

The third question – the chapter order – was the most difficult, for each chapter was disparate and more or less self-contained. After some toying with alternative sequence, I decided at last to place them in what I guessed would be Jane Austen's own order of importance in her life – which meant *seriatim* being a believing Christian, being a woman, belonging to a certain class, her upbringing, her chance of marriage, her family and her reaction to her times. My choice was a *pis aller*, far from the ideal.

This is how *Jane Austen: Real and Imagined Worlds* came to be written. While *O'Connell* was proceeding, it filled the corners of time and relieved the seasons of despair; and then at last, by the beginning of 1990, it was the only task ahead and not far off completion. It was a comparatively simple work for I have from the start eschewed, so far as possible, anything in the nature of literary criticism; and the texts on which I worked as a biographer were small in extent and number. I say 'biographer' partly because half the book was devoted to describing, as far as I could, Jane Austen's life, and partly because it is the people in the novels, and their characteristics and development, which receive the lion's share of attention in the other part.

It is therefore a highly unconventional form of history, a series of biographical essays about both actuality and the imaginative reactions to that actuality. So far, the critics, generally, have been kind about my hybrid. But perhaps this is merely because, as a reviewer of Wodehouse (P.G. not Emma!) once wrote, 'One does not take a spade to a *souffle*'!

1992

4. The Making of *Australians*: A Historical Library A Personal Retrospect

When I became head of the department of History at the Research School of Social Sciences at the Australian National University in 1976, my first task seemed to be to find some major undertaking which our department – as the only 'national' department in Australia, and the only department primarily devoted to research, could promote. Our existing offspring, or at least stepchild, the *Australian Dictionary of Biography*, already well into its second decade of distinguished work, offered an encouraging precedent.

The 1970s as well as the 1980s were an epoch of centenaries in Australia, and I had come fresh from serving on the executive committee of the multivolumed project for *A New History of Ireland* (1989). Given this combination of circumstances, it is not surprising that my first idea for the department should have been an Australian equivalent to the *New History*, to be published in 1988 to mark the bicentenary of the European settlement of that continent.

Even my small experience of the *A New History of Ireland* suggested to me, first, that even a decade's preparation would not be too long for any similar venture; second, that some mechanisms for eliminating laggard authors and replacing them in time would have to be devised and enforced; third, that a considerable annual budget ($100,000 per annum for ten years was the figure plucked from the air) was indispensable; and fourth, that auxiliary or reference volumes would form a more important element in an Australian than in an Irish scheme, because of the relative paucity, then, of source work in Australian history, and the relatively short period of time which would be covered by the history proper.

Specifically, the initial sketch plan was for eight volumes in all, four covering Australian history between 1788 and, say, 1970, with four reference books, a chronology, a historical atlas, a bibliography and a collection of historical statistics. In form, this first back-of-an-envelope scribble came remarkably close to the final outcome. But in substance the project was to change profoundly in several ways.

At this point I discovered that some sort of commemorative history for the bicentenary had been mooted earlier at the ANU by John Molony, head of the department of History in the Arts Faculty, but without evoking much response. Nonetheless, we tried again and on 8 October 1976 half a dozen of the senior historians at the university met to consider the new proposal. The crucial happening of this meeting – for the absence of a decision to smother the infant at birth can scarcely be termed a happening – was Ken Inglis's proposal that, instead of four narrative volumes, the histories should be four 'slices' of particular years: 1788, 1838, 1888 and 1938. The project was not to be an attempted summation of current scholarship, but a revolutionary type of historiography. I have a lifetime of academic meetings to remember, but this was the only occasion that I can recall when a daring, original idea was accepted with excited acclamation within seconds of its being set out.

The crucial problem, as it seemed at this initial meeting, was to prevent the project being, or even being seen as, an exclusively ANU undertaking. We wished to be truly national.

We feared that people in the state universities might resent our taking so bold and universal an initiative. But in the end we bit the bullet, and decided that while the editorial work should be devolved and distributed as widely as possible among the states, and while we should try to entice contributions from every part of Australia, the Research School would have to remain the controller of, and headquarters for, the project – 'with', as the minutes of that first meeting ran, 'all the odium but also all the advantages which this would involve'. Perhaps I might add here the final item of those minutes (which I wrote myself): 'It was accepted that the author of these notes was, in effect, the pin in the grenade, to be discarded shortly before explosion.' For good or ill, I failed to carry this point later, and became instead the chairman of the management committee.

There followed some eighteen months of wooing the historical profession, stumping the country for support, attempting to appease opponents and counter critics, and lobbying the federal government for grants. To deal with the last first, despite years of soliciting and the painful preparation of an untold number of financial estimates and submissions, we never secured a penny from any state or federal department. The basic difficulty was not ill will or scepticism about the value of the project but simply that government ministers and bureaucrats think, at most, two or three years ahead, and our time span fitted no official budget. Had we begun in 1984 or 1985 there is no doubt whatever – in my mind at least – that we would have received the government million-dollar grant that we had counted on originally. But if we had begun in 1984 or 1985 there would have been no project ready in time for the bicentenary.

It also seemed at first that we had been over-sanguine in expecting even substantial support and commitment from the Australian historical profession. True, our initial step – inviting, in February 1977, the head of every History department in the country to Canberra in order to consider and (they and God willing!) endorse the project – was smoothly taken. The atmosphere was genial. The scheme itself was warmly approved, as well as usefully elaborated, and the body turned itself into an interim management committee.

But the appearance of enthusiastic unanimity was deceptive. One or two of the departmental heads sang very different tunes when they returned to their constituents – not unlike nineteenth-century Irish MPs when they had left behind the blandishments of London and Westminster and faced the public in Clare or Mayo. In one or two other cases, departments soon made it clear that they by no means agreed with their respective heads. There were, besides, protests from particular interests, such as women's history, against their having no voice, and perhaps no sympathizers, in the interim management committee. Marxist, Foucaultist and other radical historians considered the project vitiated by the likely predominance of liberal pragmatists – 'mindless empiricists' was the phrase then in vogue. Again, how *could* the project avoid being celebratory, and what was there to celebrate in the establishment of a penal settlement and the destruction of an indigenous culture?

There was moreover a powerful school of 'senior' and conservative criticism. The very senior historians had already been excluded – not greatly to their satisfaction – by one of the first decisions which we took, namely to recruit no one as a contributor who had already passed the age fifty-five. But even some less venerable seniors decried the project as monopolistic, one deploring it as 'the sole scholarly focus of an enormous investment, both of professional and government money'. It was also decried as eccentric, concentrating on arbitrarily selected segments of time at the expense of the historian's proper procedures, which were the use of the narrative method and a linear time perspective. Finally, even some who wished us well thought that the dream of harnessing teams of historians to work to the same end by absolutely immutable dates was madness.

Although painful at the time, this gallimaufry of opposition, wrong-headedness, right-headedness, penetrating and obtuse criticism proved the utmost value in the end. Late in 1977 Ken Inglis returned to Canberra from a tour of most universities quite daunted, and even dismayed, by the receptions which our scheme had met. But in fact several of the most doubting Thomases turned out to be crucial supporters of the project later on. We were fortunate to have been baptized by fire. We were fortunate to have been taught salutary lessons in time. More precisely, the scepticism, questioning and hostility focussed our attention on points already mooted but in danger of being lost to sight in the multitude of early considerations.

First, the testing of the waters brought home to us the necessity – in Australia, at any rate – of a much more democratic structure and procedure than was customary in large-scale historical undertakings. The volumes – and especially the slice volumes, which were now termed Section A – would have to grow from below rather than be imposed from above. This meant that, within the general, overarching principles of the operation, there might be considerable variety of emphasis and very different forms of teamwork.

Later on, I shall discuss this heterogeneity. But let me give a single example of unanticipated developments immediately. The volume *Australians 1838* was in effect, bid for, some time on, by two young historians then in Perth, Alan Atkinson and Marian Aveling: their bid was eventually successful. They had been excited by the prospect which Ken Inglis had opened up when he visited western Australia during his 1977 tour; they felt that it offered much hope for the sort of history that appealed to their generation. They were deeply interested in the possibilities of the new 'history from below', fervently anti-authoritarian by instinct, and much attracted by collective forms of work. In fact, they set up an 1838 collective in 1980, open to everyone who contributed anything to the journal for 1838 studies which they had established, with the wryly pointed title, *The Push from the Bush*. This ethos and this *modus operandi* were maintained throughout the composition of their book, with much consultation, exchange of drafts, conferences and co-operative writing. Most of the chapters ended up with several authors, one with no fewer than eight contributors, all loyal to the collective's initial resolution (I quote from the volume's introduction) 'to present the minds of people living in Australia in 1838 as far as possible from inside, by recounting the language and behaviour of day-to-day situations ... going *beyond* the records of the elite so as to recreate the minds of the inarticulate and powerless'. I think readers will agree that Atkinson and Aveling have succeeded brilliantly in their purpose.

The second benefit of the douches of cold and tepid water with which we were showered in 1977 was that they confirmed the importance of devolving as much of the project as possible to other universities, and throughout the country. This was not – could not have been – as much a matter of strategic planning as of seizing opportunities as they arose. And in fact the requisite opportunities appeared. The obvious centre for *1838*, in its early years, was Perth. The ideal editors for *1888* emerged in Melbourne, and for *1938* in Adelaide and Sydney. The most important devolution of all was the appointment of Frank Crowley as general editor of the whole series of reference volumes, now termed Section B. Not only did this create another headquarters (or at least sub-headquarters) in Sydney but also it meant that Crowley's university, New South Wales, would henceforth support the project financially, on a very considerable scale. Of course, this successful dispersion of the undertaking owed much to luck; but I should like to think that the founding fathers of Canberra did something to help luck along, or at least that they recognized her when they met her in the street.

So – we were democratized and judiciously scattered about the continent long before anyone had put pen to paper. But I should also make it clear that three centralizing and controlling elements were retained: not for nothing I served, however humbly, on the *New History of Ireland*. First, the ultimate authority, the management committee, remained substantially in the hands of our History department in Canberra: the head of department was chairman ex officio. Second, we set absolute deadlines, not only for completion but also for each major stage in the production: we were, in one sense (though only one!), fortunate in having a ready-made date by which, come hell or highwater, the books would have to appear before the public. And third, we decided to use the various production stages as tests for the punctuality of our contributors and to eliminate all who failed to produce whatever was required by the specified time, and to search for replacements as soon as the malingerers (however eminent) were identified and disposed of. I cannot claim that we quite lived up to this stern resolution, but we certainly went a fair way down the audacious path.

On 28 March 1978 the interim management committee wound itself up, and the management committee proper took its place. By now, general editors – Inglis and Crowley – had been appointed for sections A and B respectively, as well as convenors (who were really proto-editors) for *1788*, *1838*, *1888* and *1938*. Besides the ANU had appointed a special assistant general editor for Section A, and the UNSW [University of New South Wales (Sydney)] a similar officer for Section B: these were full-time appointments, essentially managerial and executive in design.

All these people, with some later additions, constituted a newly formed editorial board, which would govern the content, style and method of the books, independently. The general title *Australians* was proposed by Bill Gammage at an early meeting of this board and accepted at once as a simple inspiration. Meanwhile a fifth volume, *Australians from 1939*, had been added to Section A; and although the *Atlas* and the *Guide to Sources and Historical Statistics* had been confirmed in Section B, its fourth volume, the *Handbook*, was to remain an uncertainty. Eventually it was partitioned into an *Historical Dictionary* and the chronology-cum-gazetteer *Events and Places*, the latter an unanticipated addition to the collection. Final decisions on editors, contributors and all else were due to be made by 1981, but in the interim the working parties for each volume would be laying the foundations with an eye to completion by 1985 and 1986.

In short, we had hit ourselves over the head with a bottle of champagne, glided down the slipway, and recruited many of the artificers who would labour in the still-empty hull.

For a fair while we counted on public funding, and we lived from hand to mouth for the day when the Australian Bicentennial Authority would be constituted. When the authority was at last set up in 1980, we lived for the day when it would receive federal monies for distribution. Then we lived for the day when the authority would determine its support policies and its criteria for patronage. Then – we simply ran out of days. Meanwhile, universities, in particular the ANU and University of New South Wales, kept us alive from year to year, diverting to us scraps of savings and pieces of unfilled posts. The Division of National Mapping, a federal government agency, helped us generously in the creation of the *Atlas*. The Australian Research Grants Committee gave indispensable grants towards the making of particular volumes. Finally, we received cash transfusions from our publishers in the form of advances on royalties.

In our early days we had discussed publishers in a more or less desultory way, not thinking the matter urgent and assuming that we would be sure to find a victim or band of victims. But when in 1980 we invited tenders and received submissions, it became clear that the scale, technical sophistication, unknown market prospects and concentrated publication programme daunted most Australian publishers. At this point Inglis happened to meet Kevin Weldon, an entrepreneur who published high-quality books for the mass market. Weldon was immediately seized by the idea of our national scheme. So it was no surprise that he responded with great enthusiasm when approached by the David Syme group, publishers of the Melbourne *Age*, and John Fairfax & Sons, publishers of the *Sydney Morning Herald*, to co-publish *Australians: A Historical Library*. Weldon's interest proved the turning point. We were about to enter a bigger league than we had originally contemplated.

We were now History Project Incorporated, so constituted a legal entity under the Australian Capital Territory Associations Incorporated Ordinance. I shall pass quickly over the protracted courtship and early lovers' quarrels between HPI and FSW, as the new partnership of Fairfax, Syme and Weldon came to be known. In 1982, the contract between us was finally signed and we were a married couple – at least in the sense in which Robert Louis Stevenson defined marriage, as a sort of friendship recognized by the police.

The project had been originally expected to emerge as a conventional type of multivolume academic publication, such as the *Oxford History of England* or the *New Cambridge Modern History*. It is true that we had hoped, from the beginning, to write for a more general public than such series were aimed at. It was also true that – partly for this reason and partly because the book of the future would (we thought) contain much more than the printed word – we intended that the volumes should be (I quote again from early minutes) 'richly illustrated'. But FSW's vision of potential sales for the series, so much grander than any other publisher we had spoken with, provoked us to bolder thinking about both words and pictures.

It became imperative that the volumes should be written in plain (which is far from meaning inelegant) English, and as free as practicable from the argot and jargon of the various disciplines which the project would embrace. Later, Alan Gilbert, who joined Inglis as general editor of Section A late in 1981, made this a special study. Drawing particularly upon American syntactical and grammatical research, he prepared a paper of great interest and importance for contributors. Effective presentation was another corollary of aiming at a mass market. It quickly became clear that FSW contemplated illustration upon a scale, and of a degree of sophistication, far beyond what we had had originally in mind. Our volumes have ended up with some three thousand illustrations, most of them in colour: the ratio of illustration to text is roughly one to three. Moreover, illustration was not treated as mere decoration. It was carefully interwoven with text wherever possible. These changes of emphasis added enormously to our load, and did much to make our relationship with the publisher both more complex and more intimate than we had imagined. FSW set up editorial and design systems from the start, so that from 1982 on we were working not in a vacuum but in continuous communication with our partner. At last, in November 1986, arrived the joint meeting at which we could all leaf through the first two finished books, artefacts of our common purpose.

In the heady days in 1976 and 1977 we imagined that we would end in some immense thunderclap of achievement. Instead, we have seemed to dwindle gradually into annihilation. Exhaustion has overlaid and smothered jubilation. In W.B. Yeats's words:

> Too long a sacrifice
> Can make a stone of the heart

Was it all worth while? Were those critics right who argued at the start that such a prodigious mustering and spending of intellectual resources was a mistaken, indeed a most wasteful strategy?

I can answer only for myself. I see many reasons for concluding that the game has after all been worth the candle; and I shall offer the five which seem to me most powerful.

First, in the reference books, deep foundations have been laid for Australian historiography in general. Virtually *de novo*, the project has created a series of historical statistics, a historical chronology and gazetteer, an historical atlas, an historical dictionary and a major guide to sources. This was achieved under the general editorship of Frank Crowley to 1985, and of

Peter Spearritt from 1985 to the finishing line. No one would pretend to perfection or finality for any of these volumes or part-volumes. But at least a solid basis has been laid over the entire range of reference works.

Second, the project has, I believe, integrated Aboriginal with what we may loosely term European Australian history, as never before. The planned *1788* ended up as *To 1788*, with four-fifths of its content devoted to pre-European Australia. This brilliant survey of the Aboriginal era, itself a *tour de force*, is thoroughly knit into the doom of traditional Aboriginal life, as signalled by the arrival of the British fleet in 1788. In addition – and of no less importance, I should say – each of the volumes set in later years takes up other Aboriginal themes and interweaves them with the expansion of white Australia. Again, the historiographical map seems to have been changed significantly. Already, the old automatic identification of Australian history with the settlements of the past centuries looks passé. The project itself has fiercely eschewed the celebratory note: 1988 is treated throughout as the anniversary of a revolutionary happening, not as the starting point of a neo-whig interpretation, or glorification, of a short stretch of time.

Third, the project has had a striking effect upon the historical profession in Australia. It is even arguable that it created this profession, in the sense that enterprise has forced a multitude of Australian historians into collective and co-operative interaction upon a hitherto undreamt-of scale. There were working parties of up to thirty people on particular volumes and constant traffic between one volume and another: commonly, the interchanges proceeded for several years. Paradoxically, the inevitable – indeed desirable – differences in historical presuppositions and general philosophy had – all in all – a centripetal rather than a centrifugal effect upon the participants. The *esprit de corps* growing out of the common commitment tended to bring a corps itself into being, over time. Moreover, by a further paradox, the historians themselves have been not only enriched but also stung into a greater self-awareness, by all the close and constant work with people from other disciplines, which the project practically enjoined. Among these disciplines, I would stress particularly geography and anthropology, as well as prehistory and economic history. In short, it seems to me that history in Australia has emerged from the experience immensely strengthened, structurally as well as intellectually.

Fourth, the project dragged at least those of us who needed to be dragged into the late-twentieth century. In saying this, I refer, in part, to our technical education.

Without the word processor and the disc our task would have been impossible. Our colour and design requirements called for the newest processes. All this experience of modern publishing has filtered downwards. Even if only at second or third hand, our academics should have received useful glimpses of the future.

This is perhaps also true of some more fundamental matters. As we have seen the project's objective has been to reach a very wide and varied public without the sacrifice of any principle of scholarship. This high ambition did not stop at windy rhetoric and exhortation. Gilbert's work on words reached and – we trust – exercised some degree of influence, small or great, upon our hundreds of contributors. Correspondingly, the systematic collection of non-literary forms of evidence, and the attempt to render text and illustration mutually supporting and cross-reflective, have surely made an enduring impression on our trade.

Few words have been more overworked by historians during the past twenty years than 'modernization'. But rarely if ever do we think of it in relation to ourselves. Yet the mechanics of composition, the economics of publishing and the potentiality of readership – not to add, listenership and spectatorship – have been changing rapidly and profoundly. I do not want to exaggerate the importance of the *forms* of communication. The substance of what is to be communicated is, and always will be, absolutely paramount. Nonetheless, we should know what we are about in the times in which we write; and the project has proved a technical school, or forcing-house, for many of the rising as well as the declining generation of Australian historians.

The fifth, final and (to my mind) most important reverberations of the project will, I believe, follow from the slice approach. The exclusive study of a single year is not of course without precedent. At least one distinguished book is based upon this method, and the *New History of Ireland* itself employs it. But never has it been attempted on such a scale, or by such large numbers of historians, or with such single-minded rigour. I think that one can fairly claim that, as deployed in *Australians: A Historical Library*, it is a truly revolutionary device.

Each volume group interpreted its task, and dealt with its cross-sectional layer, in a different fashion. *Australians from 1939* was practically by definition barred from slicing its half-century assignment, although its editors were also to eschew conventional narrative structures. But all the other books took individual approaches. *To 1788*, charged with 40,000 years of pre-white Australian history, could obviously not adhere to slicing proper. Even so, it was deeply influenced by the general method. In the final portion of the book, 'Sydney 1788' lent itself to and duly received an orthodox cross-sectional treatment. But what is really interesting is the manner in which much of the remainder of *To 1788* is shaped or coloured by the principle of slicing, as authors depict Aboriginal life in an actual or metaphorical 1788 – the eve of European settlement whenever that moment happened in different parts of the continent.

Australians 1838 was, as I have said, the most closely collaborative volume of all. Like coalmining, history from below lent itself to collective effort. The book has taken, as its introduction proclaims, 'a critical stance towards the social values of the past', and tried to reconstruct the Australia of its particular year in terms of so-called ordinary events in the lives of so-called ordinary people, their weddings, church-going, funerals, groupings, legal and business dealings, and the like. The very roll-call of titles of the middle chapters of *1838* – 'Families', 'Work', 'Markets', 'Meetings', 'People Confined' – is practically a manifesto of the history of the unsung and long-forgotten men, women and children, too.

The *1888* volume was *organized* upon more conventional lines, and subject to more authoritative editorial direction, than any of the others. The editors selected their own team of contributors and drove them systematically through exchanges of drafts and discussion meetings. Yet their interpretation of the slices was far from commonplace. One of the editors, Graeme Davison, has noted the influence of French historiography as embodied in the journal *Annales*. He observes of *1888*:

> insofar as we have a specific model it is perhaps the kind of fully textured detailed portrait of environment, economy, society and politics that one finds in Fernand Braudel's *The Mediterranean and the Mediterranean world in the Age of Philip II*. We aim to portray, more fully than hitherto, the regional and social diversity of Australia in 1888 and the ways in which different environments and regional economies were mediated in family structures and class relations.

Moreover, the *1888* editors were bold in selecting chapter topics. These were often quite out of the ordinary; 'Distance', 'Death', 'Capitals' and 'Energy' are examples. In fact, the Energy chapter provides an excellent illustration of what the slice approach can yield. In conventional narrative historiography the emphasis would almost certainly be placed upon the extraordinary growth in the newer forms of energy, coal, oil and electricity, during the 1880s. This is the normal patterning of the narrative. But the slice view, across the entire spectrum and at a fixed point in time, shows that horse power, in the ancient and literal sense, still easily predominated in the Australia of 1888; that the next most important source of energy was the oldest of all, human muscle; and that the rate of innovation varied widely from region to region and between the various sectors of the economy. Energy, in another sense, might well be taken as the emblem of this volume. One emerges – or at least I emerged – from reading it, dazzled by the new perspectives and tingling with intellectual excitement or liberation.

The *1938* editors took as their starting point the fact that the year itself was within the living memory of many Australians. One of the basic resources developed immediately was a collection of interviews with a sample of people who were growing up during the 1930s. In all, nearly four hundred interviews were taped. In length they varied from forty-five minutes to nine hours, and they concentrated so far as practicable on the year to which the volume was dedicated. In a sense therefore it was *recollection* itself which was sliced in this particular exercise. The immediate value of the interviews in the composition of the book varied of course from topic to topic, and according to author's inclination. But they have also a lasting value as a source, which quite transcends the specific purpose for which they were assembled. *Australians 1938* was also able to apply the slice precisely in its section entitled 'Pioneers on parade', which deals with the Australian sesquicentennial celebrations and anti-celebrations. In neither case – one profoundly hopes – do they constitute a dress rehearsal for 1988, but are rather two flies in amber fixed forever in their antique confrontation.

Even this lightning sketch should have made clear that the slice, as deployed in these books, is not a formula, not a new scholasticism, not an orthodoxy, not even a taking of sides in any great methodological debate. Its makers do not assert that the slice is the only, or the best, or even an always practicable or an always desirable mode of composing history. They accept that in Clio's, as well as in a more transcendental house, there are many mansions. They even refrain from throwing the occasional ideological brick – deliberately, at least – into any other dwelling. But, I would argue, the method has its own special value, which renders it the crown and glory of our project. I know of no more eloquent or telling elaboration of this claim than that put forward by Davidson in his paper, 'Slicing Australian history'. 'In constructing his narrative', he writes,

> the historian has the immense advantage of hindsight: he selects those facts or events which appear to favour that known outcome and he ignores those which are irrelevant to it, whether or not they seemed important to contemporaries. By focusing upon an arbitrarily chosen moment of time the slice approach acts as a corrective to the inbuilt teleological bias of narrative history. It implies that we *temporarily* abstain from the search for 'the most significant years, or the busiest or the epochal' and concentrate instead upon the routine, the ordinary and mundane. Instead of assigning significance to events in terms of a known outcome or *telos* it gently subverts the 'received notions of the rhythms or contours of Australian history'. Instead of exalting the established heroes of Australian history, it aims to rescue the struggling selector, the suburban housewife, even perhaps the landboomer's clerk, from the 'appalling condescension of posterity'.

But it would be quite out of kilter with the project to end on too celebratory or even congratulatory a note. Our authors tend to see the project as a living thing, not a dead achievement, a seedling rather than a harvest cut and garnered. Nonetheless, I, who have neither written nor edited a line in any of the volumes, may perhaps be allowed to boast on behalf of the many who spent years in this grinding work, now completed in good time to help readers throughout and beyond Australia to understand the experience of humanity in this continent from its beginnings to 1988.

1988

II
INTERVIEWS WITH HISTORIANS

5. Interview by Roy Foster for the Royal Historical Society Video Series, *Interviews with Historians**

Roy Foster: '[I see] myself as a sort of pinchbeck *ultimus Romanorum*, a last general practitioner among consultants, a chance survivor from a vanquished world.' I think one should notice in that the ironic tone amid the generally modest disclaimers because every single one of those statements is highly questionable, and many of them completely wrong. MacDonagh's work has started hares in all sorts of directions; from the debate on early-Victorian government to the morass of Anglo-Irish relations in the present as well as in the past. The point is, I think, that his genius is uniquely and urbanely to provoke an impassioned discussion, often in a very laconic way, and then to move on to another part of the field altogether – the historian as icebreaker, as he has described

* In the interests of clarity the editor has added some explanatory matter in square brackets to this transcript of the interview. He is grateful to the Royal Historical Society for permission to reproduce it.

it on one occasion, rather than ring-fencing and defending one patch of territory all one's life. And he has left his mark with, I think, brio and a very notable style, which is hardly equalled in his generation. So, Oliver MacDonagh, can I ask you as a historian to whom a sense of place means a lot in your work, something about your own origins and influences? You were born, and I think brought up, in Carlow.

Oliver MacDonagh: I was born in Carlow, not brought up there. I was brought up effectively as a boy in the west of Ireland in Roscommon, which was a tiny town of, I think, 1990 inhabitants, 1983 or -4 of whom were Roman Catholics. I can remember a great deal about its landscape, which was of a gentle kind, but the things I think which affected me most, looking back on it, were the intensity that one learnt from living in the immediate aftermath of a civil war, that politics was a really serious and divisive business.

RF: You moved on to another intense location, which was Clongowes, the great Jesuit school. Did Clongowes and the Jesuit training leave a mark on you?

OM: I think so, yes, a literary mark anyhow. The teachers I had for English were two Jesuits who were remarkably good; all my life I've had remarkably bad history teachers. And one of them was a very bad novelist himself, but he was a great patron of his charges and he got me to encourage the little flame of talent that I had, essay writing, and got my poems published in *The Irish Monthly*, which I believe, if I may say so modestly, was where Yeats's first poems were published – but there the resemblance ends.

RF: Then, University College Dublin and the L&H debating society and King's Inns and the Bar. Was that because a legal career commended itself to you or because it was an intellectual training that you thought would help your historical bent?

OM: Well, these were in the desperate 1940s and the idea was that one got a profession or an occupation. I intended to be a barrister if I could survive the three or four years of starvation without any legal connections. I did actually learn, I think; at least there were lessons there which were very useful to me as a historian. I keep remembering the emphasis in law on stating things precisely and getting the exact meaning and that nothing else would do, and working and worrying for that. And the other thing I got from it, which I think is useful for historians, was emphasis on decisions. Ideally, I think that in law you always end up one way or the other in the end, and I think an occupational danger for historians is to fudge when things become difficult and that law at least taught me to try and focus on making up my own mind in the end, if the evidence was there, of course. I'm taking that for granted.

RF: I've always thought of you as rather an Occam's razor kind of man, and I'd assumed that came from a good and strict training in the great Catholic theologians as much as in the law, but you would put your decision to strip away the inessential and to arrive at a decision down to a legal approach, or a legalistic approach, rather than a Newmanesque [one]?

OM: Well, I suppose I had my share of hand-me-down apologetics and I'm sure I learnt something from that, but as far as I can recall it was the legal training that impressed me the most on that particular point.

RF: To continue with your odyssey, from UCD you went on, as many others have done, to Cambridge. That was in the late 1940s, a time when there were a number of very distinguished historians operating there. Could you say something about the historians in your time who affected the way that you began to write history?

OM: Well, there was a galaxy of historians there. There were

[Herbert] Butterfield, [David] Knowles, [M.M.] Postan, [Denis] Brogan, who was my supervisor, Graham Plaque and Brian Wormald, and Dennis Mack Smith and other dons. This was all out of a fellowship of about fifteen, I think, and it was very exciting. The person who influenced me most in a very indirect way was David Knowles, simply because I found him so admirable an historian, so humane and exact, correct and just, and so on. Brogan was my supervisor; we rarely met but he was a delightful supervisor because he always arranged supervisions for the Reform Club, because although he lived down the same staircase for a time, he was away so much. He was a wonderful friend to have, but he was utterly uncritical when it came to research students; he would simply put a little tick like at primary school – very good – after a whole chapter, just correct your spellings and give you a torrent of other reading to do and that was all.

RF: But this gave you a free rein, presumably.

OM: Oh yes, absolutely. I have had a charmed life by being relatively uninfluenced by other historians.

RF: This is what you mean about having bad teachers?

OM: Well, I was thinking of school in that case, but in one way or another I seem to have escaped much teaching.

RF: Was [G.S.R.] Kitson Clark influential in your decision to approach the early-Victorian period in the way you did?

OM: No, he wasn't. I had hoped to have him as supervisor when I went to Cambridge, but at that time I think he had a thing about Irish subjects. Anyhow he sheered off, and Brogan, who was a sort of Statue of Liberty person, he took in everybody. So the curious result was that I didn't meet Kitson Clark until I had finished my PhD; I was five years at Cambridge before I met him. But then of course he'd read something that I had written, and I was the pioneer speaker at his famous seminar.

RF: And he encouraged you to write the book you say is for the plain reader, on early Victorian government (*Early Victorian Government*).

OM: Yes, he kept saying: 'MacDonagh you must write this. MacDonagh you must write this.'

RF: The idea being there that what you had done in your *Pattern of Government Growth* book about the Passenger Acts, and also your controversial article on the nineteenth-century revolution in government, should be delivered to a general audience.

OM: Yes, that's right, put in a broader perspective. Well, I'm sure he didn't mean the book to be, and nor did I mean it to be, simply an elaboration of the pattern of government growth; it dealt with various aspects of it.

RF: Indeed it does. It casts a wide net. It also rather eschews discussion of the controversies which emerged from your, really quite subversive, work on early Victorian government. Was this a deliberate decision on your part?

OM: I'm not a very good deliberate decider, I sort of drift into things, but I suppose it was more or less a decision. I've always disliked controversy in history; sometimes it's unavoidable and necessary, but I've a feeling that it rapidly becomes very wasteful, that people build themselves into positions and cease to hear. Taking the economy of history writing as a whole it tends to waste time and to stunt creativity. I know it's necessary that people should be put through the examination process and their work criticized. Nonetheless, the idea of spending your time writing counter [arguments] and becoming narrower and narrower and blinder to any view except your own, which probably would have happened to me, didn't appeal to me. It seemed to be a waste of time.

RF: Could it be said that you cultivate a rather urbane and lapidary style in order to avoid that kind of engagement?

OM: It could be said – you've said it – but I hope it isn't true.

RF: Well, I think it's a very good way of provoking discussion and then moving gracefully on.

OM: Well, I mean, as a fellow Irishman you know this weakness we have for epigrammaticism and paradox, and a lot of what you say may be a reflection of that epigrammaticism.

RF: One of the things that I think annoyed people in that government work was your – dismissal is too strong a word – but your scepticism about the notion of a zeitgeist, specifically a Benthamite zeitgeist, which flowed into the mind of the governing classes. Does this reflect in your approach a general distrust of that kind of model for the way things happen?

OM: Yes, I think it does. Benthamism itself is one of these concepts or bodies of ideas that people are very defensive about, perhaps offensive about as well. And I think that got under some skins, and it was that, rather than [scepticism about the] zeitgeist, as such. But I did from quite an early stage have quite an uneasiness about this attribution of trains of historical decisions, major trains, being attributed in a simple way to a body of ideas from which they seemed to 'floor' a doctrine, and all my life I suppose, really, I've had that scepticism.

RF: If I could approach your earlier work from another angle, you use, I think, in *States of Mind* with great pleasure a quotation from [George E.] Buckle, who boasts 'I write the history of England because it is normal.' I laughed out loud when I read that. Would you say that you approached the history of England through an Irish interest? What you tend to do in your early work is to show that administrative history, if that's what you call it, can throw a different light on Irish history, especially if you approach it from as wide a knowledge as you do of the English world, especially of the 1830s and 40s. Did Ireland bring you to writing

English administrative history, is what I'm asking?

OM: I don't think so, no, except in one special sense in that I was always struck by what W.L. Burn called the use of Ireland as a social laboratory, where experiments would take place that Englishmen would never agree with at the time. But the same is true, as Eric Stokes pointed out, about India and for something of the same reasons. So in that special sense, certainly, I had that at the back of my mind, but my interest in English social policy and the development of welfare institutions in the nineteenth century was, I think, an intrinsic interest not really coming from Ireland.

RF: Didn't it begin with an interest in Irish emigration?

OM: That's what set me off in the emigration offices as they were. They were run from the Colonial Office; they were all British half-pay naval officers, mostly stationed in British ports, so of course their fodder was mostly Irish emigrants. That's how I got led into it, but it took me over.

RF: The social laboratory idea, which as you rightly say was Burn's formulation, but which you added enormously to, can be approached in two ways, can't it? On the one hand, it can be seen as a sort of argument that British government in Ireland wasn't the neglectful and deliberately oppressive machine which nationalist historiography made it out to be; on the other hand, it can be approached, to quote yourself, as simply indicating that it was thought that Ireland needed a more rational, elaborate and autocratic system of repression than happier lands. Do you see your work as taking part of both those angles of interpretation or as coming down more towards the repressive than the benevolent angle?

OM: Well, that certainly calls for Occam's razor. I suppose if I had to choose, I'd come down for the more repressive version. That is what I had in mind when I quoted

Burn, but I think it's a little misleading if it suggests the element of deliberateness and planning. I think I went on to say that expedience would be rather a better word than the experiments from the social laboratory. It was the logic of the situations which arose from the position of political control and responsibility.

RF: This is your coral-reef idea, which is an image I think you used very powerfully for the way that administrative structures developed. As a very crude transposition, let's move from coral reefs to Australia, because pursuing this rather jejune notion of influence, which I still think is very important, you began in 1963 what was to be a long association, and a very fruitful one, with Australian academe. I think you went temporarily first to, was it, ANU and then Flinders?

OM: Yes, I went to a research fellowship with the ANU, not in the department of History – they wouldn't have me – but the department of Demography. At that stage I was flying under the colours, temporarily, of an emigrationist, and I did work and published something on the Irish in Australia. I wrote demographic essays partly because there were so many Irish immigrants – it's much the largest area per head of population of Irish settlement in the world; and secondly Australian demographic and population records of all kinds are superb, perhaps the best in the nineteenth century. And so it was this twin reason that drew me there, and then there was a new university being set up in Adelaide and I was asked if I would be one of the founding fathers. And it all seemed such a wonderful change from Cambridge, especially as this came in February after a really bad winter.

RF: And was it a change from Ireland as well?

OM: Well, I had sort of made that change, not deliberately, but that's the way things had fallen out. I didn't feel very much more separate.

RF: It was also in your Australian years that you produced at least two books; the two I'm thinking of, certainly, which looked at Ireland through the other end of the telescope. Instead of the highly specific administrative and governmental history, you produced two extremely wide-ranging books: one, *Ireland: The Union and its Aftermath*, as it was eventually called; and the other, *States of Mind*, a survey, really, of Anglo-Irish misunderstandings over two hundred years. Do you think you needed the distance in Australia to do that?

OM: Yes, well, I don't know if I needed it but it was certainly very useful. The other thing was that in Cambridge I was getting more and more involved, happily involved, in British history. I was for example lecturing on Labour politics and socialism and so on, as well as the ordinary British constitution in the nineteenth century, and I think that this was a break and a wrench, and suddenly my Irish interest reawoke very fully ... I think it probably dominated my time in Australia.

RF: Looking at the oeuvre, that's what it certainly seems. Is it also something, do you think, about being in an environment where Ireland is not seen as in opposition to Britain as it may have been from the Cambridge angle? Well, the Irish experience in Australia is a very enabling experience, isn't it?

OM: Well, I think that one thing that struck me early on was that the Australian population proportion throughout the nineteenth century up to 1914 and perhaps even up to 1939, was almost a mirror of that of the United Kingdom after 1801, and the Irish were, in a very muted and pale form, varying from colony to colony in something of the [same] state of exclusion to a degree, and of competitiveness, and of an incomplete group identity. All this was in a very pale and minor form, but nonetheless there was that element which intrigued me. The whole course of Australian development in the nineteenth century seemed to me to throw interesting light on at least the Home Rule Movement and perhaps the Repeal Movement as well. But in the 1880s and 1890s I believe that Australia contributed as much to the Irish National Party, the Land Leagues, and all the other organizations, as came from the United States. That's in gross figures, considering the difference in the population was about seventeen to one in terms of Irish derivation; that shows the relative significance of Irish Australia. And what Irish Australia was saying, and why it built up contacts with the non-conformist liberals, was that what Ireland should have is what we already have, here in New South Wales, or in Victoria; responsible self-government. And Parnell's appeal, especially after 1886, made a tremendous impact there. And it seemed to me that this was regarded as the apotheosis for the time being, of Australian development. It threw a very interesting light, for me, on Ireland.

RF: It's still a dimension, I think, which is under-researched and under-recognized, that imperial notion. Pressing this idea of how your work on Ireland developed in Australia – now you may well contradict me on this – but my impression from *Ireland: The Union and its Aftermath* and more especially *States of Mind*, is that in these books the gloves are coming off, in a sense; the language is more passionate, the style more audacious. If I could just give a quotation to give a flavour. When you write about late-nineteenth-century land legislation in *Ireland: The Union and its Aftermath*, you write:

> Most important of all the conception of society as operating on an essentially individualist and contractual basis in which market forces were the proper determinant of social and economic good

> had been irremediably breached. The great example of Ireland passive under British rule became in the end a paradigm of Ireland drastic. 'The man that once did sell the lion's skin while the beast lived, was killed with hunting him.'

It's different from the urbanity, or the surface urbanity of your earlier work. These are very passionate books, especially, I think, *States of Mind*. Would you accept that or do you think that I am reading something into them that isn't there?

OM: Well, you're an excellent judge – if you say it, I'll accept it. But on that particular issue, as far as I recall, what I was suggesting was, I've forgotten the context, but it probably was something to do with land legislation or something of that kind. Is that right?

RF: Yes.

OM: What I meant was that the irony whereby the pursuit for reasons of control, a forced pursuit of certain policies, in the long run ended up with Britain applying them, or suffering from them, if one saw it like that. I don't know if that came across clearly?

RF: The message that I was reading is that in the end exploitation and, if you like, oppression, received its own reward by a number of stunning historical ironies with the buying out of the landlords being one of them.

OM: That, I'm afraid, is all too generally true.

RF: Yes, I think it probably is, but it's a tone that emerges in these later works more strongly than in the earlier ones. The other thing I would like to put to you about *States of Mind* particularly is that there is a chapter in it called 'Politics Bellicose', which I think is one of the most astringent reviews ever written of the tradition of violent rhetoric and violent deeds in Irish history. But that chapter ends by allowing what you call the emotional pull of violence for Irish people. I think Occam's razor and coming down to a decision isn't happening there; there is a deliberate ambiguity.

OM: Well, I was trying to round out the picture by pointing to the ambiguity of the dualism there is in most Irish nationalists' breasts, or was at the time I was writing, which was a long time ago. I think that it's a commonplace that people have these ambiguities, these elemental tribal feelings. It depends on the amount of pressure and circumstances [to which they are exposed]. I think a chapter on violence without making this clear would be misleading. I think I end with a Boswell quotation about the Forty-Five, and about the fact that those who look at these things and expect sober rationality and calculation to last all the time know very little about human nature. I meant it as – I hope it wasn't too pompous – a reflection of human nature in this situation of violence. But that's why I put it in – what I believe. It wasn't to make a decision myself on violence; I was trying to describe the Irish nationalist reaction as I saw it.

RF: No, pompous is the last thing it is; it's pessimistic. And you move from that chapter of 'Politics Bellicose' straight into a chapter called 'Politics Clerical' and I wondered if you saw that particular theme in Irish politics as being the clerical theme, as being one way to rationalize and control these dangerous urges, which you have written about in the past.

OM: Well, perhaps yes, but also, I think, you never really know what motive you have at the bottom. But I think I'm sure one of them was to have an ironic commentary on the preceding chapter because one of the points I'm making in 'Politics Clerical' is that the Catholic clergy en masse, especially those below episcopal ranks, but not excluding the episcopal ranks by any means, were subject to the same pressures and feelings and pulls as the mass, or perhaps more so, in their being articulate and educated, relatively speaking – more articulate – and yet their tight ecclesiastical discipline, the role and influence which was pretty consistently pro-British, the canon law on conspiracy and on use of arms, all these pulling [the other way]. And I thought it a very sad, ironic situation, not to say that there aren't similar ironies if I had the knowledge and the time to do Ulster, Ulster Unionists or British nationalists. I think in that chapter I mention that, but the one that I'm picking because it is relevant to my theme is 'Politics Clerical', and 'Politics Clerical' seems to me to be a tremendous, and I don't mean tremendous in its own quality, but an intentional commentary on violence because the clergy seem to me to express it in a much more acute form and also to be subject to these dilemmas and problems.

RF: Yes, the relationship between those two themes is to me the core of that book, which is a book that I have read and reread many times. It's at the core of Daniel O'Connell's career, this tension between the use of an impulse that often declares itself in violent or confrontational acts and the firm commitment to clerical politics, and working within the system by reining in these tensions. Were you working on O'Connell when you wrote *States of Mind*?

OM: No, I'd been thinking about O'Connell, not directly, for a long time but was afraid to write – like putting your foot at the bottom of Everest. It just seems so huge, so big. I'd been collecting material for a long time but no, I hadn't begun. But what I wanted to write, what I set out to do was, I suppose, a grandiose idea. It seemed to me that there was no proper study of how a modern Irish Catholic nationalist had developed. The way to do it was to study O'Connell, both because he was a key figure in shaping it and expressing it and because he seemed to be a fine exemplar of its progress in the first half of the nineteenth century. I began with this in mind, and I began, as I always do, with the easy parts first. The easiest part was the one about his secret marriage and his hiding the marriage from the curmudgeonly uncle from whom he had great expectations, and this sort of human development just caught me and it became a biography – I just couldn't help it (*The Hereditary Bondsman: Daniel O'Connell, 1775–1829*). But I hope the underlying beat is there of these large cultural things; I didn't specify them but I hope that it came through because that was really what I meant to write about.

RF: The themes that you mentioned: the marriage, the uncle, the money, could come straight out of a Trollope novel, and creative literature, especially of the nineteenth century, preoccupies you, I think, and we'll go back to that. But, in a sense, when I look at your writing and at O'Connell, it is in some ways the inevitable subject for you. It's like a great nineteenth-century novel even in its scale; it has the themes of love, and money, and politics. Would it be true to say that there is an appeal there for you too because the period in which you have chosen to locate a lot of your work is the period when romantic and utilitarian themes are, in a sense, in a creative tension with each other? And this is true of O'Connell himself?

OM: Very true of him, yes. I think that's absolutely right; I agree with you completely. My predecessor in the research school in the Australian National University, John La Nauze, used to say 'nobody should write a biography until they're over fifty because they haven't lived enough' and I laughed very secretly at this when I heard it in my thirties. But when I came to write about O'Connell in my fifties, I could see the point because of the structure and mechanics of my life – even to having seven children and all the business which running this complex enterprise involves. And of course I saw

O'Connell at the start in Catholic terms, the second Counter-Reformation in the English-speaking world, and I saw myself as a youth in the final stage of the same historical phenomena. And I saw the Ireland in which I grew up as the epitome of that, apart from the violence, which produced exactly what O'Connell would have dreamt of; Westminster and the law courts, and Whitehall and everything transposed, but power transferred. It seemed to me that I understood all sorts of little things because I had been through the same range of experience so, although I didn't intend it like that, it became very personal; it's just that you have the secret codes, the little information that alerts you to certain things.

RF: That leads me to think of the kind of writers who attract you – creative writers. Because you use creative literature not just as jejune illustration of what's going on but as a way into *mentalité*. I think you were doing this very early; I've come across references throughout your work. You may completely contradict me on this, but it seems to me that the novelists you are drawn to – I think about Somerville and Ross, you've written about Charlotte Brontë, Peacock and most of all Jane Austen – are writers who notoriously dismiss what I think you've called in your essay on *Sanditon*, the claptrap of modernity. They are merciless parodists of fashion. Again your work on *Sanditon*, I think, shows that very clearly. Is this kind of rather astringent approach particularly sympathetic to you among novelists?

OM: It is sympathetic to me, but I think my tastes are more catholic. The novelist I read most is Trollope, whom one could hardly categorize with the others in that regard, and George Eliot, Mrs Gaskell, Charlotte Brontë, especially for *Jane Eyre*. Anyhow, you mustn't lead me into talking about novels.

RF: I won't, but I wondered how this related to your early

work, which is more politely sceptical about the notions of a Benthamite zeitgeist, as I said earlier. You seem to like a way into the nineteenth-century mentality that discounts such easy assumptions. There is another tension – I keep coming back to tensions in your work – which is one of the reasons, I think, why people read it with such profit, but there is a tension in your work from the historian's point of view between the acceptability of large patterns or not. In the Austen book you very tersely remark that historians must periodize or perish. This is to say, [must] think that the Regency can, indeed must, be seen as something entire of itself. Yet, in *States of Mind* you almost flamboyantly don't periodize. These are very thematic essays taking almost an elitist approach towards abstract issues like time, place and so forth, and swerving through two hundred years on those themes. Do you think that is an implicit contradiction?

OM: Oh no, I think it's a fair cop, I think there is a contradiction. But I suppose that if I had to say something in defence of this argument against *States of Mind* it is that I was using the whole two hundred years as a period, roaming up and down. I've never thought about it before, but if I had to mount a defence I would think you could periodize variously, you can speak of small epochs within larger ones. But this doesn't affect the generalization, periodize or perish. What I meant was you couldn't envisage history writing without periodization.

RF: We've talked about patterns in history, and the way you conceive it, and the reconciliation of different tensions. Reading the few aperçus of intellectual autobiography which you have let us have – and I think reading between the lines of, for instance, the conclusion to your Fitzpatrick book (*The Inspector General*) I'd infer that a very strong though subtle conditioning influence on you is Catholic philosophy of a traditional and rather stringent kind. You mention Duns Scotus from time to time, as well as, of course, Newman. Do you think that's accurate?

OM: Oh, I think that's accurate. The stringency suggests a greater degree of scholarship than I have in it, but it is absolutely true, yes, I have been coloured by it and I suppose always will be.

RF: But I wonder, in conclusion really, if this predisposition of yours, this intellectual training or conditioning, or whatever you want to call it, goes with a certain pessimism about human ambitions, whether Benthamite or other, as well as [about] other human frailty? Do you think you essentially cast a rather cold eye on attempts at betterment, whether in patterns of government growth, or political utopianism?

OM: I'm afraid I must plead guilty to the charge. I suppose I come down on that side, not by choice, but I suppose it's just my nature and reading.

RF: It seems to be something that comes through your work more and more strongly as it progresses, though it's tempered with your belief in what you've called humaneness, and with a very strong, as I say, conditioning in specifically Catholic philosophy. But, just to go back completely full circle, I began this interview by saying that you described the historian's function as an icebreaker to plough up the surface and leave things churning around, and then move on to a different part of the terrain. What waters would you like to have left disturbed in your wake of the various areas that you've explored?

OM: I think I'd like to have [disturbed the way we regard] eighteenth-century social reform, the sort of [issues highlighted in my] Fitzpatrick work. I'd like a great deal of effort in that field. I'm sure it's rewarding, and I think it's largely hidden. I think, as far as I know, there has been very little work in this field and I'm sure this is something where new ploughing would yield a harvest. And it would be a fascinating harvest, because one has there not only pre-Benthamism, if you like, but also the evangelical movement, the eighteenth-century Enlightenment, rationalism, if you want to put it into intellectual influences. But the tension, to use the word which you keep using, between the eighteenth-century political structures as they were evolving and the pressures, humane or statistical, to produce social change, is fascinating in the 1770s, 80s and 90s.

RF: And this is the area you'd like most to leave, as I say, churned up, rather than the rethinking of Anglo-Irish relations or the notably perceptive new angle, I think, on the relations between creative literature and nineteenth-century life and politics?

OM: Well, I thought you meant which area did I think would yield the most fruit, which area that I'd touched on was most reviewable.

RF: Vainly, I suppose, I was looking for a more self-regarding response from you. In which area do you think you've done most to leave behind that sort of churning-up?

OM: I would like to think it would be Anglo-Irish relations. I don't know whether it is, but I would like that. It's something that touches one very personally, much more deeply and acutely than the other areas.

RF: Well, I think you would be right. Thank you very much, Oliver MacDonagh.

1997

6. Interview by Trevor McClaughlin and David Myton for *The Australian Journal of Irish Studies*

McClaughlin & Myton: Professor MacDonagh, you are equally comfortable writing about Jane Austen or the Irish economy, as well as Daniel O'Connell or patterns of government growth. Can you tell us if, among your many publications, there are some that are your favourites, and can you explain why they have a special meaning for you?

Oliver MacDonagh: I suppose I'm a general practitioner, I belong to the old tradition where you simply saw a problem and if you thought you could manage it you went ahead and wrote about it, rather than specializing in one particular area. As to the favourite, one doesn't really have favourites among your hard-won children, but if I had to choose I would say *The Inspector General* or *States of Mind*. *The Inspector General* because it was a very complex book, and exciting because I was working on eighteenth-century history for the first time. I was working in an area which didn't seem to have been touched much by eighteenth-century Irish historians – social reform – and doing the biography of a very interesting eccentric humanitarian, Sir Jeremiah Fitzpatrick; and, superimposed [upon] or underlying all this, was the main purpose of the book, which was to find a testing ground for my ideas on the interior momentum of government in the nineteenth century. I went back to the eighteenth century to see how far it had [been] anticipated, and from the *lacunae*, to learn something of what had driven the nineteenth-century movement. So it was the complexity of doing all these things together which appealed to me. I must say it's a book that has received less notice than anything else I have written. Nonetheless, it's one of my favourite children. *States of Mind* I like and, of course, one also dislikes one's books for the things that one should have done that one realizes too late aren't there. My relative liking for *States of Mind*, then, is because it is a 'think-book'. It takes the history more or less for granted and it thinks about it and discusses it and its implications. It is also cast in a form that I rather enjoy, that is, circling round a topic with essays on it, all of which I hope illuminate, more subtly than is normally the case, the central theme. I don't know why I enjoy that form, but it's something which is a challenge and it leads to a more effective demonstration of the argument, when it comes off, than straightforward, bullying statements.

M&M: Most of your works have been described as having been written in a very elegant style and, indeed, *States of Mind* has been admired for its breadth and its elegance. Do you think the present crop of historians pay as much attention to style and elegance in their writing as perhaps they ought?

OM: I think the best ones do – probably a circular answer to the question. For me style is what the old catechism used to call 'the outward manifestation of an inward grace' and it is the inward grace, I believe, which comes through with the best people. These are generally the people who think cleanly and clearly, who are after exactitude in what they want to say and convey. I also think that history is, in the old-fashioned sense of the word, rhetoric: rhetoric in the classical sense whereby once you are convinced of an argument, or want to put forward an argument, or a thesis, or an account, you do so in the most effective and persuasive way. You do it with your audience or a readership in mind. That's what style is about, I think. If you think of it as decoration on a wedding cake, of course, that's nonsense and self-defeating; it's what springs from within and the way in which the thought patterns that lie behind it, the precision and exactitude of them, are worked out.

M&M: With your reference to rhetoric, is there something of the Jesuits in that?

OM: I think the emphasis on the Ciceronian model was well gone by my time [laughs] ... but I suppose something lingers. Besides, at university in my time as an undergraduate in the late 1940s you spent so much time debating formally and practising these skills. I did mean to be a barrister and got as far as being called to the Bar, but then I got diverted to history and Cambridge.

M&M: *States of Mind* would have been written about the time of the Bobby Sands hunger strike in 1980–1; did you find that the political circumstances of the day impinged upon your writing?

OM: I really wrote it because I got an idea one day walking down the street in Cambridge about the difference between the Irish and the British ideas of time, and it grew from there. It lay in my mind for a decade or more. I came back to it as something I had wanted to work on, so really it had nothing to do with that particular situation. Of course when I redid it I added a chapter that gave something on Northern Ireland. 'England's Opportunism, Ireland's Difficulty', I think it's called.

M&M: In a sense it's a reflective historian who's making a contribution to a public debate, is it not?

OM: Yes.

M&M: It's been described as a masterpiece ...

OM: I wish they'd said that about all my books. [Laughs]

M&M: Do historians generally not participate in public debate or make known to a wider public the benefits of their knowledge? By and large, historians are very rarely public figures. Do you think that historians should contribute more to public debate?

OM: I believe the question is largely one of temperament. Some historians feel that it's a matter of duty to use their knowledge for the enlightenment of the public and policy generally. I'm sceptical of this. I think it's all too easy to slide into propaganda; you probably already have an axe to grind if you have the urge to do that. I'm very chary of sliding into polemical positions instead of keeping your eye on the ball, the ball being the struggle to get as near as you can to the ever-elusive truth.

M&M: You have little truck with post-modern, post-structuralist French philosophers, Derrida, Lyotard and the like, who tend to write in a very obtuse manner, and yet if you struggle with them there is a kernel of interest, is there not? Your kind of history would not be the same kind of history as that? Historians now write in many different ways. It's almost impossible to keep on top of it all.

OM: I would think that is very true. A couple of days ago I got an example of this. Someone sent me a paper he'd written on popular poetry and its impact on nineteenth-century politics and especially on O'Connell. When I wrote about O'Connell it was in total ignorance of this new genre. There's a lot to be learnt. But in terms of general theory I'm afraid I'm what used to be called, insultingly, a mindless empiricist. What I mean is that I really feel no need myself for a theory of history. Just practising it is enough to fill my day. I'm afraid I look at this selfishly and ask: does this teach me anything? Foucault, for instance, I find I learn nothing from; that sounds very arrogant but it's just a statement of fact; it's no criticism of Foucault. One is, after all, a carpenter with a limited number of tools and if one starts using all the tools in the world you're not going to get anywhere.

M&M: What was the allure of literature, of Jane Austen?

OM: I had a bad back, I was in bed for a week and reading Jane Austen's letters and also some of her novels. With *Emma*, I started jotting down the details of the heroine's social traffic, and that's how it began. It issued in a paper eventually on social traffic in *Emma* and in Jane Austen's own life. Then, using my circling method, I did six or eight chapters on different aspects of Jane Austen. I like using the essay to put a different light on something, looking at different angles, hoping it's a subtle creation and not slap-bang assertion. I also started a book on Trollope that was the same general type, but a different form. I've got two or three chapters done; I don't think I'll ever finish it. It's looking at one novel per chapter as a means of illustrating mid-Victorian life. The last chapter I did was on *Orley Farm*. Instead of going on about the forgery and the sin, I took the commercial travellers and the Bar as two exemplars of mid-Victorian jingoism, as an insight into that period.

M&M: There's an interest in fiction in your work?

OM: Yes. I did better at English than I did in history at university but I was never tempted to take it up. I found I could argue plausibly from so many different points of view. But history is a hard mistress.

M&M: Our next questions are prompted by the assumption

that an historian and a professor of history are often two different things. They are questions about your experience in 'professing' history. You came into Flinders as foundation professor of History in 1964. Why did you come to Australia?

OM: Well, it was accidental. It had been half-arranged that I was to go to Berkeley in California for a sabbatical for six months – I'd knocked up six months in Cambridge credits – and the invitation was slow in coming. Meanwhile I got, out of the blue, an invitation to come to the department of Demography at the Research School at the Australian National University, not as an historian, but as a demographer, and I said snap to that because time was short. Of course, what happened a week later was that Berkeley came through, but meanwhile I was bound for Australia instead of the west coast of the United States. While I was here, Peter Karmel, the vice-chancellor of Flinders, as he subsequently became, met me at University House and apparently liked me. He brought me down to Adelaide, and I rang up my wife – she was back in Cambridge – and I said I had been offered this, what do you think about it? And she said as long as it's not Cambridge I'll go anywhere [laughs]. At that stage we had five children in what was still a bachelor world at Cambridge – dining in three times a week, formal dinners at home, trying to keep the children quiet upstairs – so it was still very much a bachelor world, this was the 1950s, early 1960s. Subsequently, we have been often back to Cambridge and she's completely reversed her position – she loves it now, but at that stage, in those conditions, it was very different.

M&M: It gave you an opportunity to translate your vision for a history department in a new country into practice. What did you try to set up at Flinders and do you think that it succeeded?

OM: I went to Flinders with one rather dreadful condition precedent, and that was that English and history couldn't be taken together. The difficulty was, at Adelaide University a large proportion of the arts undergraduates were going to be teachers, and a large proportion of would-be teachers were taking English and history. So they decided that on the new campus these two would be divided and they belonged to different schools, and were the cores of two different schools. So that cut out a good deal of my own particular interests. Nonetheless I thought that the model, which was much in vogue at the time, was Asa Briggs's plan for the University of Sussex. I looked into this and found that really things weren't at all [suitable] there in a key respect for us: that you moved between schools and had subjects from different schools. You could have a composite degree, whereas the idea at Flinders, which I had erroneously thought was the idea of Sussex, was that each school should be essentially autonomous. So within those limits I set out to work out a history syllabus which would take into account the talents of the various people we were able to recruit. I liked the idea, which didn't really work out as well as it should, of having, say, a course on revolutions, which would have six major revolutions, each done in three weeks (or political crises, dealing with the English Civil War or whatever it might be) and building up units so that you could involve everyone on the new staff, so that each would have a segment to do, and expose to the admiring youth the great talents we had collected. The idea was autonomy within the school and to provide by gobbets, to use the old-fashioned word, a sampling of different periods in the first year; then students would go on to pick from these for larger, more intense study in the second and subsequent years.

M&M: Are there achievements you look back on and remember more fondly than others in your career as administrator? Are there occasions which mean more to you than others?

M&M: I suppose in my professorial days, in the 'sere and yellow leaf', the happiest experience was in the Research School of Social Sciences at, and partly because of, the generosity with which we were treated in those days but largely because of the people who were there. There were only a handful of core people, such as Ken Inglis, Allan Martin and Barry Smith, but they were just wonderful historians and colleagues. We got a constant stream of what we thought were the brightest and best in our fields from all around the world. Those were glorious days. Among the achievements, which weren't so happy but which we struggled through, was the nine years or so over the Australian bicentennial history, which was a tremendous achievement in the end. It was my idea at first, but my idea came from the [*A*] *New History of Ireland*. I suggested it and meant that to be my solitary contribution. I wasn't an Australian historian; I knew nothing professionally about Australian history at that level. But I'm afraid that I didn't get away with it. I was made chairman of the management committee and that meant a lot of administration. But it was a great achievement. There were four hundred academics in the end involved in it, and really they restored one's faith in academics; not that I'd ever lost it [laughs]. There was so little vanity. Moreover we got away with something: it was a daring early decision. I didn't realize how daring we were when it was suggested. But we decided that nobody who was over the age of, I think it was fifty-five, it may have been fifty-two, would be involved, and this left out all the good and the great [laughs]. When I look back on it, it *was* a very daring decision. They were good enough about it, the older generation; I don't know how I would have felt if I had been over fifty-five.

M&M: You are an Irish historian, but you are Australian as well, someone who has lived here a long time and developed an interest in Australian history and the Irish in Australia. Can you tell us of your involvement in that area?

OM: I am an Irish historian with a British dimension. In the sorts of fields I've worked in it's not really been meaningful to look only at Irish history. The division between the two is unsatisfactory but that's by the way. I became interested in Australian history through the invitation I got to the department of Demography in the Research School at ANU. My first work had been on emigration, even my work on government involved emigration, and I knew that Australia was the country, apart from Sweden perhaps, with the best demographic statistics as well as a huge proportion of Irish immigrants. I was attracted to the department of Demography, having done some work already on this. So, Australia was attractive to me as a research project. It happened that I ended up going back to Canberra and, though I didn't continue my demographic work, I felt a tremendous responsibility to play my part in flying the Irish flag in Australia. I tried to do this by organizing meetings in Irish-Australian studies. With Bill Mandle, my counterpart at Canberra University, we had three or four of these meetings or conferences at two-year intervals. They did a lot to set up Irish-Australian studies in Canberra. I'm glad to say they are flourishing far beyond our humble beginnings.

M&M: Does being a migrant change the way we look at Irish history? Is there a difference between being Irish in Australia and being Irish in Ireland?

OM: There is so much individual difference in that experience that I wouldn't like to generalize about it except that to say that impressions fade and things become sentimentalized, as anyone knows. Obviously there is a difference. I remember saying once that as soon as the – it was about American immigration – moment the emigrant put his foot on the ship and the sails were unfurled, he was an Irish American. It begins from that moment. It's so varied individually I wouldn't attempt to generalize about it.

M&M: If we may be so bold, are you working on something now?

OM: I'm pretty incapacitated. I find it very hard to work. I am writing a book. It's autobiographical, of my childhood in the west of Ireland in the 1930s. Again I'm using my oblique method. None of my books has ever been deliberately decided; they're like Topsy, they just grow. I'm writing essays about different aspects, hoping that it will all come together. If you counted it up, I suppose I'm about two-thirds of the way through. The only library I use is in my head, my memory, which isn't very reliable. Fortunately, I have a good friend, John Ritchie, head of the *Australian Dictionary of Biography*, who responds to my frantic requests for something that appeared in *The Irish Times*, which is on microfilm in the National Library. It's a marvellous exercise doing this, very humiliating too; you realize how little you remember. I might give the book the same title that I gave my essay on Irish rugby [which appeared in *Best Australian Essays*, Bookman Press, 1999], *Clouds of Glory*.

2002

III
STYLE AND SUBSTANCE: THE BUSINESS OF WRITING HISTORY

7. 'One of my Favourite Children': Introducing *The Inspector General**

From the Preface

This book is a biography, though one with the rather grave biographical defects of being practically confined to twenty years of its subject's life and to a single form of his activity, the official. But the twenty years are rich in matter, and the tumultuous nature of the man and of the times were such that the account of his career is almost a species of clerk's *Gil Blas*.

It is also a study in central administration, though again with serious deficiencies. In part, these arise from lacks in private records; in part, from 'lacks' in the governmental and parliamentary structures of the day whereby even such matters as the text of unenacted Bills, House of Commons debates or annual inspectorial reports enjoined by statute, are missing

* The biography of Sir Jeremiah posed particular difficulties of evidence and interpretation, which MacDonagh discussed in the Preface, in the opening chapter of the book ('In Search of Sir Jeremiah') and in the closing chapter ('Meanings'). These difficulties also led him to attempt an imaginative reconstruction of Fitzpatrick's life, and to consider its implications for his own earlier work.

now. Moreover, a nineteenth-century historian is chastened to discover how many elementary biographical and institutional facts, readily accessible in his own time, remain obdurately hidden for even the 1770s and 1780s. Yet there is compensating profusion and colour in the Georgian caches which have here and there survived, in joyous contrast to the reticences and emasculations in Victorian files and printed papers; and several of the very 'lacks' in the eighteenth-century political and administrative systems provide keys to understanding the nature of later governmental growth.

This last is important. For if the book has ended as a sort of historiographical centaur, half-human and half-institutional, that is because it proved impossible to relegate Fitzpatrick to a subordinate role. Yeats once complained of George Moore's 'terrible gift of intimacy'. If the gift is to be deplored, Fitzpatrick stands condemned. He buttonholes, he grasps attention, he can somehow speak directly across two hundred years. So at least I have found. If caught like me, the reader may be occasionally exasperated by the tireless iteration and unflagging passion – but never to the point where any of that 'terrible' immediacy would be foregone. To find such a man was, however, an unconventional delight. The subject was chosen originally, not because of him, but for what it might contribute to an understanding of the genesis of the modern state, and particularly if paradoxically, for what it might contribute to a better understanding of the nineteenth-century revolution in government ...

In Search of Sir Jeremiah [Chapter 1, in full]

In the Anglo-Saxon analogue of life, a bird flies from the night into a lighted hall, veers this way and that, and then vanishes into the darkness from which it came. It might almost serve as an analogue for this book as well. A single penny-candle worth of information breaks the darkness which surrounds Fitzpatrick before he was knighted in 1782. All we know for certain is that he married an Elizabeth Fitzgerald in November 1770. His end is almost equally mysterious. A handful of letters from, and one concerning, him; an attempted intervention at a public meeting; a deed of assignment, and his will, are the only surviving traces of the last eight years of his life, after his unsought retirement from the public service. His administrative career also fits the image. Parts of it were brilliantly illuminated, and parts remain in shadow, as Fitzpatrick swung left and right in his headlong passage. But perhaps a better metaphor for his official life would be the Roman candle: a racing fuse, a blaze, petty explosions, showers of sparks and at the last a black and empty shell – or rather several of them, for Fitzpatrick burned briefly in many fields.

We know where he was born, Kilbeggan, Co. Westmeath, in the Irish central plain; but not when. *Circa* 1740 is the best guess which I can make. His marriage took place in 1770; in 1798 he spoke sadly of his advanced years; his portrait of 1801 suggests a man of sixty. His family too is practically unknown. It is certain that his parents lie buried in the Old Relic graveyard (from the Gaelic *reilig*, a burial ground), abutting the road between Kilbeggan and Tullamore. But although most of the tombstones can be read, theirs, with characteristic Fitzpatrickian perversity, must be among the number which have fallen down or become indecipherable with weathering. We can infer that the elder Fitzpatricks were Catholics. The churchyard lies in the shadow of the ruined Durrow Abbey, and such places were used by Catholics as burial grounds in the eighteenth and early-nineteenth centuries to elude the funeral rites of the established church. We may also infer, though less confidently, that they were people of some substance, for it was generally these who were buried in monastic grounds. Beyond these fragments, we know nothing of Fitzpatrick's ancestry.

His schooling and medical training lie in equal darkness. He knew French and was a practised Latinist. Possibly he could read, if not speak, Italian. But his quite extensive Italian reading might have been in translation rather than the original. Undoubtedly he possessed a good working knowledge of mathematics and of the contemporary natural sciences, both chemistry and physics. But there is no evidence of literary training in his work, beyond a gentleman's acquaintance with the Bible and a capacity to write both chaste and ornate prose, given the licence of eighteenth-century grammar, spelling and punctuation. What are we to make of all this in terms of illuminating his education? Unfortunately, it excludes nothing. The evidence is compatible with a hedge school, a grammar school or private tutors. It was possible, though of course more difficult, to receive as good a grounding in classics and mathematics in surreptitious classes in hay-barns or ditches or from wandering 'professors' as any regular 'academy' might provide. If Jeremiah's parents were Catholics, the illicit hedge school or itinerant teacher was the more likely source of his early education. But we cannot put it any stronger, for many Catholic children attended the grammar schools of the established church.

His medical training is equally obscure. There is no record of his attending any British, Irish or Dutch college of physicians or surgeons – the standard channels of qualification in the mid-eighteenth century. Yet he practised as a physician, and described himself on all formal occasions, and was always described officially, as 'MD'. It is of course conceivable that he was, medically speaking, an impostor, or that his doctorate in medicine was furnished by one of the German universities, perhaps at that time engaged in the business of selling higher degrees without examination or close enquiry. But neither supposition is at all likely. To look no further, he made many bitter enemies in Dublin, where he was well known, and later in the army medical service in Great Britain; and none would have hesitated to charge him with quackery, or worthless qualification, had there been the slightest ground for such a challenge.

The most likely explanation is that Fitzpatrick read medicine on the continent. In Ireland, the third quarter of the eighteenth century was marked by the rise of a Catholic middle class. With landownership barred to almost all Catholics by the penal legislation of 1691–1709, and the law, church and army altogether closed, they naturally turned to trade and the demi-professions such as medicine for economic and social advancement. Not that they had a free run of either commerce or medicine: important parts of each were fenced off for the benefit of Anglicans. Nonetheless from 1750 onwards Catholics became numerous and prosperous in the 'open' sectors. They may even have been predominant numerically by 1775. Thus given Fitzpatrick's Catholic parentage and probable 'comfortable' background, medicine was a natural choice for a career; and for an eighteenth-century Irish Catholic the study of medicine meant, almost invariably, study in France or Italy. Some came through the medical schools of Padua or Bologna, and a few doubtless attended Strasbourg or Montpellier; but most were Paris-trained. The best guess is, therefore, that Fitzpatrick qualified in medicine in Paris. This receives some slight measure of corroboration from his familiarity with the administrative systems and other aspects of life in the French capital, although it is also true that almost everything which he wrote of Paris could have been gathered readily enough from books and journals. Possibly he studied in more than one European centre. Certainly, he claimed to have visited hospitals all over the continent in his early life.

By the early 1780s Fitzpatrick was practising as a physician in Dublin: his address, Jervis Street, may suggest a connection with the nearby hospitals, Simpson's and the Charitable Infirmary. But where did he practise in the preceding fifteen or twenty years? It may well have been Dublin from the start. There are however one or two faint indications that he had lived in Kilkenny earlier in his career. Certainly he knew that city better than any other in the province. His marriage throws no light upon this question. In the settlement his wife's residence is set down as Dublin: unfortunately, his own does not appear. But all her property in prospect lay close to Kilbeggan, and all the trustees but one – the former prime serjeant, Anthony Malone – lived within twenty miles of the little town. Several of the trustees were her own relations. Thus, although Elizabeth Fitzgerald was a Dubliner in 1770, nothing in the marriage was incompatible with Fitzpatrick living elsewhere, for their common origin in Westmeath is the *prima facie* explanation of their acquaintanceship. The settlement does, however, throw a little light on other things. It tends to confirm Fitzpatrick's Catholic background, for Malone was the lawyer chiefly used by well-to-do Leinster Catholics. It also tends to confirm his middle-class milieu, first, in that there was considerable property to be settled, and second, in that Elizabeth was evidently an educated woman: her signature is fluent and elegantly formed.

So far we have been dealing in the obscurity in Fitzpatrick's life. But there are also mysteries, in particular his religion and the reason for his knighthood. Such evidence as we have up to 1782 certainly indicates a Catholic origin and upbringing. But no open Catholic or even known nonconformer to the established church would have been knighted in 1782. Moreover, various of his reports to the Irish parliament in the 1780s imply his attendance at Anglican services. Of course this in itself presents no difficulty. In the third quarter of the eighteenth century the stream of prudential conversions from Catholicism in Ireland quickened considerably. But there is no record of Fitzpatrick conforming; and contrariwise he was spoken of as a concealed papist – if anything – in 1789. Moreover, he was remarkable among late-eighteenth-century advocates of the penitentiary system in giving a negligible role to religion in the reformatory process. Possibly this expressed a general scepticism, or scepticism about the capacity of prison chaplains to touch men's hearts or change their courses of behaviour. But it may also have expressed a covert opposition to the state religion, for only clergymen of the established church would have been appointed to penitentiaries in Ireland in the 1790s. This view receives some support from Fitzpatrick's tentative suggestions that Catholic priests might be employed as a species of supernumerary chaplains for their co-religionists. His army career throws no light upon the problem except in two negative respects. First, although Fitzpatrick's appointment as inspector general of health for the land forces in 1794 was militarily unique, his effective rank was that of colonel; and to commission a Roman Catholic at that level would then have been in breach of the anti-popery laws, in an area in which they were still firmly upheld. On the other hand, his voluminous writings upon the care of the army sick and soldiers' morale and comfort contain no reference whatever to religious instruction, solace or ministration.

When we reach his years of retirement, after 1802, a similar ambiguity, or ambivalence, persists. In 1808 he was present at and attempted to address a meeting of the Catholic Committee – a body of Catholic aristocrats, landed proprietors and professional men – in Dublin. Although this is not conclusive evidence, it strongly suggests that he was by then sailing openly under Catholic colours. Tangentially, his will, drawn up a year later, reveals close – not to say, militant – Catholic connections. Among the beneficiaries was Hugh Fitzpatrick, the Catholic bookseller and a leading member of the 'radical' Catholic faction, who was to be imprisoned four years later for publishing an anti-government tract. It seems clear from the context that Hugh was either the nephew or (much less likely) the grand-nephew of Sir Jeremiah. Another of the beneficiaries was Patrick Vincent Fitzpatrick, at this time a youth, but later to become O'Connell's political manager and a prime organizer of the Catholic Emancipation campaign of the later 1820s. He too was a collateral descendant of Sir Jeremiah, almost certainly a grand-nephew. It is tempting, in retrospect, to inject positive

Catholicism into Sir Jeremiah from these links with the Irish Catholic *avant garde*. But the main beneficiary of the will was Sir Jeremiah's grandson, Jeremiah Tisdall, the fruit of a union between his daughter, Elizabeth, and John Tisdall of Ardee, a member of a leading Ascendancy family. From this it seems probable that young Tisdall and his other grandchildren by the same marriage were born into the Anglican ranks.

What type of religious indentikit should we construct for Fitzpatrick from this medley of indications and implications? This seems to be the best that can be done: that Fitzpatrick was born and educated well into manhood as a Catholic; that he then, tacitly at least, conformed to the established church, while perhaps developing into a deist or some equivalent in belief; that he nonetheless retained a vestigial identification, at least, with the depressed community from which he had sprung; and that as his life closed in and the sects in Ireland became re-polarized he reverted to the church in which he had been reared. This reconstruction has the additional merit, slight though it may be, of keeping in step with the general march of religious ideology and commitment in Ireland. The young among the Catholic middle class and aspirants to social rank or professional advancement conformed to Anglicanism in considerable numbers in the 1760s and 1770s. The years 1775–95 were marked by the rapid spread of indifferentism among the literate in Ireland, and by the rise of the sentiment that true religion (or humanity) transcended the ecclesiastical poles. From 1795 onwards, from a variety of causes, sectarianism and passionate religiosity returned to Ireland with redoubled force; the 'middle ground' contracted; and conversions to Anglicanism among the educated, and religious admixtures in families, fell away. Men – even the technical atheists and apostles of progress – had to choose their sides; and not a few of the conformers of the 1770s and 1780s returned to Catholicism in the new century. Fitzpatrick would certainly have been no curiosity in the land had he followed this general pattern.

At any rate, inconclusive though it may be, speculation about his religion is worthwhile. It is still the first question to be asked about any Irishman. It is also one of the first questions to be asked about any social reformer of the late-eighteenth century. But most important of all an Irish Catholic boyhood amid the fears and repressions of the 1740s may provide the key to Fitzpatrick's extraordinary reticences in all the torrent of explanation and expostulation in his public life. It may even help to explain his rare but sharp shafts against his English betters and their order, as something akin to the ambivalence which Kramnick detects in Burke:

> Torn by personal misgivings about his own place in society, some of his basic inclinations seem, in fact, to have been not far removed from those of the very radicals against whom he thundered.

Fitzpatrick's knighthood in 1782 is much more simply and blankly a mystery than his religion. His 'elevation' early in August in that year belonged to what would now be termed a list of resignation honours. The Duke of Portland, who conferred the knighthood, was on the point of leaving the Irish lord lieutenancy. It is true that two other Dublin physicians received the same title at the time. But unlike Fitzpatrick they had official standing. It is also true that Portland's chief secretary was another Fitzpatrick, Colonel Richard, the crony of Charles James Fox, and the younger brother of the Earl of Upper Ossory. Immediately, it is tempting to guess that Jeremiah was an illegitimate connection of this family, being hurriedly pushed up a rung or two while the noble Fitzpatrick had still some power in Dublin Castle. But the parents buried in the Old Relic graveyard seem to close off this avenue of conjecture once for all. On the other hand, there might have been a Catholic branch of the Upper Ossory family to which Jeremiah belonged, and he might have been useful to his hypothetical relative, the chief secretary, during the four months of the Portland administration in Ireland. Doubtless this may seem a farfetched explanation, although many Ascendancy families did have Catholic tails. But any other explanation seems more farfetched still. That Jeremiah performed some dark but valuable political service for Dublin Castle in 1782 might appear to offer a more substantial quarry for speculation. But not only is there no grain of evidence that he did, but also it seems impossible even to conceive of any political service which he might have rendered at all commensurate with a knighthood. Similarly, his career as social reformer or administrative philanthropist had not yet begun in 1782. At most, the foundations for it were being laid, out of sight. So this road, too, is closed, and we are left with either the mystery absolute or an airy construction resting on a mere coincidence of name and common region of origin – though possibly we might add to these the general principle that, in a question of eighteenth-century politics, family connection is the first place to look in seeking to explain an advancement.

The two decades 1783–1802 are the years of light. We know that Fitzpatrick was practising as a physician in Dublin up to 1786, though with increasing absences from the city when voluntarily he undertook inspections about the country. In 1786 prison and other inspections became his full-time occupation, in which he continued until the end of 1793. He then took up army medicine, at first as a succession of ad hoc tasks, and later, in November 1794, as a properly appointed officer. In the summer of 1794 and again in 1794 and January 1795 he visited the British army in the course of its successive retreats in the Austrian Netherlands and Holland, but otherwise spent most of 1795 and of the first half of 1796 dealing with various calamities at Plymouth. Thereafter Portsmouth was his main base, although he also worked for considerable periods at and around Southampton with occasional forays to east-coast ports and the Thames. From 1797 he appears to have spent more and more time in London where he had maintained an office almost from the start, and where in July 1802 he received the dire news that, like many officers in the wake of the Peace of Amiens, he would soon be out on half-pay.

Although there is much that is obscure about his whereabouts and activities during these two decades, the broad outline is clear enough and there are also many phases in which his doings, virtually day by day, can be recorded. Strangely enough, it would seem that he never returned to Ireland from the day that he sailed with sick troops from the Cove of Cork to Plymouth, merely to tend them during the voyage, to the day of his enforced retirement from the service. One cannot be categorical about this. Various periods during these nine and a half years are not sufficiently accounted for to preclude absolutely a visit to his homeland. But his increasingly agitated – and unheeded – requests over the years to be sent to Ireland for one piece of business or another tend to support the inference that once caught up in army matters, he was held fast in the services without a break. He might as well have been a pressgang's prey, although it is also true that he was a most willing, not to say eager, victim.

As I have said above, the evidence of Fitzpatrick's life in retirement is sparse. In almost every instance what survives relates to one or other of his hobby horses. Even in powerlessness, the 'reforming' habit proved ineradicable. It is not clear where he lived from 1802 onwards – or rather all that is clear is that he was residing alternately in London and in Dublin. The 'Lady Elizabeth', as he sometimes called his wife, died in Ireland sometime shortly before July 1809 predeceased, it would seem, by the two children of the marriage, Elizabeth and John. But when Sir Jeremiah's own death came in February of the following year, he was living at 'his apartments in Frith-street', London. Evidently, he made a final translation once his wife had died.

When J.B. Yeats the elder was asked to identify the essential difference between the English and the Irish, he replied that every Englishman had rich relations and every Irishman poor ones. Sir Jeremiah's will provides mild confirmation of this grand dictum. Among the bequests was one of £110 to his grand-niece, Ann Kelly, 'to purchase a life annuity to prevent her becoming miserable and wanting the necessaries of life'; and another of £100 to Ann's brother, John, to purchase him a similar annuity. A niece-in-law and her four daughters were to receive £10 each, 'but to her that is deformed in the chest in order to get her a trade', £5 more; while to the future organizer of victory, P.V. Fitzpatrick, £12 to buy Malone's edition of Shakespeare and 'a set of geographical maps of the best kind' was bequeathed. Other Fitzpatrick relations received more substantial sums, up to £200, but it is clear from their addresses, Thomas Street, Capel Street and Petticoat Lane in Dublin, that these were people in trade, at a comparatively modest level. One general impression of Sir Jeremiah which emerges from his will is that of the successful member of a long-tailed upwardly mobile and moderately respectable tribe. Another is that of a feeling heart and sensitive conscience. Apart from his bequests to grand-nieces and -nephews, he left £120 each to his former servants, remembered old debts (including one owed by his son, John, presumably dead for some time), and was concerned that a woman who had, at his request, made clothes for small boys in the Penitentiary or Bridewell of James's Street should not be out of pocket if the government had failed to settle her account. The will also makes it clear that Sir Jeremiah was tolerably well-to-do. The cash legacies amounted to approximately £1000; a residue of unknown amount was, at any rate, notionally allotted; there were many carriage horses to be distributed among his nephews; and the income from rentals of lands owned in Westmeath and King's County, divided between the two principal heirs, Jeremiah Tisdall and Jeremiah Fitzpatrick, grandson and godson respectively, may well have exceeded £1000 per annum. At a hazard, his annual income in his last years may be put at about £1400, quite enough to make him a very substantial man in Ireland (particularly in Catholic Ireland), though still far from the category of 'rich'. It is to be noted that the bulk of his money, deriving from land, appears to have come to him through his wife. This might help to explain how he could afford the career of philanthropy from the mid-1780s onwards: possibly Elizabeth came into the inheritance foreshadowed in her marriage settlement about this time.

Fitzpatrick's career as a public servant may fairly be described as philanthropic, despite the fact that he was a salaried officer from its formal commencement. In his early years as inspector general of prisons in Ireland, the expenses of running his 'department', which he had to meet, exceeded his stipend; and even later, if matters mended at all, he cleared at best £200 a year – meagre compensation for the abandonment of a profession. Certainly the inspectorship of army health was a more rewarding occupation. But again his pay, £730 per annum, must have been considerably higher than his net income from his employment. He was forced to meet some of the costs of his office – precisely how much is uncertain, as the matter was lengthily disputed and the outcome unrecorded. He suffered greatly moreover from another of the misfortunes of the eighteenth-century public servant, delays and arrears in payment; and years of putting up in English inns and lodgings, for which he received no compensation, must have eaten heavily into his earnings. In short, his army career, while not run absolutely at a loss, cannot have been a profitable substitute for private practice.

In some respects, Fitzpatrick was far from the stereotype of the mid-Georgian public servant. He worked, not few and occasional hours, but day and night in crisis. In place of the fee'd parasite, he was the salaried official. So far from appropriating, he himself sometimes paid for government supplies. There can be little doubt that he was incorruptible, even if he were sufficiently a man of his time to look upon the malversation of other public servants resignedly. Only once was an observation made which might conceivably be construed as a charge that he manufactured jobs for his own advantage. In June 1791 he appeared in a mid-year squib in the *Freeman's Journal* under 'the Art of Humbugging by Sir J- F-p-k'. But, as Shaw once remarked, one of Dublin's marks is a 'certain flippant futile derision and belittlement which confuses the noble and serious with the base and ludicrous'. Many of Dublin's other leading men were made to stand in still less flattering lights in the lampoon; and in any event Fitzpatrick was a *bête noire* of the reactionary Irish Anglicans by that time. On the other hand, it cannot be denied that the system of patronage and personal influence was – and doubtless had to be – his natural air. Such posts and power as he attained could not have been won unless he had been adopted by great men; and to some extent his successes in office depended on the continuance of such a backing. Conversely, he himself may have patronized others in his Lilliputian way. In particular he was accused, probably with good reason, of trying to push the fortunes of his indigent fellow-countrymen in England. Certainly, his governmental world was poles apart from one of 'merit', competition and examination; and certainly he was marked by the supposedly Irish characteristic of attachment to persons rather than 'principle'.

There remains a question, which opens into broader matters: was Fitzpatrick a government agent, in the political sense? As has been said, one cannot even think of any useful role which he might have played during the crises of 1780–2. But he did provide the Irish government with political intelligence in 1792–3. He later called upon the Earl of Westmorland, who had been lord lieutenant at the time, to confirm 'my capability of obtaining early and true information, since the time of the formation of the Catholic Convention [1792]'. But the information provided appears to have been general and innocuous. It was knowledge of Catholic opinion, and of the influence and status of various prominent Catholic 'Individuals of each County, City or District within the Kingdom', which Fitzpatrick put at the service of the Castle.

Such information might have had its political uses – for example, in briefing Hobart and Nepean as to the respective characteristic sticking points of the members of the Irish Catholic delegation whom they met in London early in 1793. But we need not regard this as sinister. In the early 1790s, most educated Irish Catholics, especially of the older generation, still looked to Britain for deliverance. Many of them feared that by pressing for too much too soon the Catholic Convention might frighten London off, while at the same time creating appetites at home which could not possibly be satisfied, but would issue finally in revolutionary violence and bloody suppression. Moreover, we must note that it was the British element in the Irish government that Fitzpatrick was attempting to enlighten. The corollary of Catholic trust in the British parliament in 1792–3 was distrust in the Irish, and in particular distrust of the Anglo-Irish office-holders in Dublin Castle. It might well have seemed important to Fitzpatrick to provide London with an alternative view of the Irish situation to that furnished by the Ascendancy faction. Whether he was asked to report or volunteered to supply information – there is no evidence either way, but the second course would certainly have been in character – he was probably doing no more than the cautious Catholic party (which at that stage included the entire episcopate and most priests) would have approved.

On 3 May 1797, after he had served in England for over three years, Fitzpatrick proposed collecting political information during a visit of inspection of the Irish ports. He observed that 'for some months back' this had been

> a wished for object of mine; indeed from the Moment I heard of the intended French Invasion in that Country; but more particularly, – when I found that a disappointed party was determined, at every risk to render the Catholic Body dissatisfied, to answer their own Views.

The 'French Invasion' was Hoche's (and Tone's) expedition which after maddening delays had reached Bantry Bay on

21 December 1796, only to fail to land its army. The 'disappointed party' was the United Irishmen, already losing its northern Presbyterian base and turning to the Catholic peasantry for a substitute. Fitzpatrick had good reason for his concern. The French were soon to attempt an invasion once again, and the 'disappointed party' was certainly maintaining its efforts to embroil the Catholic masses.

Fitzpatrick's primary aim, in proposing to visit Ireland, was, he laid, to counsel the Catholics against the United Irishmen and to open Catholic eyes to the perils, for them, of violence and conspiracy. But he also hoped 'by the confidence reposed in him ... [to] receive the best information and make proper use of it'. Clearly he envisaged some form of subterfuge, if not espionage, for he spoke of 'keep[ing] clear of suspicion' and later, travelling 'inadvertently as it should have appeared'. What he hoped to discover is not made plain. The only indications contained in his letters suggest the projected landing place and the Irish exiles most likely to participate in the next French invasion.

In the event Fitzpatrick's proposal came to nothing, although he pressed it more than once on Huskisson and Dundas. Perhaps they felt that the qualities which he himself had prescribed as indispensable for such a mission, 'judgement' and 'delicacy', were not his forte. But he also asserted roundly that certain native members of the Irish administration had determined that 'unprejudiced, accurate and true accounts ... [of] that distracted, disturbed Country' should not reach London. This was not altogether implausible. Fitzpatrick might have been exaggerating the divergence between British policy and Ascendancy interests at this particular stage. But as yet the gap between the two had by no means closed. In fact mid-1797 marked the crisis here, for it was now that the revolutionists were beginning to make serious inroads amongst the Irish masses; it was now that the Orange Societies were swelling monthly in numbers, menace and official favour; and it was now that the militia were sowing the seeds of the next year's rebellion in Leinster by their gross brutality and exactions in the course of stripping the peasantry of arms. Whether or not it actually played a part in frustrating Sir Jeremiah's scheme, there was unquestionably a faction in Dublin Castle eager to drive the British government and the Irish Catholics into conflict.

When the Wexford rising did take place in May 1798, Fitzpatrick became frantic in his endeavours to be sent to Ireland. Even as late as 12 June, when the rebellion had been practically crushed, he begged, vainly, 'in the Name of Charity, Humanity and Policy' to be despatched: 'much time has been lost – every day I get essential information from that unhappy country'.

How is all this to be evaluated? On the face of it it might seem as if he were offering himself as an informer. But this would probably be a misreading of the business. Fitzpatrick was not being moved by fear or greed. He had no access to secret information. His Irish knowledge was either four or five years old, or distant gossip. In short, though he may have deceived himself, he could scarcely have deceived anybody else, in pleading information-gathering as a justification for government sending him on a tour of Ireland in 1797 or 1798.

The truth would seem to be that he found absence and inaction unendurable when his country and community were in their supreme crisis. Of course this feeling was augmented by his self-importance. But the prime notes in his importunity were the desperate need to turn the Irish Catholics – 'the poor deluded peasantry' – from their fatal course, and his horror of the impending blood bath. When the slaughter actually began, in May 1798, his voice rose to the pitch of agonized impotence. Irishmen far to the left of Fitzpatrick politically, and with far less natural sympathy with the common people, were reacting in essentially the same fashion. Tone, writes his principal biographer,

> was shocked to find such old friends as Griffith and Plunket taking an active part among the forces of the Crown. Perhaps he did not know that even Burrowes and Stokes had joined the yeomanry. So indeed had someone else of whom

> Tone had probably never heard, but of whom the world was to hear a great deal – no less a patriot than Daniel O'Connell. The fact is that the state of mind of large numbers of educated Irishmen of liberal views was by no means what Tone supposed it to be. It was entirely possible to hate the ascendancy system, to despise religious intolerance, to long to better the lot of the poverty-stricken masses, even to have sympathized at one time with the French Revolution, and yet to shrink from civil war and to feel that the French had lost all title to be considered deliverers of mankind.

A decade later Fitzpatrick flickered again upon the Irish political scene. 1808 was a fateful year in Irish Catholic politics, marking the beginning of the rise of O'Connell to the leadership of the emancipation agitation and the supersession of the aristocrats by the professional men as controllers of the movement. The most interesting development of all was a *volte face* by the Irish prelates. In secret negotiations with the Irish executive in 1799, their representatives had agreed to an unlimited government veto on appointments to vacant sees. By 1808, partly from middle-class lay pressure, partly because the emancipation tacitly promised them in 1799 had been denied, and partly because of the continuation of full Protestant ascendancy in Ireland after the Act of Union of 1801, almost the entire body of bishops had swung around to condemn every form of interference by the crown in appointments to the Irish Catholic church.

The critical meeting held in Dublin on 19 January 1808 ended in defeat for the conservatives. But there had been a struggle during the meeting, and an unsuccessful attempt by Fitzpatrick to propose a moderating amendment. As published two days later in the newspapers, his proposal amounted to a species of inverted veto. The diocesan chapters were to nominate the candidates for the bishoprics, the Irish executive to approve them (or otherwise) and the papacy merely to robe the *faits accomplis* in canonical form.

Although Fitzpatrick's burked motion had no further public effect than to provoke some newspaper correspondence, it may have been otherwise behind the scenes. An unsigned letter of 31 January from Dublin Castle, directed to Lord Liverpool, then Home Secretary, and possibly written by Sir Arthur Wellesley himself, as Irish Chief Secretary, contains this interesting passage:

> Sir Jerome Fitzpatricks publication produced an alarm among the Bishops ... They had a meeting on Monday last (the 25th) & it is supposed they were to consider Sir Jerome's proposition. But it is not known what passed – one of them had previously called on Sir J. & represented the injury or inconvenience to the Clergy if he persisted in agitating this subject & in engaging the Lay Catholics to take it up ...
>
> It is considered by some that Sir J. is set on by Governmt.
>
> If the Laity thought they could carry their points they would readily engage the Clergy & succeed in making them adopt some measure like Sir J.'s. The Pope would for the good of the Catholic cause agree to it even in his present circumstances.

It seems clear that Fitzpatrick had not been 'set on by Governmt.': the communication was an intragovernmental one. It also seems clear that the writer did not really grasp the nature of the conflict within the Catholic agitation: his 'Laity' was the cisalpine, loyalist, aristocratic faction, which was on the point of losing control of the movement in Ireland to the Gallican, nationalist, middle-class thrusters epitomized and marshalled by O'Connell. Fitzpatrick's resolutions expressed substantially the views of the waning aristocratic element. If he were acting as anybody's mouthpiece, it was theirs.

But there is no reason to suppose that he was speaking on behalf of others. His sentiments were typical of the Catholic lay conservatives even as late as 1808. But we should remember that these had been 'advanced' sentiments in an earlier generation. In fact, there is consistency in Fitzpatrick's various political interventions or attempted interventions over nearly a quarter of a century. From first to last he spoke the language of a liberal Catholic of *c.*1775. That is, he looked to the British government for relief; he regarded the Anglo-Irish members of the executive as inherently inimical to Catholic claims; and he was increasingly alarmed and dismayed by the growth of Catholic radicalism in and after the 1780s. Fitzpatrick's behaviour was also consistent from first to last. He was on all occasions (to use his own ironical self-description) 'Sir Jeremiah-the Busybody', pressing himself into others' business, often absurd in his pretensions and maddening in his prolixity and persistence. But this was merely the dark side of Sir Jeremiah the compassionate man. Given his reading of Irish Catholic politics, his periodic drives to involve himself in their working-out were no less feeling than meddlesome. Predominantly, it seems to have been the prospect of suffering, of blood and death, which rendered him, so to say, a man possessed. Nor was this 'possession' solely tribal. In June 1798 he had pleaded passionately to be given a hand in the setting-up of field hospitals and ambulance services in the wake of the crown forces during the Leinster campaign.

Perhaps he did really see himself as a political agent at certain junctures. Perhaps he even had at some time or other a specific political principal, though this seems unlikely. But his 'politics' were immediate and crude. We need probably say no more than that anything was liable to be taken on as his concern when the prospect of pain or popular degradation met his inconstant eye.

So much for Fitzpatrick's disposition and situations for the present; the rest can be left to show themselves in his administrative career. But what of his intellectual equipment and the body of his ideas and inclinations? His published writings draw on 27 other authors, the great majority of them men of science or medicine. Priestley, Harington, Black, Lavoisier and MacBride are his main sources for general chemical theory, Robert Boyle and William Hooper for air compression, Stephen Hales for air putricity, and the physicians Ramazzini, Mezery, Tissot and William Buchan for the practical relationship of all these to preventive medicine. He made much greater use, however, of the works of the great eighteenth-century military and naval doctors, his near contemporaries Sir John Pringle, Donald Monro and James Lind. From them he derived the belief that the main generator of all 'fevers and fluxes' was the exhalations from human and animal excrement, with fetid air, marshy locations and damp the next most important causes. They agreed that camp, gaol, cottage and the rest of the fevers of the poor were essentially but different names for the same infectious disease – typhoid, as we should say; and they allowed that such factors as poor housing, overcrowded rooms, dirty clothing, scanty and ill-balanced diet and bad water must predispose or contribute towards the outbreaks. Fitzpatrick's approach to public health was based upon these writings. His theoretical carapace of humoural physiology and phlogistic chemistry does not appear to have had any bearing on his practice. At any rate, his struggle for sanitation, ventilation, space, cleanliness and better food, drink and clothes was not a wasted or irrelevant undertaking.

His other authorities were few. There are a handful of references to chronicles recording the circumstances of gaol fevers. Only two sources, Beccaria and Eden, are employed for general criminology, although he also draws on Eden extensively when writing upon the penitentiary system. On the slave trade, Wilberforce's concepts and plans, doubtless as publicly reported, impressed him deeply. But Howard was by far the greatest influence upon him outside the field of medicine proper. *The State of the Prisons in England and Wales* (1777) largely determined Fitzpatrick's view of prison reform. He added many details of his own, and differed from Howard on a few minor questions and on one matter of significance – the role of religion in the gaols. But by and large he was a faithful and open disciple. 'The second Howard' – an accolade he was frequently awarded – had itself a second meaning.

Thus Fitzpatrick dealt for the most part in other men's ideas, although he discriminated intelligently amongst them, and modified his own conclusions with experience. He was however an inventive person in a characteristically eighteenth-century way. When faced with a practical mechanical difficulty he would not have dreamt of delegating the search for a solution to an 'expert'. Instead, he devised and sketched endlessly – ventilation mechanisms, smokeless lanterns, folding beds. No less was he an administrative gadgeteer – planning diet schedules, designing hospital wards, arranging office hierarchy, composing draft legislation. At the same time, his instinct was to reduce the data from which all these were drawn to order and simplicity: he kept creating new forms of tabulation as he went along. His statistics were the only innovations in which he took much pride. The rest were put down to mere natural reaction to a stumbling-block and (very rightly in most cases) common sense. Nor was it very remarkable that he should have seen nothing extraordinary in this. It was the day of the Franklins and the Benthams, even if few of the second rank of devisers showed Fitzpatrick's fertility or range. Similarly with his habits of quantifying and searching for the most economical and readily comprehensible forms of classification. For it was also the day of the first literary and philosophical associations, bent on gathering and arranging independent social and medical statistics, the data which might make 'improvement' practicable.

In general philosophy, however, he was a man of his time in a much more commonplace fashion. The Enlightenment touched Dublin late and feebly; and Fitzpatrick was steeped in its clichés rather than conscious of its deeper implications. His cosmic optimism was facile. Again and again he looked back complacently on vanished barbarism. Curiously enough, current miseries, cruelty and exploitation – his constant professional concerns – never struck him as incompatible with the age of beneficence. On the contrary, he spoke of them repeatedly as strange, shameful survivals from 'the darkened centuries', all the more necessary to uproot because they contrasted so disgracefully with the general advance. Of course, the sunlit uplands of the present had been won by knowledge, magnanimity and the softening of manners. Of course, ignorance and superstition (whether from prudence or not, he never added priestcraft and aristocracy) were still forces of the fading night, and the most powerful restraints on further progress. It must be said, however, on Fitzpatrick's behalf that most of these expressions of simple faith belonged to the years 1782–93, one of those delusory phases of convergence and amelioration which have interrupted the turbid flow of Irish political history. Retrospective satisfaction and prospective hope would not perhaps have seemed quite so callow in Dublin then as they were to look only five or ten years later.

The blessed trinity which Sir Jeremiah invoked most often, in the prayers for action which composed much of his official writing, was Economy, Policy and Humanity. Sometimes Common Sense was added. In arguing that the various social reforms which he proposed were economical, he did so in no candle-end-saving sense. When he thought that an improvement should be made or a need supplied, he gave money little consideration. He did emphasize from time to time that this or that innovation would cheapen the governmental process, and he occasionally showed a species of housewifely pride in 'using up' unwanted scraps of labour or materials. But essentially his economical arguments were on a grander level. For example, his unceasing opposition to sending ill, old or decrepit soldiers overseas was based on the financial waste implicit in their uselessness, their need for support and their proneness to infect the remainder with disease. Similarly, lack of investment in hospitals or clothing or food for the troops was presented as a most costly form of cheeseparing; it reduced the effectiveness of the army so drastically that the net loss ran into hundreds of thousands of pounds in the worst years. Nor were Fitzpatrick's arguments on the social costs of 'economy' confined to the circumstance of an army at war. High among the evils flowing from overcrowded and insanitary prisons was the danger of spreading contagious diseases into the community at large – expensively in all senses. Of course there were other fields in which he could not so easily call up 'Economy' to his support. For example, it was difficult in the 1790s – perhaps it still is – to convince anyone that neglecting soldiers' wives or the insane would cost society dearly. We may infer from his excursions into such fields as these – certainly it would be true – that economy was not the driving force in Sir Jeremiah's various campaigns. At the same time his hatred of waste was genuine, and his concept of waste at once more generous and more penetrating than that of the great majority of his Victorian and Edwardian successors.

The concept of 'Policy' Fitzpatrick never defined. But he probably meant by it the political equivalent of his Economy. Repression and illiberality were as injurious to the cause they were supposed to serve, public and social order, as blinkered parsimony in government was to true economy. In other words, Fitzpatrick was a moderate and gradualist reformer, arguing that greater equity and equality and judicious change were the best security of established society. He might have smiled at Foucault's aphorism, 'The first task of the doctor is therefore political: the struggle against disease must begin with a war against bad government,' as a Wildean extravagance: soberly, he would have thought it an inversion of the truth. He was certainly anti-radical. He would uproot nothing, although there was a great deal that he wished to modify. True perhaps to a Catholic upbringing in the 1740s and 1750s, he remained fearful of democratic action and agitation. Conversely his faith in the ultimate good will of government – of Westminster, that is, not Dublin Castle – was practically boundless. But there are two qualifications to be made. He feared mass activity as more terrible for the masses than for the classes. Irish experience had branded deeply in him the knowledge of the peasant suffering which followed every challenge to their masters. Secondly, every so often one is startled by some savage phrase in his writing, seeming to show, for the moment, a burning hatred of the powerful. It is almost as if the slack has shifted and an incandescent glow in the interior been suddenly revealed. But this comes and goes so swiftly that it may be an illusion, after all.

Economy, Policy, Humanity: for Sir Jeremiah the greatest of these was certainly Humanity. It was the argument most commonly and most confidently deployed. What was economical, or what politic, in particular cases might be disputable. What was humane was taken to be self-evident; and it needed no justification beyond itself, for was not humanity the very mark of his more enlightened time? Fitzpatrick's supporting self-image was that of a heart responding generously, and boundlessly, to human suffering. Sympathy for the miserable welled irrepressibly in the breast, and impelled one headlong into battle to alleviate and console the wretched.

Can there be a species of pathetic fallacy between a man and a book? Although it seems improbable that he ever read Henry Mackenzie's *The Man of Feeling* (1771) and although he may never have so much as heard of its existence, Fitzpatrick's administrative career is strangely reminiscent of the novel. The bureaucracy of sensibility may seem an absurd conflation. Yet it would not be inaccurate as a categorization of Sir Jeremiah's view of his role, or even of the considerable majority of his undertakings, and like the man of feeling, he was repeatedly being diverted by new calls upon his commiseration. Of course, the parallel is not to be closely pressed. Fitzpatrick was not absorbed by the moral beauty of his own reactions. He was not essentially concerned with inducing an emotional condition in himself or in his readers. Without exception his cases for compassion were inherently pitiful, to any generation or to any class; and without exception they concerned the most helpless and abandoned in the community. Nonetheless sensibility was important to his work, and in a subjective as well as an objective sense. It provided him with endorsement and validation for his tireless importunity; it maintained his impetus in the teeth of failure and rejection; it kept finding him new fields for struggle as soon as or even well before he had reached his limits in the old.

In a sense then Fitzpatrick was an ideologue of his time. Almost every commonplace of the day, from the reign of reason to the man of feeling, found its way repeatedly into his writings, informal as well as printed. But this is not to say that ideology shaped what he did or attempted. In the first place, he was no theoretician; he dealt in shibboleths and the surfaces of ideas. Secondly, the concepts which engaged him were not readily reducible to administrative rules of thumb. In itself, the general notion of enlightenment suggested nothing about the mechanics of government; that of sensibility would never of itself produce a principle of social regulation. Finally, his ideology was in certain respects anti-ideological in tendency. At any rate, it could masquerade as the absence of ideology. Feeling, common sense, the practical responses to the specific difficulty – in such terms did men like Fitzpatrick interpret their own courses of action, and look on them as 'natural' and independent of philosophy. On the other hand, serene faith in the *Aufklarung* and the certainty that one was fighting not merely the good but also the winning fight were an inexhaustible resource for the early social reformer. Sir Jeremiah's world-picture – a patchwork of contemporary thought and sentiment – did not teach him how to sail. But it somehow seemed to conjure up, in foul weather and fair, the wind which drove him onward.

Meanings [Extracts from Chapter 13]

Among the many dissimilarities between the present author and Byron is waking up one morning to find himself infamous. Not long after the publication in 1958 of my paper, 'The nineteenth century revolution in government: a reappraisal', it was assailed, first from one quarter and then another, until it presented – and doubtless still presents – a St Sebastian-like appearance, with the arrows angled from widely different directions. One critic argued that it was a Tory tract, partly it would seem because it attacked the Whig interpretation of British administrative history – forgetting no doubt that Butterfield's 'Whig interpretation' was not at all about Whigs as such, but about the cast of mind which glorifies particular historical sequences leading to the present. Another argued, incontrovertibly no doubt, that in the field of motivation it is impossible to prove a negative, in particular that one can never prove that men were not influenced in their actions by this or that belief, even if those actions could be satisfactorily accounted for without such a reference. Some raised the cry of 'taking the ideas out of history', others that of diminishing the role of the individual, and yet others the cant of 'explaining the how but not the why'. The paper was attacked for erecting a single instance into a general law; for confining doctrinal membership to those who openly expressed their adherence to a doctrine; and even for not being applicable to a period which it specifically repudiated. Perhaps Dr Valerie Cromwell was right when she said that the paper's leading cause of offence was its supposed attempt to devalue the contribution of the utilitarians, and especially of Bentham and his immediate disciples, to English social reform and the general liberal achievement.

Like the cuckolded husband, the misunderstood author is not a grateful character to play. Friends may present him with long faces, but usually only to his own. Nor is the part of controversialist much happier or more profitable to perform. It may help in the building of one of those academical set pieces which, like the syllogistic exercises of the medieval schools, provide gymnasia for undergraduates. But unless the case is one of misused or neglected evidence, historical 'controversies' seem inherently prone to end in thickets of definition and counter-definition, and in the imputation of unstated stances. Rarely is light increased, sweetness never. Sooner or later, the world at large wishes a plague on both houses, and moves on to other fields; and the ultimate consequence may be a halting rather than an advance of knowledge and interest alike.

At any rate so it seems to me; and instead of attempting to explicate and defend the old, this book has tried to improve upon it by carrying its concepts on to fresh ground, in the double hope of refining the first and mapping some little of the second. This appears to be all the more sensible a course because most of if not all the real points at issue in the 'debate' are extra-historical, being either epistemological or more generally philosophical. At the same time, it will surely not void a self-denying ordinance to outline the argument of 1958. For one hopes that the readership will be by no means confined to those who have the article at their fingertips, while one fears that many have 'read' it only at second-hand.

What did 'The nineteenth century revolution in government' (or better still the paper as qualified and elaborated in the last two chapters of *A Pattern of Government Growth*) actually say?

Its first concern was to make clear that such a revolution had taken place. Doubtless, the increase in state activity appeared very small when regarded retrospectively from the mid-twentieth century. Relatively, however, the growth from 1801 to 1900 had been prodigious. But it was the qualitative rather than the quantitative changes which were presented as revolutionary. It was the rapid transformation of central government from 'antique' to recognizably 'modern' modes and conduct which earned the change so drastic an appellation. Further, it was assumed that this change was concentrated into the half-century, 1825–75, and the subsequent attempt to construct an explanatory sequence was limited to these specific years.

No one in 1958 would have disputed that national government altered profoundly in the nineteenth century. But at that time the alteration had been little considered in its own right by historians. To notice and to name it seemed in itself worthwhile. Moreover, in so far as it had hitherto been analysed, this was mainly in the work of A.V. Dicey, a lawyer and student of political ideology and *mentalités*, whose terms of reference were almost exclusively ideas, sentiments, statutes and legal decisions. Such factors as industrialization, urbanization, developments in science, technology and medicine, the recruitment and procedures of the civil service, the relationship of political and administrative 'reform', or the influence of Irish or Indian precedent, had received small attention. Not least, the interior momentum of bureaucracy, once launched upon a particular course of social 'betterment', had gone virtually unrecognized.

The article attempted to draw these additional factors (and especially the last) into the definition and general description of the 'revolution'. In particular, it tried to arrange and evaluate them by means of a 'model' of the process of governmental growth. The 'model' (clothed in protective inverted commas!) was not of course meant to be of either the predictive or universal type, but rather a heuristic device. It did not necessarily describe any specific – let alone all – administrative development. But it was hoped that by abstracting and ordering the most general tendencies of the day, a means of measuring the particulars might be provided. It was meant to be an historical tool, not an historical template. But historians as a class are not to the forefront in distinguishing the tin-opener from the contents of the tin: hence, many of the essay's later troubles ...

The late-eighteenth-century inspectorate as conceived and performed by Fitzpatrick, and discussed in *The Inspector General*, is not to be evaluated according to its degree of conformity or otherwise to its later, 'successful' counterpart. True, in the search for explanations and causes of the early and mid-Victorian offices, it is important to gauge the measure of their anticipation by half a century or more. But it is also vital to place Sir Jeremiah's achievements – or those of any other period – into their contemporary setting, political, social, governmental, economic and sentimental. Once this is done, both the contemporary expression of the eternal inspectorial impulse and the contribution of discoverable individuals to releasing, advancing and moulding it, can be fairly estimated.

It would be cold, I think, to end a book devoted to one man upon the note of abstract reasoning. Not that it is mandatory to throw philosophy from the window to enable a person to come in at the door. Duns Scotus, for one, achieves the reconciliation between the singular and the genus in terms to which historians should instinctively respond. Of course, generality is valid, not to say necessary, to organize experience in the mind or on the page. But every phenomenon, every stretch of past reality, has its own inimitable form and markings, and every human actor his own 'particular glimpse', and every life its own 'most special image'. Haecceity holds the delicate balance. The great press of events and 'inexorable' social movement are, paradoxically, unique in each of their innumerable historical expressions.

This element of quiddity is, needless to say, all the more powerful where a single individual sustains so much of a protracted endeavour by himself as did Fitzpatrick. But it would be altogether wrong to leave him struck forever in the attitude of an Atlas, or a Hercules, or any antique deity: Don Quixote is a more fitting prototype. Once when Shaw lay close to death (though typically he was to live for half a century more) he wrote an article declaring that his hearse should be drawn by all the animals which he had not eaten. Humans are not particularly grateful; but – in the same strain – if no more than one in ten of all the murderers, Rightboys, prostitutes, inebriates, assaulters, insolvents, charity children, madmen, transportees, settlers, soldiers' wives, soldiers' families, widows, naval ratings, East Indian fusiliers, French priests and Hanoverian mercenaries, whose sufferings Fitzpatrick tried to lessen, had drawn his funeral carriage, even London itself might have been astonished by the train.

1981

8. *Apologia pro Vita Sua: In Vita Mea Vedemecum*[*]

Irishmen are, I suppose, as prone as anybody else to thoughts that do often lie too deep for tears. But rarely have they thoughts that do lie too deep for words. This is one of those rare times for me, for I am overwhelmed by a sort of embarrassed disbelief. I feel that I am almost the last historian who should be marked out for an honour of this extraordinary kind. I had no teachers; I have no disciples; I founded no school; I possess no theory of history; I am master of no field; from time to time, I catch a horrid vision on myself as a sort of pinchbeck *ultimas Romanorum*, a last general practitioner among consultants, a chance survivor from a vanquished world. More and more, two cherished lines from the seventeenth-century Gaelic poet, David Ó Bruadair, toll in my mind, '*Is mithid domhsa bann do bhaile ... ó táid eigse an ché in a gcadladh.*' (It is time for me at last to foot it homeward ... for the poets of the world lie sleeping.)[**]

But this, I need hardly tell you, makes all the more precious the ill-deserved tributes with which you load me. Best of

* A response to the papers of a conference held in his honour, and later published as, *Ireland, England and Australia: Essays in Honour of Oliver MacDonagh*.

** This quote was misattributed to Geoffrey Keating in the original.

all, it brings home to me that I am mysteriously blessed with one of the only two things said to be worth the wear of winning. I mean, of course, the love of friends. You must forgive me if I attempt no thanks or particularization where so many have given me so much. My wondering gratitude truly does lie too deep for words or tears or explication. May you never find me out. I keep thinking of Cardus's description of Patsy Hendren, scurrying between the wickets, clutching his bat with both hands against his chest (like the slum child he once had been) as if in fear lest the big boys would remember who he really was and seize the bat from him, and expel him from the game. I know exactly how Patsy felt. Please do not think of my deserts, but in your charity let me go on playing.

It chanced that two years ago I was asked to speak on Newman's *Apologia pro Vita Sua*. It was a book that had been with me as a schoolboy, that had helped to shape me then, and since. Nor is this surprising. Not for nothing did Newman choose as his motto, *Cor ad cor loquitur*, Heart speaks to heart. At first, I faced the difficulty that I was after all simply a professional historian. But as – like Newman himself – I pondered on the problem of how to come to grips with an elusive subject, I gradually realized that the *Apologia*, the book itself, was the work of a fellow-craftsman. The answer seemed clear: I should try to evaluate it as a piece of history; and what I propose to lay before you now is the product of my endeavour.

In this company, I need not, I am sure, explain how the *Apologia* came to be written. It was the culmination, in April 1864, of Newman's four-month struggle to compel Kingsley to withdraw his allegation that 'Father Newman' taught that truth for its own sake 'need not be and on the whole ought not to be' a virtue with the Roman Catholic clergy. But behind the immediate occasion of Newman's great outpouring lay more than a decade of apparent defeat and disappointment. The Achilli trial for defamation, which he lost, had clouded the early 1850s. For seven years thereafter, Newman had striven to institute a

Catholic University in Dublin before he threw up the task as hopeless. In 1857 he had been commissioned by his cardinal, Wiseman, to edit a new translation of the Scriptures, only to have an entire year's labour wasted when the English bishops proved as apathetic towards this project as the Irish bishops had proved towards the Dublin university. He had been promised a bishopric, but neither the brief, nor any explanation for its failure to appear, ever came from Rome. He was a deeply attached Oratorian, and his sister-congregation, the London Oratory, broke away, rancorously, from his own community in Birmingham, greatly to Newman's humiliation. His attempt to set up a first-rate Catholic review, *The Rambler*, collapsed when (as he said himself) 'the Bishop put his extinguisher' on the venture. Even his own post-1845, post-conversion to Catholicism writings seemed (to himself, at least) so many failures. 'O My God,' he wrote in a private memorandum, 'I seem to have wasted these years that I have been a Catholic. What I wrote as a Protestant has had far greater power, force, meaning, success, than my Catholic works.' This is the true background to the composition, between 21 April and 2 June 1864, of the *Apologia pro Vita Sua*, when the dammed-up waters broke, and the sublime tide flowed forth, at last.

Newman's *Apologia* belongs to that rare category of books of which it can be truly said that they are solitary and unique achievements, and that there is nothing in all literature with which they can properly be compared. The *Apologia* is often spoken of as an autobiography, but this is wrong. Newman tells us nothing of his life or family circumstances, except what bears directly on the particular part of his spiritual *aeneid* which he wishes to disclose. As Meriol Trevor puts it, the reader 'sees the child who played hide and seek with Angels ... but knows nothing of the leader of the Spy Club, the composer and actor of comedies, the boy who rode a pony, played the fiddle, read novels in bed and was fond of mince pies'. Again, despite its title, the *Apologia* neither proclaims nor defends a thesis. Almost obsessively, it avoids arguing any case at all beyond that of the writer's own integrity. It concerns itself only incidentally, even if most effectively, with landscape and locale. Its five chapters are unevenly divided, one dealing with a thirty-three-year span, another with eighteen, a third with only two. Although he was to live for more than a quarter of a century, Newman believed in 1864 that he was not far from death. The book begins, 'As men draw close to their end they care less for disclosures.' Yet it is far from being a systematic reminiscence or the summation of a great career.

However, no more exact writer ever breathed and, as we should expect, Newman himself provides the precise description of what he is about. The sub-title of the *Apologia* is rarely noted, but it is vitally important to understanding the author's purpose. It sets out neatly what he aimed to do: to provide 'A history of his religious opinions'. So, too, each chapter heading, with one exception, reads 'A history of my religious opinions between X and Y'. 'I will draw out', he had declared beforehand, 'the history of my mind.' In this book, Newman, divine, poet, novelist, preacher, polemicist, philosopher, logician and devotionist, turns himself into an historian. As ever, he proved a master in a chosen role.

It is the truth, almost universally ignored, that it takes a true historian to write history. Of course, history writing can be calibrated along a very lengthy scale. It is an activity, in the same sense as water-colouring or opera-singing are activities. Just as the first may range from the merest Sunday dauber to J.W. Turner and the second from the last row of the chorus in *Iolanthe* to Maria Callas, so, too, history writing ranges from the self-taught genealogist to Edward Gibbon. But I am speaking now of serious, pretentious history: and here, as you all know, the delusion that anybody can do it is sadly common. I discovered this painfully for myself when once I wrote a history of a brewery. This led me into reading many histories of companies written by retired accountants, and of brewing science written by superannuated chemistry professors. All too often these proved innocently mendacious, childishly triumphalist, disorganized and uncritical, neither brief nor correctly dated. The trite point I try to make is that, contrary to the popular assumptions, history writing is a very difficult and demanding business; and to find that Newman can produce a masterpiece in this genre, as well as in so many others, at virtually first attempt – for his work on the Arians and Monophysites is really historical theology rather than history proper – all this fills the professional – this professional, at least – with awe at the breadth and penetration of his genius.

Of course, in many ways he came to his task forearmed. For one thing, he was a stylist of the first water. This again is often misunderstood. Style in history is commonly regarded as an ornament or decoration; it may even be denigrated as showiness or affectation. Nothing can be further from the truth, and especially so in the case of Newman. With him, style is the literary outpouring, the outward and visible sign, of his prodigious mental energy and power. The majority of the *Apologia* is concerned with niceties of ancient heresies and the stands of now-obscure clergymen and clerical factions. Without Newman's burning intensity of thought, without his precision of phraseology and marvelous capacity to personalize and vivify whatever he takes up, it would long ago have dwindled into a dead book, a mere interesting literary curiosity.

Secondly, Newman possessed already two other essential pieces of the first-rate historian's equipment. He could describe, with the sparest economy and clarity, both places and people: I distinguish these because they seem to me two separate gifts. For an instance of his power to evoke a local atmosphere, we need look no further than the famous last sentences of Chapter 4, where he deals with his break with Oxford:

> Trinity [that is Trinity College, Oxford] had never been unkind to me.
>
> There used to be much snap-dragon growing on the

> walls opposite my freshman's rooms there, and I had for years taken it as the emblem of my own perpetual residence even unto death in my University. On the morning of the 23rd I left the Observatory. I have never seen Oxford since, excepting its spires, as they are seen from the railway.

As to Newman's capacity to depict personality and mind, let me use his contrast between the cautious Cambridge don, Hugh Rose, and the impetuous Hurrell Froude, as my sole example.

> Mr Rose had a position in the Church, a name, and serious responsibilities; he had direct ecclesiastical superiors; he had intimate relations with his own University, and a large clerical connexion through the country. Froude and I were nobodies; with no characters to lose, and no antecedents to fetter us. Rose could not go a-head across country, as Froude had no scruples in doing. Froude was a bold rider, as on horseback, so also in his speculations. Mr Rose said of him ... that 'he did not seem to be afraid of inferences'. It was simply the truth; Froude had that strong hold of first principles, and had keen perception of their value, that he was comparatively indifferent to the revolutionary action which would attend on their application to a given state of things; whereas in the thoughts of Rose, as a practical man, existing facts had the precedence of every other idea, and the chief test of the soundness of a line of policy lay in the consideration whether it would work.

Thus, Newman was already half a historian when he began his history. He was a master of style, description and characterization. But he proved to be an *anima naturalitur historica*, into the bargain. The supreme quality in a historian is, I suppose, the capacity to discern the decisive moments or stretches of change, as well as its causes. Almost instinctively, Newman constructs his narrative about the turning points in his religious development. In 1816, when he was fifteen years old, he underwent an evangelical-like conversion. In one sense, this was *the* critical experience of his life. He was henceforth committed to God: for a time indeed in the Calvinistic sense for – as he himself puts it – 'I considered myself predestined to salvation.' But he is too fine a critic to notice only the palpable and the obvious. He points to two other pieces of reading in the same year which were to affect him profoundly for the next quarter of a century. First, in 1816, he was also introduced to patristic studies, and from them learnt what he called the principle of Antiquity; and second, through Isaac Newton's work, *On the Prophecies*, he came to see the Pope as anti-Christ, and the Church of Rome as the embodiment of this spiritual or rather anti-spiritual force.

When he shifts the scene to Oxford in the 1820s, Newman displays another facet of the historian's art. Decisive change is not always sudden or attributable to a single influence. Sometimes it is the consequence of a very slow development, only retrospectively apparent. Later in the *Apologia*, Newman speaks of such a thing in another context. 'For who can know himself,' he asks, 'and the multitude of subtle influences which act upon him?' Well, if anybody can, Newman could. With great delicacy, and discriminating carefully among the people and events colouring the progress of his thought, he shows us both his retreat from the brink of liberalism, and his growing interest in defining the nature and standing of the Church of England, during the 1820s. He also assembles for us, like a stage producer, the *dramatis personae* of the future Oxford Movement, with brilliant lightning sketches of the religious ideology of Pusey and Keble, as well as a considerable number of speculative ecclesiastics of the second rank.

As a sort of background accompaniment, Newman makes clear, without ever addressing it directly, his own politicization, as he comes to track back political and theological liberalism to their common source. Again, it is only a professional perhaps who can value properly the extraordinary skill with which Newman indicates his gradual movement into new positions between 1822 and 1830. The central problem has become the nature of Anglicanism, with Antiquity, on the one hand, and the anti-Christ in Rome, upon the other, beginning to act – so to speak – as markers, left and right, on the new glide-path.

In his third chapter, covering the years 1833 to 1839, Newman varies his historical method constantly. At several points he provides careful summaries of his ecclesiastical position. Particularly striking is his delicate dissection of his own defensive network at the moment when the Oxford Movement finally took shape: Keble's Assize Sermon of 14 July 1833 is generally accepted as its beginning. These passages in the *Apologia* may fairly be described as static analysis, a halting of the story to clarify its unfolding to that date. Conversely, Newman turns to swiftly flowing narrative when he wishes to set out the rapid growth, and convey the youthful excitement, of the agitation. He is particularly effective in doing so because he centres the story upon himself, and frankly displays his own ruthlessness and self-confidence in action, which enemies might readily decry as arrogance or vanity. A typical passage runs:

> Nor was it only that I had confidence in our cause, both in itself, and in its polemical force, but also I despised every rival system of doctrine and its arguments too ... Owing to this supreme confidence ... there was a double aspect in my bearing towards others, which it is necessary for me to enlarge upon. My behaviour had a mixture in it both of fierceness and of sport; and on this account, I dare say, it

> gave offence to many; nor am I here defending it.
>
> I wished men to agree with me, and I walked with them step by step, as far as they would go; this I did sincerely; but if they would stop, I did not much care about it, but walked on, with some satisfaction that I had brought them so far ... I was not unwilling to draw an opponent on step by step, by virtue of his own opinions, to the brink of some intellectual absurdity, and to leave him to get back as he could. I was not unwilling to play with a man, who asked me impertinent questions. I think I had in my mouth the words of the Wise man, 'Answer a fool according to his folly,' especially if he was prying or spiteful. I was reckless of the gossip which was circulated about me; and, when I might easily have set it right, did not deign to do so. Also I used irony in conversation, when matter-of-fact men would not see what I meant.

Yet again Newman builds some of his third chapter about his own writings between 1833 and 1839, and in particular about three books, *The Prophetical Office of the Church*, *Lectures on Justification*, and *Romanism and Popular Protestantism*. These books furnish the nodal points in his history of his own development during the six years of plenty. Between them, they show at once the molten thought in flow and its hardening successively, into new theological shapes. Between them, they also led the way to Newman's final position as an Anglican, where he presents the Church of England as the *Via Media* between Rome and Biblical Protestantism, as a form of Catholicism which had been virtually lost in England itself for the past century and a half, yet remained the underlying reality – awaiting, like the Sleeping Beauty, the kiss of recognition which would restore her to waking and moving life.

We are now approaching the half-way mark of the *Apologia*, and as we have progressed the key word, Antiquity, has been thrust increasingly upon us. Antiquity was Newman's shorthand for the Primitive Church, the touchstone of doctrinal orthodoxy and ecclesiastical legitimacy. He rested his *Via Media* upon it, and in fact his early work on the Arians, published in 1832, had helped to turn his theological speculations in that direction. Hence the powerful dramatic effect of his account of taking up the study of the Monophysite heresy during the summer of 1839. As he read up on the subject, he suddenly glimpsed a correspondence between Anglicanism and Monophysitism rather than one between Anglicanism and Antiquity. It seemed a passing though disturbing doubt. As he writes later, 'I had seen the shadow of a hand on the wall. He who has seen a ghost cannot be as if he had never seen it. The heavens had opened and closed again. The thought for a moment had been – the church of Rome will be found right after all – and then it vanished. My old convictions remained as before.' But within two months the ghost re-appeared, when Newman's attention was drawn to St Augustine's Judgment against yet another body of heretics, the Donatists. '*Securus judicat orbis terrarum,*' Augustine had written, 'The judgment of the world is conclusive.' What if 'the world' meant nothing more or less than Rome? Again, but most lastingly, he was shaken. Augustine's words seemed, as he writes, to 'pulverize' the theory of the *Via Media*. 'They decided ecclesiastical questions on a simpler rule than that of Antiquity. Nay, St Augustine was one of the prime oracles of Antiquity; here, then, Antiquity was deciding against itself.'

Having brought the, reader to this brink, Newman leads him off tangentially for a time. In fact, his finest general reflections upon his age occur in Chapter 3. Without employing the term itself, he expounds the effects of the Romantic Movement on early-nineteenth-century England, considering it as a reaction, in the religious no less than the literary field, to the dry and superficial modes of the preceding generations. For example, he writes of Scott, that he

> turned man's, minds in the direction of the middle ages. 'The general need,' I said, 'of something deeper and more attractive, than what had offered itself elsewhere, may be

> considered to have led to his popularity and by means of his popularity he re-acted on his readers, stimulating their mental thirst, feeding their hopes, setting before them visions, which, when once seen, are not easily forgotten, and silently indoctrinating them with nobler ideas, which might afterwards be appealed to as first principles.'

Correspondingly, Newman devotes considerable space to current politics in this chapter, and reveals himself to have been a passionate and narrow partisan. Again, his anathema was Liberalism in all its forms, O'Connell was his *bête noir*. 'I had', he says, 'an unspeakable aversion to the policy and acts of Mr O'Connell, because as I thought, he associated himself with men of all religions and no religion against the Anglican Church, and advanced Catholicism by violence and intrigue.' To an English Catholic who proffered an olive branch in 1840, he responded, 'Break off with Mr O'Connell in Ireland and the Liberal party in England, or come not to us with overtures of mutual prayer and religious sympathy.'

Artistically, the function of these apparent digressions is to bring home the fact that from late 1839 to 1841, Newman could no longer justify his continued commitment to the Church of England, except in anti-Roman terms. 'I had', as he confesses, 'no longer a distinctive plea for Anglicanism unless I would be a Monophysite,'; the *Via Media* was in ruins. His other fundamentals, his belief in the dogmatical, episcopal and sacramental systems, were better realized already in the Catholic Church. All that was left to keep him within the Anglican fold was Rome's doctrinal and devotional excesses and her unscrupulous and self-interested traffic with the political liberalism of the day.

I have no doubt that Newman realized, instinctively, that this oblique approach to the gathering crisis in the Oxford Movement, and in his own spiritual fate, would be more telling than bald recitation and assertions. It conveys marvellously a sense of clouds gathering in from every corner of the sky, and of his being driven to pin everything upon a frantic, even hysterical, opposition to his life-long anathemas in politics and religion. It also sets the stage for what – melodramatically perhaps – may be nominated, his last stand. I mean, of course, the notorious Tract 90, which he published in the spring of 1841.

The Tract argued that the 39 Articles, which formed the basis of Anglican belief, were compatible with ancient Catholic teaching, whatever their framers may have intended. As Newman sets out his argument, 'infants are regenerated in Baptism, not on the faith of their parents, but of the Church, so in like manner I would say that the Articles are received, not in the sense of their framers, but (as far as the wording will admit or any ambiguity requires it) in the one Catholic sense'. Rome was still rejected, in part for its accretions of dogma, but primarily for what Newman called its 'dominant errors', that is, the superstitious practices it encouraged among the faithful and its unsavoury conduct of its worldly business. In particular he was repelled by the devotions to the Blessed Virgin and the saints which the papacy sanctioned; while he also adhered steadfastly to the idea that only through the English church could the English nation be acted on. (Incidentally, we should never forget Newman's intense Englishness and his inbred sense of the superiority of his own country.) Something of these antipathies and predelictions – his distaste for pious practices and his feeling that they jarred on the English character – were to remain with him all his life. Even when writing the *Apologia* in 1864, after almost two decades as a Catholic, he confessed, 'Such devotional manifestations in honour of our Lady had been my great *crux* as regards Catholicism; I say frankly, I do not fully enter into them now; ... They may be fully explained and defended; but sentiment and taste do not run with logic: they are suitable for Italy, but they are not suitable for England.'

Newman intended Tract 90 to be what he himself called the crucial test. In a sense the entire chapter has been preparing us for this experiment of life and death. He makes this clear, though with that characteristic understatement and restraint which charms rather than bullies us into an appreciation of what was at stake. The experiment was certainly decisive. The Tract was met with a storm of angry repudiation and condemnation, at first in Oxford and then throughout the entire country. 'I was quite unprepared for the outbreak,' Newman writes,

> and was startled at its violence. I do not think I had any fear. Nay, I will add, I am not sure that it was not in one point of view a relief to me. I saw indeed clearly that my place in the Movement was lost; public confidence was at an end; my occupation was gone. It was simply an impossibility that I could say anything henceforth to good effect, when I had been posted up by the marshal on the buttery-hatch of every College of my University, after the manner of discommoned pastry-cooks, and when in every part of the country and every class of society, through every organ and opportunity of opinion, in newspapers, in periodicals, at meetings, in pulpits, at dinner-tables, in coffee-rooms, in railway carriages, I was denounced as a traitor who had laid his train and was detected in the very act of firing it against the time-honoured Establishment.

In short, official Anglicanism had rejected Newman decisively.

Newman's final Anglican chapter, Chapter 4, covering the years 1841–5, is, as he says himself, a death-bed scene. He professes that it will therefore prove uninteresting to the reader, 'especially if he has a kind heart'. It will be the story, he continues, of 'a tedious decline, with seasons of rallying and seasons of falling back'.

How does Newman deal with the technical problem of holding the reader's attention while he describes gradual, scarcely perceptible steps on what had now become his path to Rome? He does so by rendering the chapter documentary, in the main. Most of it consists of direct quotations from Newman's correspondence, almost all of them dated precisely, so that we can mark off for ourselves the minute gradations in his passage from the Church of England. The device is excellent, though only because of the superb and never-failing literary and intellectual quality of Newman's writing, even when only dashing off letters on the run. The resultant effect is one of great intimacy and immediacy. Newman also avoids the difficulty of attempting to convey the slow fading, over four years, of faith in the defensibility of one system of belief, and the piecemeal disintegration of the hereditary predispositions and antipathies, which had held him back from final commitment to another.

The extreme brevity – in fact, starkness – of the actual *narrative* in this chapter is also telling. By this means, by merely linking and annotating his successive quotations, Newman avoids anything in the nature of sentimentality, or even overt emotion, in recounting the high drama of his conversion, and of his break with the world and the companions-at-arms of his youth and early manhood. It is in this bare and simple fashion that he describes his final spiritual expiry – and rebirth:

> I had begun my *Essay on the Development of Doctrine* in the beginning of 1845, and I was hard at it all through the year till October. As I advanced, my difficulties so cleared away that I ceased to speak of 'the Roman Catholics', and boldly called them Catholics. Before I got to the end, I resolved to be received, and the book remains in the state in which it was then, unfinished.

Similarly, with the pathos of his farewells:

> I slept on Sunday night at my dear friend's, Mr Johnson's, at the Observatory. Various friends came to see the last of me; Mr Copeland, Mr Church, Mr Buckle, Mr Pattison, and Mr Lewis. Dr Pusey too came up to take leave of me; and I called on Dr Ogle, one of my very oldest friends, for he was my private Tutor, when I was an Undergraduate. In him I took leave of my first College, Trinity, which was so dear to me ... kind to me both when I was a boy, and all through my Oxford life.

The remainder of the *Apologia*, which Newman entitles 'Position of my mind since 1845', is at first sight of no direct concern to the historian. Newman himself says as much. 'From the time that I became a Catholic,' he begins, 'of course I have no further history of my religious opinions to narrate.' Yet I consider that this chapter is impregnated by modes of thought especial to (although of course by no means exclusive to) the Catholic, or at any rate, to the Christian, historian. I suppose that many of my fellows would deny that any such being exists, and I confess that this is altogether an opinion of my own, and perhaps nebulous and tentative at that. Nonetheless, it is how things seem to me.

There is, of course, a sense in which one who grows up in a predominantly and intensely practising Catholic society understands its workings in a way which no outside scholar, however acute and laborious, can ever recapture. It was late-nineteenth-century Russian economic historians such as Vinogradoff who were most successful in reconstructing English peasant society in the early middle ages. The reason is obvious: they were familiar with a substantially similar society from boyhood. Correspondingly, a Catholic bred in the intricate pattern of feasts, fasts and devotions, and the moral and spiritual assumptions of a traditionally Catholic country, has an instinctive grasp of what moved people and shaped their traffic and interactions in, say, fourteenth- or fifteenth-century communities, which were, in many vital respects, its counterparts. When for example I read the *Paston Letters*, time after time I feel at home in my childhood once again.

But I am speaking of something more than this merely mechanical advantage or idiosyncracy when I use the phrase 'Catholic or Christian historian'. I am speaking of basic standpoints or presuppositions, which may – or at any rate should, in logic – determine an entire approach. In his final chapter, Newman – so it seems to me – implies as much when he writes of the towering facts which have shaped his whole view of reality from the beginning. Simply, his master-ideas are that God exists, but that the world shows no reflection of its creator. These are elaborated in what to me is the greatest single sentence in the English language, as perfect in form and sound as any of Mozart's compositions.

> To consider the world in its length and breadth, its various history, the many races of man, their starts, their fortunes, their mutual alienation, their conflicts; and then their ways, habits, governments, forms of worship; their enterprises, their aimless courses, their random achievements and acquirements, the impotent conclusion of long-standing facts, the tokens so faint and broken of a superintending design, the blind evolution of what turn out to be great powers or truths, the progress of things, as if from unreasoning elements not towards final causes, the greatness or littleness of man, his far-reaching aims, his short duration, the curtain hung over his futurity, the disappointments of life, the defeat of good, the success of evil, physical pain, mental anguish, the prevalence and intensity of sin, the pervading idolatries, the corruptions, the dreary hopeless irreligion, that condition of the whole race, so fearfully yet exactly described in the Apostle's words, 'having no hope and without God in the world', – all this is a vision to dizzy and appal; and inflicts upon the mind the sense of a profound mystery, which is absolutely beyond human solution.

The possession of a sense of the being and constant presence of God, which is, in Newman's words, 'as certain to me as the certainty of my own existence', should certainly have its effect on a historian's viewpoint. First, God's omniscience should render that historian immune from historical relativism or (if I may so phrase it) historical flippancy. It should mean that he believes that there is an ultimately knowable, and known, truth about all human phenomena. He will never reach it, but the fact that it is there should drive him both to pursue it ceaselessly and to bring to his work a deep, unwavering seriousness of purpose.

Second, a conviction of God's omnipresence, His standing outside and above our earthly time frame, should instil in the mind of the historian so infused a deep respect for all past happenings and departed people. There is no innate superiority in existence here and now. To God, all pasts, all presents and all futures are contemporaneous. In Ranke's phrase, 'Every generation is equidistant from eternity.' All this may seem very trite; but it is commonly forgotten when we come to judge our forerunners and predecessors. Theoretically, my Catholic historian should be, almost *ipso facto*, secured against this crass and vulgar error because he or she has glimpsed – or should have glimpsed something of the God's eye-view of life. In practice, he or she is often the most contemptuous of all of the benighted Catholicism of the twelfth or the sixteenth or the nineteenth century. But this is common-or-garden inconsistency, not a defect of his or her profession, in either sense of that particular word.

Third, there is man's alienation from God, described in incomparable English by Newman in the passage which I have just quoted – there is the Fall and its consequent tangle of cross-purposes to be considered. The historian gripped by such a teaching has been handed a clue to the fundamental dualism of his enterprise. For history writing at its highest – so it seems to me – proceeds at two levels, that of actual happening and that of unrealized potentiality. Historical judgment, even historical evaluation, depends on the measurement, normally the silent or tacit measurement, of the first against the yardstick of the second. Moreover, a thorough grasp of what Newman calls the 'heart-piercing, reason-bewildering fact' that 'the human race is implicated in some terrible aboriginal tragedy' – this should furnish the breadth of mind and depth of sympathy of which our calling stands so much in need. Such, at any rate, is my own particular concept of the duty which we owe the dead – dead institutions, dead ideas and dead cultures no less than the faithful and unfaithful departed.

I think that every Newman scholar would agree that his

cast of mind was profoundly historical, and that it is no coincidence that history should have played a crucial part in his conversion. It was by measuring the contemporary churches and systems of theology against those of the early Christian centuries that he was led, step by step, to see his own religious position in fresh lights.

Now, by 'a historical cast of mind', I mean one which is instinctively drawn to the phenomena of change and development. Again, it is no coincidence that the word 'development' recurs constantly in Newman's writings and even in the titles of his work. Equally revealing is Newman's constant preference for the concrete and the personal. The historian's bent is naturally towards the unravelling of events – their nature, causation and interplay – and the sources and consequences of human motivation.

Thus it is far from a surprise that Newman should have chosen a historical method in dealing with Kingsley's charges. At first reading, he confessed, 'I almost despaired of meeting effectively such a heap of misrepresentation and such a vehemence of animosity.' Then the natural forces of his mind regrouped and began to measure Kingsley's pamphlet, *What, then, does Dr Newman mean?* quite coolly. 'He asks what I *mean,*' Newman noted,

> not about my words, not about my arguments, not about my actions, as his ultimate point, but about that living intelligence, by which I write, and argue, and act ... My perplexity did not last half an hour. I recognized what I had to do, though I shrank both from the task and the exposure it would entail. I must, I said, give the true key to my whole life; I must show what I am that it may be seen what I am not, and that the phantom may be extinguished which gibbers instead of me. I wish to be known as a living man ...

The answer was, in short, to write a history of himself, but only of himself in one particular light. It was not his achievements or vicissitudes, his personal fortunes or even his spirituality, which he would try to recount to the world, but solely the course of what he himself humbly termed his religious opinions.

This decision made, all Newman's innate historical powers sprang into place. The book cannot have been planned in the conventional sense of planning. To write 80,000 words in eight weeks, standing at a lectern day after day, once for fifteen hours on end, with fully half one's materials uncatalogued and one's sources to be checked against others' recollections at many points – to perform such a prodigious physical and mental labour left no moment for premeditation or reflection. Moreover, by his own account, he did not dare to afford himself time for thought lest his heart falter or his resolution crumble. 'And who can suddenly gird himself', he wrote,

> to a new and anxious undertaking, which he might be able indeed to perform well, were full and calm leisure allowed him to look through everything that he had written, whether in published works or private letters? Yet again, granting that calm contemplation of the past, in itself so desirable, who could afford to be leisurely and deliberate, while he practises on himself a cruel operation, the ripping up of old griefs, and the venturing again upon the 'infandum dolorem' of years, in which the stars of this lower heaven were one by one going out? I could not in cool blood ... attempt what I have set myself to do. It is both to head and heart an extreme trial, thus to analyse what has so long gone by, and to bring out the results of that examination. I have done various bold things in my life: this is the boldest: and, were I not sure I should after all succeed in my object, it would be madness to set about it.

But once he began every instrument in the entire orchestra of history writing was ready at his hand. We have seen how chapter by chapter, and section by section within each chapter, he called upon different pieces and combinations of pieces, to achieve precisely the effect he sought. He was also in possession from the beginning, of an unfailing symphonic sense.

Although the printer's boy may have been waiting at the door to carry off his copy to the publisher – on at least one occasion this was literally the case – Newman instinctively proportioned and interrelated the paragraphs and sentences with a view towards the impact of a totality. As he wrote, he was governed by basic historical predispositions – rooted in his own nature and intellectual inclination. He saw reality in organic terms, as change, decay and growth. He saw the past as fully the equal of the present, and the dead as deserving no less care or justice than the living. He understood that though historical truth may not be wholly discoverable in this existence, it is vital to believe that it is there. He exploited the great paradox that although each age and movement is unique, history contains a series of repetitions.

No doubt, the *Apologia* is inimitable. Newman's formula would end in chaos in other hands. Yet it remains, to me, historian's history *in excelsis*. Of course, the book is many other things besides – it is a theological and ecclesiastical analysis, a memoir of a great upheaval, a testimony of love and friendship; it is sustained rhetoric of the highest order, it is passion frozen like the action on the Grecian Urn. But however long this list, it should somewhere say that Newman's *Apologia* is also one of the glories, as well as a supreme exemplar, of the historiography of our modern age.

1990

Oliver MacDonagh: List of Published Writings

The Papers of Oliver MacDonagh are deposited in the National Library of Australia, MS 4806.

1947 'The Irish Catholic clergy and emigration during the Great Famine', *Irish Historical Studies*, v, 20 (September 1947), 287–302.

1954 'The regulation of the emigrant traffic from the United Kingdom 1842–1855', *Irish Historical Studies*, ix, 34 (September 1954), 162–89.

1955 'Emigration and the state, 1833–1855: an essay in administrative history', *Transactions of the Royal Historical Society*, 5th series, 5 (1955), 133–9.

1956 'The L&H in the 1940s' in James Meenan (ed.), *Centenary History of the Literary and Historical Society 1855–1955* (Tralee 1956), pp. 283–92.

'Irish emigration to the United States of America and the British colonies during the Famine' in R. Dudley Edwards and T. Desmond Williams (eds), *The Great Famine: Studies in Irish History 1845–52* (Dublin 1956), pp. 319–88.

1958 'The nineteenth century revolution in government: a reappraisal', *The Historical Journal*, i, 1 (1958), 52–67.

'Delegated legislation and administrative discretions in the 1850s: a particular study', *Victorian Studies*, ii, 1 (September 1958), 29–44.

1961 *A Pattern of Government Growth 1800–60: The Passenger Acts and their Enforcement* (London 1961).

1962 'The anti-imperialism of free trade', *The Economic History Review*, 2nd series, xiv, 3 (1962), 489–501.

1964 'The origins of porter', *The Economic History Review*, 2nd series, xvi, 3 (1964), 530–5.

1967 'Coal mines regulation: the first decade, 1842–1852' in Robert Robson (ed.), *Ideas and Institutions of Victorian Britain: Essays in Honour of George Kitson Clark* (London 1967), pp. 56–86.

1968 *Ireland* (New Jersey 1968).

1970 *The Nineteenth Century Novel and Irish Social History: Some Aspects*, The O'Donnell Lecture, National University of Ireland (Dublin 1970).

1973 Introduction to *Emigration in the Victorian Age: Debates on the Issue from Nineteenth Century Critical Journals* (Farnborough 1973).

'The nineteenth century college: rise, decline and resurgence' in E.E. Rich (ed.), *St. Catharine's College Cambridge: Quincentenary Essays* (Cambridge 1973), pp. 248–65.

'Sea communications in the nineteenth century' in K.B. Nowlan (ed.), *Travel and Transport in Ireland*, Thomas Davis Lecture Series (Dublin 1973), pp. 120–33.

1974 'The Irish in Victoria, 1851–1891: a demographic essay', *Historical Journal* (Australian National University), x–xi (1973–4), 120–33.

'The contribution of O'Connell' in Brian Farrell (ed.), *The Irish Parliamentary Tradition*, Thomas Davis Lecture Series (Dublin 1974), pp. 160–9.

'The last bill of pains and penalties: the case of Daniel O'Sullivan', *Irish Historical Studies*, xix, 74 (September 1974), 136–55.

1975 'The politicisation of the Irish Catholic bishops, 1800–1850', *The Historical Journal*, 18, 1 (1975), 37–53.

'Government, industry and science in nineteenth century Britain: a particular study', *Historical Studies* (University of Melbourne), 16, 65 (October 1975), 503–17.

'O'Connell in Politics' in 'The O'Connell bicentenary supplement', *The Irish Times*, 5 August 1975.

1976 'The Irish Famine emigration to the United States', *Perspectives in American History*, x (1976), 357–446.

1977 *Early Victorian Government, 1830–1870* (London 1977).

Ireland: The Union and its Aftermath (London 1977).

'Highbury and Chawton: social convergence in *Emma*', *Historical Studies* (University of Melbourne), 18, 70 (1978), 37–51.

1979 'Time's revenges and revenge's time: a view of Anglo-Irish relations', *Anglo-Irish Studies*, 4 (1979), 1–19.

1980 'Pre-transformation: Victorian Britain' in E. Kamenka and A.E.S. Tay (eds), *Law and Social Control* (London 1980), pp. 117–32.

'O'Connell in the House of Commons' in D. McCartney (ed.), *The World of Daniel O'Connell* (Dublin and Cork 1980), pp. 45–53.

1981 *The Inspector General: Sir Jeremiah Fitzpatrick and Social Reform, 1783–1802* (London 1981).

'Ambiguity in nationalism: the case of Ireland', *Historical Studies* (University of Melbourne), 19, 76 (April 1981), 337–52.

1982 'O'Connell and repeal' in M. Bentley and J. Stevenson (eds), *High and Low Politics in Modern Britain* (Oxford 1982), pp. 4–28.

1983 *States of Mind: A Study of Anglo-Irish Conflict 1780–1980* (London 1983).

Irish Culture and Nationalism, edited, with W.F. Mandle and P. Travers (Canberra 1983).

'Irish culture and nationalism translated: St Patrick's Day in Australia, 1888' in *Irish Culture and Nationalism*, pp. 69–83.

'The Victorian bank, 1824–1914' in F.S.L. Lyons (ed.), *Bicentenary Essays: The Bank of Ireland 1783–1983* (Dublin 1983), pp. 31–50.

1985 'What was new in the New Ireland forum?', *Crane Bag*, ix, 2 (1985), 166–70.

1986 *Ireland and Irish Australia*, edited, with W.F. Mandle (London 1986).

'The Irish in Australia: A general view' in *Ireland and Irish Australia*, pp. 155–74.

1987 'The Church in *Mansfield Park*: a serious call?', *Sydney Studies in English*, 12 (1987), 36–55.

'*Sanditon*: a Regency novel?' in T. Dunne (ed.), *The Writer as Witness: Literature as Historical Evidence* (Cork 1987), pp. 114–32.

'Emigration from Ireland to Australia: an overview' in C. Kiernan (ed.), *Australia and Ireland 1788–1988: Bicentenary Essays* (Dublin 1987), pp. 1–9.

1988 *The Hereditary Bondsman: Daniel O'Connell 1775–1829* (London 1988).

'The Making of *Australians: A Historical Library*. A personal retrospect' in *Australians: The Guide & Index* (Sydney 1988), pp. 1–9.

'The British coal mines inspectorate, 1850–1872' in J.J. Eddy and J.R. Nethercote (eds), *From Colony to Coloniser: Studies in Australian Administrative History* (Sydney 1988), pp. 88–102.

'Ireland as precursor: Jebb's concept of colonial nationalism and the crisis of Anglo-Irish relations in the era of revolution, 1775–1783' in J.J. Eddy and D. Schreuder (eds), *The Rise of Colonial Nationalism* (London 1988), pp. 94–108.

'Late eighteenth century government and expertise: the case of Sir Jeremiah Fitzpatrick' in R.M. MacLeod (ed.), *Government and Expertise: Specialists, Administrators and Professionals, 1860–1919* (Cambridge 1988), pp. 242–54.

1989 *The Emancipist: Daniel O'Connell 1830–1847* (London 1989).

'The age of O'Connell 1830–45'; 'Politics 1830–45'; 'Ideas and institutions, 1830–1845'; 'The economy and society 1830–45' in W.E. Vaughan and T.W. Moody (eds), *A New History of Ireland*, vol. v

(Oxford 1989), pp. 158–68; 169–92; 193–217; 218–41.

Irish Australian Studies: Papers Delivered at the Fifth Irish-Australian Conference, edited, with W.F. Mandle (Canberra 1989).

1990 'Apologia pro Vita Sua: In Vita Mea Vademecum' in F.B. Smith (ed.), *Ireland, England and Australia: Essays in Honour of Oliver MacDonagh* (Canberra and Cork 1990).

1991 *Jane Austen: Real and Imagined Worlds* (New Haven and London 1991).

1994 *O'Connell and Parnell*, Parnell Lecture (Cambridge 1994).

1995 *Sharing of the Green: Modern Irish History for Australians* (St Leonards 1995).

1998 (with S.R. Dennison) *Guinness 1886–1939: From Incorporation to the Second World War* (Cork 1998)

1999 'Clouds of glory' in Peter Craven (ed.), *The Best Australian Essays 1999* (Melbourne 1999).

2000 'Clouds of glory' and 'Words without end', *The Irish Review*, 26 (Autumn 2000).

Index

INDEX

INDEX